THE WAR OF 1812

The War

THE CHICAGO HISTORY OF AMERICAN CIVILIZATION

Daniel J. Boorstin, EDITOR

of 1812

By Harry L. Coles

THE UNIVERSITY OF CHICAGO PRESS
CHICAGO AND LONDON

The University of Chicago Press, Chicago 60637
The University of Chicago Press, Ltd., London

Paperback edition 1966
Printed in the United States of America
93 92 91 13 12

ISBN: 0-226-11349-3 (clothbound); 0-226-11350-7 (paperbound)
Library of Congress Catalog Card Number: 65-17283

Editor's Preface

Few events in American history have been so diversely judged as the War of 1812. In its time, some New Englanders contemptuously called it "Mr. Madison's War"; recently, some historians have dignified it as "The Second War for American Independence." Despite the fact that its events cast up one of the most popular leaders of the century, and that the National Anthem was composed during one of its battles, it has not attained romance in our history books or become a fertile source of folklore.

But the very facts which have made the War of 1812 obscure in every sense of the word also give it peculiar significance for the twentieth-century student of American foreign policy and military strategy. Many of the issues which would later face the United States there appeared on a smaller stage. Political issues were never more entangled with economic issues. In the offensive against the Creek Indians in the southwest there was even something resembling what would later be known as total war. It was hard at the time, and is not much easier now, to say precisely why the war was fought, what were the truly decisive battles, by whom the war was really won, or what were its most important consequences.

This subtlety of issues also helps explain why the war has commanded some of the most interesting and flamboyant talents ever spent on the writing of American history. Even before the war had become a battleground for scholarly monographs, it had been made a spectacle of grand conflict by eloquent historians writing multivolume works. Henry Adams, Admiral Mahan, and Theodore Roosevelt had made the war a parable of American policy even before the specialists of the new profession of American historian had begun its more academic debates. When we read about the War of 1812, then, we are witnessing a drama in which men who shaped American history in our own century found some of their guiding principles. And we are seeing how the American past itself, in the hands of historians, becomes an instrument for shaping the present.

If we follow the interesting clues that Mr. Coles has given us in this volume, we may be justified in calling the War of 1812 "The Sobering War." Not only because the blunders and defeats of that war had a sobering effect on the men of its generation. It did occasion some sensible administrative reorganization of the federal military forces, and it did sweep away some illusions, even if it was not sufficiently sobering to persuade Americans generally of the weakness of their old militia system, or to convince them that they could not, without long planning and preparation, defeat the armed forces of Europe. From a twentieth-century perspective, this is a sobering war in still another sense. The relatively small scale of its operations, the confusion of its causes, and the uncertainties of its conclusions—all these make a story in which we may see the ambiguities of international conflict drawn more vividly than in the larger, more passion-laden battles which had more sharply etched consequences.

The "Chicago History of American Civilization" aims to make each aspect of our culture a window to all our history. The series contains two kinds of books: a chronological group, which provides a coherent narrative of American history from its beginning to the present day, and a topical group, which deals with the history of varied and significant aspects of American life. This book is one of the topical group, which includes, among others, Howard H. Peckham's *Colonial Wars* and *War for Independence* and Otis A. Singletary's *Mexican War*.

DANIEL J. BOORSTIN

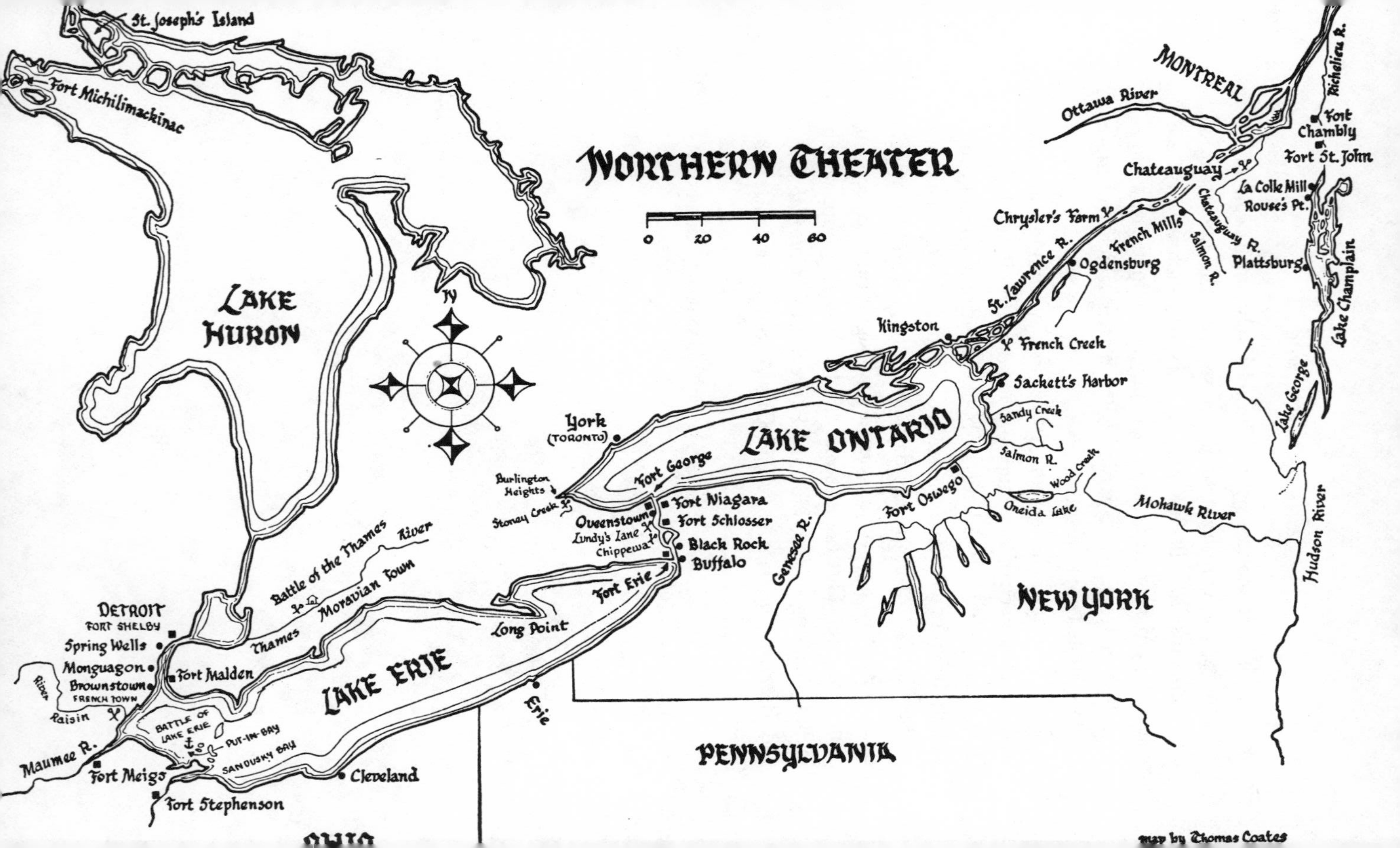
NORTHERN THEATER
0
20
40
60
N
St. Joseph's Island
Fort Michilimackinac
LAKE HURON
MONTREAL
Ottawa River
Richelieu R.
Fort Chambly
Fort St. John
Chateauguay
La Colle Mill
Rouse's Pt.
Chrysler's Farm
French Mills
Chateauguay R.
Salmon R.
Plattsburg
Lake Champlain
St. Lawrence R.
Ogdensburg
Kingston
French Creek
Sackett's Harbor
Sandy Creek
Salmon R.
Wood Creek
Oneida Lake
Fort Oswego
Mohawk River
Lake George
Hudson River
LAKE ONTARIO
York
(TORONTO)
Fort George
Burlington Heights
Stoney Creek
Fort Niagara
Queenstown
Fort Schlosser
Lundy's Lane
Chippewa
Black Rock
Buffalo
Genesee R.
Fort Erie
NEW YORK
Battle of the Thames
River
Moravian Town
DETROIT
FORT SHELBY
Thames
Long Point
Spring Wells
Monguagon
Brownstown
FRENCH TOWN
Fort Malden
LAKE ERIE
Erie
River
Raisin
BATTLE OF LAKE ERIE
PUT-IN-BAY
Maumee R.
SANDUSKY BAY
Fort Meigs
Cleveland
Fort Stephenson
PENNSYLVANIA
map by Thomas Coates

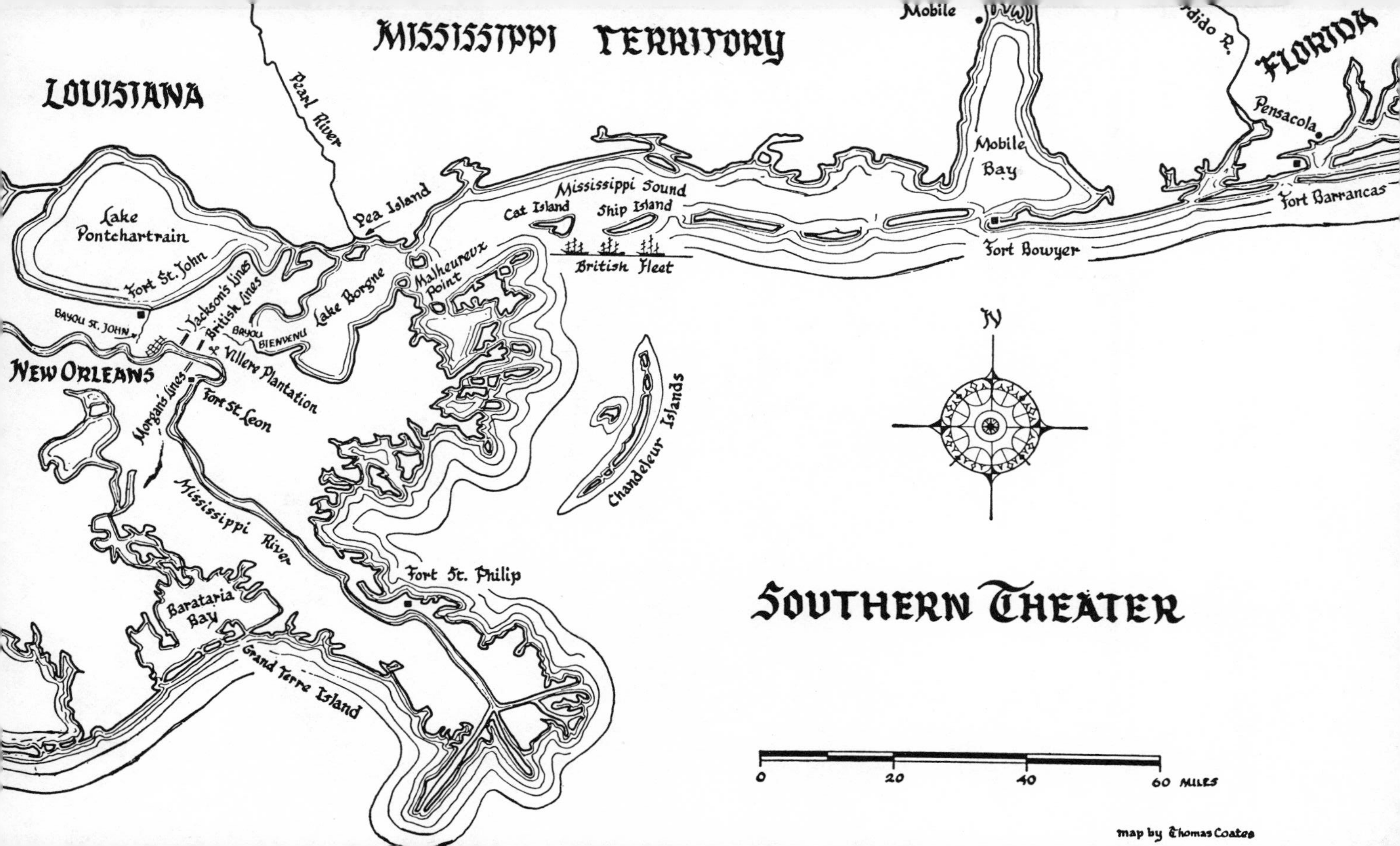

SOUTHERN THEATER
MISSISSIPPI TERRITORY
LOUISIANA
FLORIDA
Mobile
Mobile Bay
Pensacola
Fort Barrancas
Fort Bowyer
Mississippi Sound
Cat Island
Ship Island
British Fleet
Pearl River
Pea Island
Lake Pontchartrain
Fort St. John
Bayou St. John
Jackson's lines
British lines
Bayou Bienvenu
Lake Borgne
Malheureux Point
Villere Plantation
New Orleans
Morgan's lines
Fort St. Leon
Mississippi River
Chandeleur Islands
Fort St. Philip
Barataria Bay
Grand Terre Island
N
0
20
40
60 MILES
map by Thomas Coates

Table of Contents

Illustrations

MAPS

PLATES

I

Prologue to War

The War of 1812 resulted from the unsuccessful efforts of the United States to maintain its interests and its honor in a world divided into two armed camps. Both in its origins and in the way it was fought, the war was an outgrowth of a general European conflict that raged from 1793 to 1815, with one brief recess, 1801–1803.

From the founding of the American Republic peace was a cornerstone of its foreign policy. Though President Washington had serious difficulties with both the chief antagonists, Great Britain and France, he somehow managed to maintain the neutrality of the United States. President John Adams had little difficulty with England, thanks to Jay's Treaty, but he was obliged to engage in an undeclared naval war with France. Under the efficient leadership of the Federalists both the army and the navy were built up to respectable, if not formidable, forces. But while preparing for war John Adams worked for peace and, disregarding the advice of some of the militarists in his party, he made a treaty with France in 1800 that cost him a second term.

After Jefferson became President in 1801 France and England concluded the Peace of Amiens; and the Republicans took relish in quietly dismantling the military system of the Federalists. When general war broke out again in 1803 Jefferson attempted to maintain the neutral rights of the United States not by force, but rather by diplomatic negotiation and economic coercion. The same general policy was pursued by President Madison when he assumed office in 1809. By the autumn of 1811, however, a widespread, though by no means universal, demand for war arose. During the session of 1811–12, Congress passed certain measures providing for military preparation while President Madison made some last-ditch efforts to bring about a peaceable solution. Unable, however, to accomplish anything on the diplomatic front, President Madison finally recommended a declaration of war against Great Britain which was passed by Congress in June, 1812.

THE EXPERIMENT OF ECONOMIC COERCION

The reasons for the coming of the war are many and complicated. And though historians are by no means in agreement on the relative weight to be attributed to various factors, they have in general discussed two sets of causes: maritime grievances and western aims. Let us examine the maritime grievances first.

In writing about the American Civil War, one historian has said that it was a struggle involving right vs. rights. This concept has considerable validity when applied to the War of

1812. In resisting Napoleon, whom many regarded as the devil incarnate, Englishmen honestly thought they were fighting for the liberties of the entire world. Ironically, as the struggle became longer and harder, liberties were increasingly suppressed in Britain while the sense of world mission became ever more potent. Since Britain fought for the right, it was plainly the duty of other nations, particularly the United States, which owed its very existence to Britain, to subordinate national goals to the interests of the struggle which was being waged in behalf of mankind.

But if Englishmen felt that right was on their side, Americans talked about their rights. Though there was some shifting in emphasis and in detail over the years, the United States adhered fairly consistently to certain broad principles. One of these was summed up in the slogan, "Free ships make free goods." England could not countenance this doctrine in all its implications. Had she done so she would have permitted French-owned goods to move unmolested on American ships. One of the problems involved the definition of contraband. The United States wanted the list limited to those articles that would directly help the French war effort. It was, of course, to England's interest to make the list as broad as possible. Americans contended, furthermore, that the only legal blockades were those that named specific ports or areas and stationed ships off the coast to seize ships as they attempted to enter or leave. England proclaimed blockades of hundreds of miles of coastline and did not hesitate to capture ships on the high seas presumed to be headed for a blockaded port. The British never insisted that paper blockades were legal; to have done so would have created precedents not to their long-term interests. They contended that their blockades, while sweeping, were enforceable and therefore legal.

Likewise on the question of search and seizure, there were differences not so much on theoretical right as on the way the principle was carried out. The United States, while admitting the right of a belligerent to stop a neutral to search for contraband, contended that visit should be confined to examining the ship's papers. The British captains, on the other hand, apparently felt that they had the right to turn everything inside out, in the manner of a customs inspector. No cargo, however, could be condemned except by an Admiralty Court.

Impressment, on the other hand, involved not only the right to search for deserters but the right of any officer of the Royal Navy to make a decision on the spot. Whenever conditions seemed to warrant it, the British government issued Orders-in-Council authorizing the Lord High Admiral or the Commissioners of the Admiralty to issue press warrants to officers of the navy. These officers in turn were expected to keep their ships manned—no easy task in view of the conditions prevailing in the Royal Navy. Poor food, hard work, and harsh discipline caused British sailors to desert by the thousands. A British seaman wishing to place himself under the protection of the American flag could do so legitimately by taking out naturalization papers. Often, however, deserters simply obtained "protection" papers, which could be purchased, sometimes for as little as one dollar. In view of the heavy traffic in fraudulent papers, it is little wonder that the British refused to recognize any form of naturalization. "Once an Englishman always an Englishman" was the principle on which the press gangs operated. Britain never claimed the right to impress native-born Americans or to search naval vessels for deserters, but her captains, in view of the exigencies of the manpower situation, sometimes made "mistakes." Though the British government would rectify mistakes, it took months and sometimes years to trace an American who had been illegally seized. Americans not only regarded impressment as inhumane, they also considered the practice an insult to the sovereignty of the United States. No nation that allowed its citizens to be seized and carried off into virtual slavery could consider itself truly independent.

American fortunes with regard to both ships and seamen ebbed and flowed according to developments of the European war. For a couple of years after the renewal of war Napoleon entertained hopes of invading England. On October 21, 1805, however, the British fleet defeated the combined French and Spanish fleets off Cape Trafalgar. England's supremacy on the seas was once more established, not to be seriously challenged for a century. Abandoning his hope of invading England, Napoleon faced east with the determination of tightening his grip on Europe. In 1805 he defeated the Austrians at Austerlitz, in 1806 the Prussians at Jena, and in the summer of 1807 he crowned his conquests with the Treaty of Tilsit with the Russians. An invincible naval power now confronted an all-conquering land power.

Unable to get at one another directly, each side attempted to bring the enemy to terms by means of economic strangulation. By an Order-in-Council of May 16, 1806, known as Fox's Order, the British proclaimed a blockade of the European coast from Brest to the mouth of the Elbe but announced that it would be strictly enforced only from the mouth of the Seine to Ostend. Napoleon replied with his Berlin Decree of November 21, 1806, whereby the British Isles were declared in a state of blockade and no vessel coming from or touching at a British port would be received in any port controlled by France or her allies. The British answered with a series of Orders-in-Council. The most important, issued November 11, 1807, proclaimed that all vessels trading with places from which the British flag was excluded were subject to capture unless they first put in at a British port, paid a fee, and obtained a certificate. Napoleon's pretensions reached their utmost extent in the Milan Decree of December 17, 1807, which announced that any vessel submitting to search by an English ship or paying a fee to the British government would be liable to seizure. By the spring of 1808, Napoleon's continental system, as he liked to call it, was in operation over the whole mainland of Europe except Sweden and Turkey. In this situation, the United States was caught between the upper and nether millstones; neutral commerce simply could not be carried on without violating the restrictions of one or the other of the antagonists. Was there any way whereby the United States could preserve both its neutrality and its neutral rights? Jefferson thought there was, and the "Chesapeake" incident gave him an opportunity to test his idea.

On June 22, 1807, a vessel of the U.S. Navy, the "Chesapeake," set sail from Norfolk, Virginia, and when she was about ten miles to sea was hailed by the British frigate, "Leopard." Assuming that the British ship was merely asking him to carry dispatches to Europe, Commodore Barron allowed a British officer to board. This officer produced a copy of an order from Vice-Admiral Sir George Berkeley, Commander-in-Chief of the American station, to search the ship for deserters. Though his guns were not yet in firing order, Commodore Barron refused, whereupon the "Leopard" subjected the defenseless "Chesapeake" to a ten-minute cannonade that killed three men and wounded eighteen. After firing a single shot in honor of his flag, Commodore Barron submitted to the search. A second boarding party removed four members of the crew, all of them allegedly deserters.

When the "Chesapeake" hobbled back to Norfolk with her tale of woe, the response was immediate and loud. Protests from all parts of the country denounced the incident as an outrageous violation on American sovereignty. American opinion not only supported but demanded war.

Though he issued a proclamation forbidding supplies to British ships, President Jefferson did not want the situation to get out of control. What he really hoped to do was to capitalize on the war feeling to force a diplomatic settlement. "They have often enough . . . given us cause for war before," he wrote his minister, James Monroe, in London, "but it has been on points which would not have united the nation. But now they have touched a chord which vibrates in every heart. Now . . . is the time to settle the old and the new." Monroe was to demand not only restoration of the seamen taken from the "Chesapeake" but also, as security for the future, "the entire abolition of impressment from vessels of the United States." Since the British never claimed the right to search American naval vessels, they offered to indemnify the wounded and the families of the killed. Though reparation was eventually made, it was tardy and in poor spirit: the "Chesapeake" incident remained an open sore until 1812.

In December Jefferson learned that the British had issued a fresh proclamation reasserting the right to search merchant vessels to recover British seamen and that Napoleon was enforcing his Berlin Decree with great harshness. Since diplomatic bluff had not worked, some other means of inducing the great powers to alter their maritime practices must be found. Instead of war, Jefferson resorted to economic pressure and launched one of the boldest experiments in the history of American foreign policy. In December, 1807, he recommended, and Congress passed, the Embargo Act which forbade any ship of the United States to sail from a U.S. port for any foreign port.

What were Jefferson's motives and objectives? Although economic pressure was by no means new, never before—and never since for that matter—had a President seized the American economy root and branch to wield it as an instrument of policy. It must be remembered that antipathy to war was deeply rooted both in national tradition and in Republican doctrine. All the founding fathers, whether Federalist or Republican, agreed on a policy of non-involvement in European conflicts. They felt that a period of isolation was desirable in order that the United States achieve and maintain freedom of action, freedom to choose, as Washington put it, war or peace as their interests might dictate. The founding fathers disagreed, however, on the best means of achieving this freedom of action. The Federalists had given their answer: adequate preparation for war. The Republicans could not accept this because armies and navies meant encouraging militarism, contracts for private business at public expense, and high taxes, all of which they loathed. Republican doctrine demanded an alternative to war.

Just after the "Chesapeake" incident Jefferson urged restraint upon the governor of Virginia. "Let us see," he suggested, "whether having taught so many other useful lessons to Europe, we may not add that of showing them that there are peaceable means of repressing injustice, by making it to the interest of the aggressor to do what is just." How could the aggressor be made to see that it was in his own interest to do what is just? The European war had reached a point of stalemate where each side was trying to bring the other to terms by means of economic strangulation. The United States, as the largest consumer of British manufactures and as the world's largest neutral carrier, occupied a unique position in a delicate balance of power, Jefferson reasoned. By cutting off England's market and by denying both the West Indian colonies and the home islands much needed goods, Britain could be brought to terms. Here was an instrument of policy far more potent than any military build-up. There was another aspect of economic coercion that appealed strongly to intellectuals such as Jefferson and his Secretary of State, James Madison: the embargo maintained the options. Even if it did not accomplish all its hoped-for objects, presumably the embargo left the alternatives of limited or all-out war open to the President.

Though all parts of the country and all segments of the economy were affected by the embargo, the New England shipping interests felt the impact most directly. It was not long before many coastal towns were scenes of desolation. In the South, with cotton falling nearly 50 per cent in price, many planters were ruined or nearly so. The only part of the country that actually benefited was along the Canadian border where a thriving smuggling trade arose.

That the embargo brought the domestic economy to near paralysis there can be little doubt. Did it likewise have a profound effect on those countries it was supposed to coerce? France seems to have been helped more than hindered by the measure. In fact, the embargo complemented France's continental system. Napoleon said repeatedly that, though he preferred that the United States declare war against Great Britain, the embargo was the next best thing. England lost a part of her American market but this was offset temporarily by the opening of alternate markets in the Spanish colonies, hitherto closed to the British. Loss of supplies, which the authors of the embargo had thought would be particularly effective, caused some inconvenience but no crucial shortages in Britain. When William Pinkney, the American minister, tried to use the embargo to wring concessions from the British government, he met with a perfect squelch. "The embargo is only to be considered as an innocent municipal regulation which affects none but the United States themselves," George Canning, the foreign secretary told him. "His Majesty does not conceive that he has the right to make any complaint of it; and He has made none. . . ."

The noble experiment undertaken with such high hopes accomplished nothing diplomatically but it nearly succeeded in turning the American people against one another. The southern and western congressmen supported the embargo, not because they had much faith in its effectiveness but because of party loyalty. As might be expected, the most vociferous protests came from New England. Town meetings remonstrated with the government, local courts refused to enforce federal law, and occasionally violence broke out. In later years Jefferson said that he felt the foundations of government shaken under his feet by the New England townships. In other words, policies designed to avoid a foreign war brought the country to the verge of civil war. One of the last things Jefferson did before retiring from the Presidency was to sign a bill repealing the embargo.

The repeal of an old law and the accession of a new President might have provided the occasion for a new departure in foreign policy, but such was not the case. By refusing to prepare militarily the Republicans failed to preserve the options. Limited or all-out war were less realistic alternatives in 1809 than in 1807, because the Army and Navy were even weaker and the embargo had sapped the internal strength and unity of the nation. The only feasible option was to continue the policy of peaceable coercion. This was done in the form of the Non-intercourse Act of 1809 which opened up commerce with all the world except France and England and their dependencies. The President was authorized to suspend the operations of the act in favor of either belligerent that repealed its restrictions on American trade.

As a coercive measure, non-intercourse was no more effective than the embargo. In fact, relations with Great Britain steadily deteriorated. The British minister to the United States from 1806 to 1809 was a young man, David M. Erskine, who earnestly desired an accommodation. Erskine received fresh instructions from his government authorizing him to negotiate an agreement providing for the repeal of the Orders-in-Council *only* on certain conditions. One of these conditions was that the United States should agree to allow the Royal Navy to enforce American regulations against France. Disregarding the letter of his instructions, Erskine negotiated an agreement that failed to secure specific promises. Not realizing that the Erskine agreement might be repudiated, the Americans congratulated themselves on the success of their policies, and merchants blithely sent off their ships in the expectation that the agreement would be approved. Their high hopes were dashed when they learned that the agreement was rejected and Erskine rebuked and recalled.

Canning then proceeded to heap insult upon injury. In Erskine's place he appointed Francis James Jackson, who got his nickname, "Copenhagen," from the fact that he had delivered the ultimatum to the Danes that preceded the bombardment of the capital city by the British. This arrogant servant of King George III, accompanied by his haughty wife who was a Prussian baroness, came to the United States, where they proceeded to wreck what was left of good will between the two governments. "Copenhagen" Jackson was soon declared *persona non grata* to the United States.

In a mood approaching desperation, the Americans attempted to find a way out. They still could not bring themselves to accept war as a solution, both because the United States was less than ever prepared and because the French seizures had caught up with and even surpassed British interference with commerce. Was there any form in which economic pressure might be made to work? After long debate Congress took the old Non-intercourse Act and turned it inside out. The new law, known as Macon's Bill No. 2, restored trade with all the world but offered to renew non-intercourse against England if France repealed her decrees. Likewise if England would repeal her decrees, the United States would restore non-importation against France. Economic coercion had originally been undertaken with the idea of securing concessions while at the same time preserving neutrality. By the time of Macon's Bill No. 2 a subtle transition had taken place. In return for concessions the United States was really offering an alliance.

Macon's Bill No. 2 presented an opportunity for shady dealing that Napoleon quickly took to his advantage. On August 5, 1810, the Duke of Cadore, foreign secretary of France, sent to John Armstrong, the American minister, a note saying that the Berlin and Milan decrees were being revoked on the understanding that Britain would revoke her Orders-in-Council, or the United States must cause her rights to be respected. Stripped of its studied vagueness, this meant that England must abandon the advantages gained from her control of the sea or the United States must declare war against England and become an ally of France. Despite the fact that Macon's Bill No. 2 required evidence of genuine repeal, President Madison chose to accept Cadore's note at face value and on March 2, 1811, Congress officially renewed non-importation against Great Britain.

Historians have repeatedly said that Madison was duped, hoodwinked, and bamboozled by Napoleon. The critics who have dealt so harshly with Madison have failed to appreciate the desperate straits to which he reduced. It seems unlikely that he was taken in. By pretending, however, to regard the note as genuine, he hoped to win concessions from Britain —not sweeping concessions, necessarily, but some relaxation, even if only of a face-saving kind. When the American minister in London informed the government that the French had repealed the Berlin and Milan Decrees the British demanded proof. Repeated efforts to get some evidence of repeal came to nothing. Soon American policy became hopelessly ambivalent. In London the United States was insisting that repeal was genuine, while in Paris they pleaded in vain for evidence of such repeal. President Madison is to be criticized not so much for his original gamble as for persisting in a position that became increasingly untenable.

The War of 1812

In spite of the fact that relations with both France and Great Britain continued to deteriorate, the Eleventh Congress did nothing to prepare for war. The financial strength of the country was in fact weakened by the refusal of Congress to recharter the Bank of the United States and also its refusal to adopt Secretary of the Treasury Albert Gallatin's plans for new taxes which were designed to make up for the loss of revenue that would result from the non-importation of British goods. Naval appropriations were slightly increased over 1810 but provided for no significant increment of strength. A bill to raise a military force of fifty thousand volunteers was allowed to die. Though nothing was done to prepare for war, there were men in the Eleventh Congress who expressed their growing exasperation at the old policy of peaceable coercion. Those advocating sterner measures, however, lacked effective leadership.

For a year after Jackson was pronounced *persona non grata*, the British cabinet did nothing about replacing him. Since they likewise did nothing looking toward a change of policy, in January, William Pinkney, who for five years had represented the United States ably and patiently at the Court of St. James, asked for an audience of leave. Lord Wellesley, the British foreign minister, not wishing a war with the United States let Pinkney know privately that a new minister would soon be sent to Washington. When Lord Wellesley was good enough to let the American representative know also that there would be no substantial change in policy, Pinkney left London on February 28, 1811. He was not replaced until after the war.

The new British representative to the United States, Augustus John Foster, was a young man of excellent political and social connections. He was authorized to settle the "Chesapeake" affair in a way to please the Americans, but to make no other major concessions. By the time Foster arrived the U.S. Navy had avenged the "Chesapeake" affair in its own way and the British minister only found new problems added to the old.

When the United States resumed trade with France under Macon's Bill No. 2, the British sent ships to hover off American harbors. Two of these vessels, the "Melampus" and "Guerrière" lay off New York in the spring of 1811, capturing American vessels and impressing seamen. On May 16 Commodore John Rodgers, commanding the frigate "President," sighted a vessel which he thought was the "Guerrière." Since he carried standing orders to protect American shipping from unlawful interferences, he approached the unidentified vessel, but it was dark before the ships were within hailing distance. After a confused exchange of hails the ships began firing. Who fired first, it is impossible to say. The British vessel turned out to be the "Little Belt," not a frigate at all but a corvette, rated at twenty guns. After an exchange lasting forty-five minutes the "Little Belt" ran away, but she was much damaged and thirty-two of her crew were killed or wounded. In reporting the encounter, both captains claimed to be innocent victims of aggression, and their partisans on both sides of the Atlantic took up the hue and cry. The "Little Belt" incident helped to prepare the psychology of war.

Hampered by instructions that left little leeway for negotiation and by the increased ill feeling that had been stirred up before his arrival in the United States, Foster accomplished nothing. Talks with both Madison and with Secretary of State Monroe went on during July, but they only convinced the Americans that the alternatives were submission or war. At the end of July President Madison withdrew from the heat of

Washington to vacation at Montpelier, but not before issuing a proclamation calling Congress into session in November instead of the usual December.

THE ROAD TO WAR

In the elections of 1810–11 nearly half of the incumbents lost their seats. Energetic candidates often denounced what they considered the do-nothing policies of past Congresses and promised a bold new approach to foreign policy. In some cases old men were replaced by young ones. But neither in the average age of its membership nor in the percentage of new members was the twelfth Congress especially different from other early Congresses. What distinguished the new Congress was the quality of its leadership.

One of the leading lights of the new take-over generation was Henry Clay. Born and educated in Virginia, Clay had moved to the West as a young man and had both drawn from and contributed to the vibrant, go-ahead spirit of that region. Though only thirty-four years old in 1811, he was no novice in politics. Schooled in the rough and tumble of the frontier, he had served parts of two terms in the Senate of the United States. Switching to the House, Clay was elected Speaker in his first term and proceeded immediately to make something of the office. Heretofore the Speaker had been merely a presiding officer; by appointments, patronage, and clever management Clay made it a position of true party leadership.

So incommodious was the capital city of the early nineteenth century that most congressmen did not subject their families to the inconveniences of its crude facilities. Instead they became bachelors for a portion of the year and lived in one or another of the city's numerous boardinghouses. Clay shared his quarters with a group that was described as "the stongest war mess in Congress." This group, and others of like mind, have gone down in history as the "war hawks." The term was coined by the Federalists, who wished to imply, of course, that their opponents were heedlessly and recklessly determined on war. Roger Brown, in his recent book, *Republic in Peril,* maintains that "no Republican ever really answered this description." He suggests furthermore that the phrase, "war hawks of 1812," be relegated "to the realm of partisan misunderstanding and historical mythology." The same author admits, however, that "men did wax belligerent, they did ignore or minimize the evils of war, and they did predict quick and easy victory." Through long usage the term has lost much of its original sting and it is used here as a matter of convenience to designate those Republicans who took a lead in advocating new and stronger measures that led ultimately to war.

In making his committee assignments, Clay made little effort to reflect the views of the minority party, the Federalists, or even the wide spectrum of views within his own party, the Republicans (Democrats of a later day). He boldly packed the most important committees with war hawks. Peter B. Porter, a Connecticut Yankee who had moved to the Niagara frontier and settled at Blackrock, near Buffalo, was made chairman of the Foreign Affairs Committee. He was to be assisted by twenty-nine-year-old John C. Calhoun, recently elected on a pro-war platform in South Carolina; Felix Grundy, an Anglophobe from a frontier settlement at Nashville, Tennessee; and John Adams Harper, a thirty-two-year-old firebrand from New Hampshire. The committee also included two moderate Republicans who generally went along with the majority, a sole Federalist, and John Randolph of Roanoke, an old-line Republican unalterably opposed to war. Other committee chairmanships included Langdon Cheves of the strongly pro-war delegation of South Carolina, Naval Affairs; David R. Williams of South Carolina, Military Affairs; and Ezekiel Bacon of Massachusetts, Ways and Means. Though some of these men, notably Williams and Porter, were to disappoint Clay, they were selected with the hope of carrying out a new departure.

The eagerly awaited message of the President must have been something of a disappointment to the most ardent spirits. True, the President rehearsed the catalogue of grievances that had been a part of annual messages since 1805 and added the additional ones of the past year, but his conclusion had a Delphic quality: "With this evidence of hostile inflexibility in tramping on rights which no independent nation can relinquish, Congress will feel the duty of putting the United States into an armor and an attitude demanded by the crisis, and corresponding with the national spirit and expectations." If the President's message was not exactly a clarion call, it did indicate a willingness to go along with stronger measures.

The necessities of the times as they were felt by the Committee on Foreign Relations were set forth on November 29. After reviewing Britain's misdeeds over the years, the report recommended bringing the army up to authorized strength, adding ten thousand regulars and fifty thousand volunteers, arming merchantmen, and outfitting existing warships. By December 19 every one of the committee's resolutions had been carried by comfortable majorities. The reasons for the heavy pro-war votes were various. A wing of the Federalists, led by Josiah Quincy, voted for the resolutions because they felt that war would be disastrous, would result in the repudiation of the

Republicans, and would put the Federalists in the position to make the peace. Many moderate Republicans voted for the resolutions in the hope of inducing a change in British policies. Their motive, in other words, was not to fight a war but to deter one, and it was in this hope that the "Hornet" was sent to Europe laden with the resolutions, the newspapers advocating war, and the record of the debates in Congress.

It was one thing to pass resolutions and quite another to make actual preparations. When the administration urged that the regular army be filled up to its authorized strength of ten thousand and that an additional force of ten thousand regulars be raised to serve for three years, the suggestion was met by some, including John Randolph, with the ancient arguments on the dangers of a standing army. Senator William B. Giles of Virginia, who harbored personal animosities against both Madison and Gallatin, followed a different tactic. On December 9 he introduced a bill that called for twenty-five thousand regulars to serve for five years. Giles's object was not to raise an army but to embarrass the administration. He knew that twenty-five thousand men could not be raised, and even if it were possible, the support of such an army was beyond the financial and administrative means of the country. The Federalists supported Giles, also in the hope of discrediting the administration. But the war hawks called their bluff, voted for the bill, and it became law on January 9. The size of the army on paper was therefore increased to thirty-five thousand men.

After dealing with the regular army to its satisfaction, the House considered a bill authorizing the President to accept fifty thousand volunteers, to be officered by state authorities, and called into service by the President when needed. Immediately the question arose whether the President had the authority under the Constitution to send the militia outside the boundaries of the United States. Even some of the most ardent war hawks argued that he could not. It was decided finally to omit mention of the question, and the bill was approved on February 6, 1812. Having raised the constitutional problem and failed to resolve it, Congress accentuated an inherent weakness of the military system of the United States

Congress gave only partial support to Madison in his efforts to improve army administration. The War Department consisted of the Secretary and a chief clerk who had under him several other clerks engaged in such routine business as the allowance of military pensions, military bounty lands, and Indian trade. Under Republican rule no provision had been made for staff officers and the Secretary corresponded directly with the commanders of the various army garrisons and detachments. The commanders in turn looked after the feeding, clothing, and housing of their troops. In other words the Secretary had no professional advisers, either civil or military. President Madison, in April, 1812, attempted partly to remedy the situation by asking Congress to provide the War Department with two assistant secretaries. Nothing came of the suggestion. Congress, however, did approve the establishment of a civilian Commissary-General of Purchases and a Quartermaster Department which had the responsibility of procuring and purchasing all military stores and articles of supply, camp equipage, and transport. An Ordnance Department, established in May, had the function of inspecting and testing all ordnance, cannon balls, "public powder," and the like.

The navy received even less consideration than the army. Langdon Cheves brought in a bill for the construction of twelve ships of the line and twenty frigates. Despite all their talk of maritime rights, a majority of Republicans were still unwilling to support a navy. Even some of the most ardent war hawks argued that since a relatively small American navy could not hope to challenge Britain's supremacy on the seas, naval appropriations were useless. In vain did Henry Clay argue that the navy could defend New Orleans through which the produce of the west must pass to market. The navy bill was defeated by a vote of 62 to 59.

Senator James A. Bayard, a guileless Federalist from Delaware, said of the war hawks: "I shall consider the taxes as the test, and when a majority agree to the proposed taxes, I shall believe them in earnest and determined upon war." The test came in February, 1812, when Ezekiel Bacon introduced a series of resolutions that called for doubling of import duties, for laying a direct tax of $3 million on the states, and for the levying of excise taxes. After much debate Congress passed the resolutions, but the taxes were to go into effect only if war was declared and were to be continued no longer than one year after the return of peace.

From one point of view, the war measures were woefully inadequate either as deterrents of war or as genuine preparation for fighting. From another point of view Clay and his followers had accomplished a great deal since Congress met in November: they had forced the abandonment of peaceable coercion and had laid the groundwork for a policy backed by force. Though many Republicans had voted for measures short of war in the belief that they were preserving their freedom of action, retreat now would be difficult if not impossible.

During these months President Madison's leadership was hesitant and uncertain. The old story that Clay and his associates finally brought the President around to their point of view as the price for their support of his re-election in 1812 is not true. Probably Madison made up his mind that there was only war or submission in the summer of 1811 after he found that Foster had nothing new to offer. Still he was unwilling to take a strong pro-war stand. This was partly owing to his Republican scruples—the Constitution left the war-making power to Congress. But also Madison seems to have clung to the hope that some development would make war unnecessary. "Our President though a man of amiable manners and great talents," said Calhoun, "has not I fear those commanding talents, which are necessary to control those around him . . . He reluctantly gives up the system of peace."

Constantly prodding the administration, in March Clay suggested a thirty-day embargo to be followed by a declaration of war. Secretary of State Monroe went to the Hill to confer with the Foreign Affairs Committee. He informed them that he still considered the country ill prepared and that the war legislation was largely "an appeal to the feelings of foreign governments." Though he did not oppose the embargo, he suggested it be extended to sixty days in order to allow time for the "Hornet" to return with news of European developments. In the Senate the embargo was extended to ninety days and went into effect April 4. One of the last excuses for delay was removed when the "Hornet" returned on May 22. The vessel brought supplementary instructions to Foster, but they merely repeated what the British had said time and again before: obviously the French had not repealed their decrees and "America can never be justified in continuing to resent against Us that failure of Relief, which is alone attributable to the insidious Policy of the Enemy." Faced with what seemed to be final refusal of any concession, Madison began composing his war message.

Before the die was finally cast, there were various last-minute developments that threatened to divert the Republicans from their course. In the spring of 1812 Napoleon stepped up his war against American trade by seizing a large number of ships principally engaged in the grain trade with the Iberian Peninsula. Often the ships were burned at sea and the crews thrown into French jails. For years the Federalists had charged that the Republicans were sycophants of Napoleon. To remove the imputation, a few Republicans advocated what was sometimes called a triangular war with both Great Britain and France. Some who opposed war took this stance also in order to expose the whole movement as an absurdity. Responsible Republican leaders admitted that ample cause for war with France existed, but they pointed out also the sheer lunacy of trying to fight the whole of Europe. Great Britain's provocations took precedence and the United States should deal with one enemy at a time. "We resist the enterprises of England first," explained Jefferson, "because they first come vitally home to us."

President Madison submitted his war message on June 1. Reviewing Anglo-American relations since 1803 in roughly chronological order, the document was an indictment of British policy under five main heads. First was impressment. Madison has been criticized by Henry Adams on the ground that "this was the first time that the Government had alleged impressment as its chief grievance, or had announced, either to England or America, the intention to fight for redress." The President put impressment first, not because he necessarily thought it was the chief grievance, but because it was the oldest. It is true that the United States did not press the point in negotiations just before the war. But relative silence was the result of a conviction that it was hopeless to pursue the issue rather than indifference toward it. Furthermore, American consular agents had carried on a steady correspondence with the Admiralty about the matter and the practice had by no means abated. It has been conservatively estimated that from 750 to 1,000 men were taken every year from 1809 onward. Next in Madison's catalogue was the practice of British cruisers hovering near American ports and harassing entering and departing commerce. Third were the blockades that were, said Madison, illegal even according to definitions issued by the British themselves.

Fourth were the Orders-in-Council. Assuming the purpose of the message was to arouse sympathy in Britain and indignation at home, it was here that Madison made his most telling point. It has become certain, Madison charged, "that the commerce of the United States is to be sacrificed, not as interfering with the belligerent rights of Great Britain; not as supplying the wants of her enemies, which she herself supplies; but as interfering with the monopoly which she covets for her own commerce and navigation." Though the charge may seem extreme, Madison was saying no more than some Englishmen were saying themselves. George Canning, a staunch adherent of strict blockades, charged in Parliament that the Orders-in-Council had been transformed from a blockade into "a measure of commercial rivalry." This had been done through the use and the abuse of a system of special licenses. The Board of Trade had the power to issue licenses exempting ships and cargoes from the effects of the blockade. It is not difficult to see that the interests of the empire might be well served by a judicious use of such power. The issue of licenses, however, became honeycombed with favoritism, corruption, and fraud. Many an Englishman who would have supported his government to the death on impressments and legitimate blockades blushed at the traffic in special licenses.

Madison's fifth, and only non-maritime grievance, referred to the renewal of Indian warfare on the western frontier. No specific charge was made, but the President found it difficult to believe that the latest uprisings were unconnected with British officers and agents in Canada whose past activities among the Indians were well known.

The House passed a bill on June 4 declaring war by a vote of 79 to 49. On June 17 the Senate passed the declaration by a vote of 19 to 13 and the President signed it the next day.

In a war filled with irony, nothing was more ironical than the timing of the declaration. From April to June the British, who had remained adamant for nearly a decade, moved toward conciliation, while the Americans, who though they had been patient under extreme provocation, hastened toward war. Since 1807 England had been ruled by the Tories and since 1809 Spencer Perceval had been Prime Minister. Under Perceval the war against Napoleon had been prosecuted vigorously and, in general, the shipping interest had been favored over manufacturing. Beginning in 1810 a depression hit the manufacturing areas of the British Isles, and Parliament was soon besieged with petitions for repeal of the Orders-in-Council. On April 21, 1812, the British government announced that if France would publish an official repeal of her decrees, the cabinet would withdraw the Orders-in-Council. The Duke of Bassano, Cadore's successor, responded by handing the United

States minister to France, Joel Barlow, a paper that came to be known as the Decree of St. Cloud. Dated April 28, 1811, the document was supposedly an official revocation of the Berlin and Milan Decrees. No one had seen or heard of the document before but the French minister maintained it had been in effect for a year. Soon after this strange piece of paper crossed the channel, on May 11, Spencer Perceval was assassinated by a lunatic. After a cabinet crisis lasting nearly a month, Lord Liverpool agreed to form a new government from the remnants of the old. The new government did not want to be burdened with the Orders-in-Council. They knew Napoleon's St. Cloud Decree was a forgery, but since it suited their purpose they accepted it as evidence of genuine repeal. On June 23 the Orders-in-Council were, with certain conditions, revoked.

The repeal of the Orders-in-Council is often regarded as a belated triumph for economic coercion. Such was the case only to a limited extent. A depression, resulting primarily from the loss of the European market, began in 1810, at a time when American restrictions had been lifted under Macon's Bill; it continued and probably was aggravated by the reimposition of American non-importation in March, 1811. Fearing a permanent loss of trade through the growth of American manufactures, the British merchants brought pressure for repeal. If non-importation had only limited effect in inducing a change of British policy, American military preparations had even less. The threat of war simply was not believed. In February, 1812, a consular agent in London reported to Washington that the general opinion was, ". . . we do not mean to go to war, notwithstanding all our preparation; and the idea of our taking Canada is laughed at."

Prologue to War

THE PROBLEM OF CAUSATION

For nearly a hundred years after the outbreak of the War of 1812, American historians took Madison's message more or less at face value. That the war was brought on by Great Britain's impressment of American seamen and her Orders-in-Council seemed self-evident. With the rise of a more critical and professional generation of historians near the end of the nineteenth century, the causes were probed more deeply. For one thing, the nature of the vote on war began to be examined critically. Why should a war for maritime rights be opposed by the Northeast whose rights were allegedly being ignored, and supported by the South and West which had neither ships nor sailors?

During the course of the debate on the war, John Randolph accused his opponents of a variety of base motives. Among other things he charged: "Agrarian cupidity, not maritime right, urges the war." Louis M. Hacker, in an article published in 1924, took up the hint thrown out by Randolph. Pointing out that American agriculture was terribly exploitative, he maintained that by 1812 most of the good lands in the Old Northwest, with the exception of the prairies, were exhausted. Since the prairies at that time were considered unfit for cultivation, the land-hungry farmers wanted the good lands of Canada. This thesis was soon attacked by Julius W. Pratt, who showed that there were still plenty of good agricultural lands left, exclusive of the prairies. Though agreeing that western aims were important, Pratt felt there was a better foundation on which to base the case.

The true picture of western aims, as Pratt saw them, was set forth in his book, *The Expansionists of 1812*, published in

1925. Pratt states that war was declared as a result of a sectional bargain between the South and the West. A general desire to annex Canada had existed since the War for Independence, and this desire became strongly activated with the outbreak of Indian unrest all along the western border in 1811. "The rise of Tecumseh, backed, as was universally believed, by the British, produced an urgent demand in the Northwest that the British be expelled from Canada. This demand was of primary importance in bringing on the war." The South was indifferent about Canada but wished to annex Florida for a variety of strategic and economic reasons. By linking Canada and Florida together in a general program of expansion that would maintain a rough equilibrium in the sectional balance, enough votes were mustered for war.

Based on much original research and written with great clarity and perception, Pratt's book was, and is, widely influential. Although he was careful to say that he was dealing with one set of causes only (western aims), his explanation has often been accepted as the whole story. Before Pratt's book the western aims were sometimes noted as contributing causes; after his book was published, they were often accepted as the main, and sometimes as the only, real causes.

Emphasis on western factors soon received further confirmation from another source. In 1931 George R. Taylor published two articles on prices and economic conditions in the Mississippi Valley in the period just prior to the war. Agreeing with Pratt that the Indian menace was a contributing cause, he pointed out that this matter was of concern to only restricted areas of the West. The whole area, on the other hand, was affected by agricultural prices. Taylor showed that prices had declined in the period before the war and that a general economic depression had hit the whole area. Hitherto it had been assumed that westerners had talked about maritime rights and national honor only to shield their expansionist ambitions. Taylor showed the real connection between western problems and maritime rights. Though the westerners were not sailors and did not own ships, they produced goods that were carried in ships. And though the real causes of economic distress lay primarily within the area, the western farmers and planters blamed British restrictions on neutral commerce for their ills and eventually supported a war to obtain relief.

The timely addition of economic motives in the early thirties immensely strengthened the position of what we might call the western school of causation. Though they differed greatly among themselves, their case now rested on four legs: land hunger, the Indian menace, northern and southern expansionism, and economic depression. For several years the western school gained ground steadily and almost succeeded in ousting the old school of maritime grievances. But just when victory seemed complete, a reaction set in. In recent years the pendulum has been swinging back in favor of maritime causes. In 1941 Warren H. Goodman published an article in the *Mississippi Valley Historical Review* which, after reviewing various interpretations that had been offered down to that time, concluded: "One can no longer doubt that nineteenth century writers overestimated the significance of maritime matters, but contemporary historians are perhaps committing an equally serious error in the opposite direction." He maintained that there was need for a comprehensive account, based on sources, to synthesize the various sets of causes.

The defect of which Goodman complained was soon remedied. A comprehensive survey had in fact already been completed but was probably unavailable at the time Goodman completed his study. In 1940 A. L. Burt published a book entitled *The United States, Great Britain, and British North America from the Revolution to the Establishment of Peace after the War of 1812.* Burt was probably more familiar with the documentary record on both sides of the controversy than any writer since Henry Adams. After tracing the many complicated threads of the story of Anglo-American relations, he examined the Pratt thesis in some detail and concluded by rejecting it outright. Swinging back to maritime grievances, he found the real causes of the war in the cumulative frustration of the American government.

The path hewn by Burt was followed by Reginald Horsman, who in *Causes of the War of 1812*, published in 1962, evaluated both sets of causes. Horsman develops in detail an idea merely suggested by Burt, that in the plans of the war hawks Canada was to be seized as a hostage rather than a prize. While rejecting Pratt's thesis of a sectional bargain on expansionism, he accepts western concern over the Indian problem and depression as contributing causes. The fundamental cause, however, was the British maritime policy which hurt both national pride and the commerce of the United States.

The economic arguments, originally put forth by Taylor and generally accepted by Horsman, received further confirmation in an article by Margaret Kinard Lattimer, which appeared in 1956. Using the same concepts that Taylor had applied to the Mississippi Valley, Miss Lattimer found that the South too was suffering from declining prices and general depression. Pointing out that South Carolina was even more directly dependent on the European trade than the West, she concluded that "whether or not fighting a war with England was the logical step, the South Carolinians of 1812 were convinced that a war would help."

The Taylor-Lattimer thesis remained unchallenged until 1961, when Norman K. Risjord published his article "Conservatism, War Hawks, and the Nation's Honor." Taking a look at the Middle Atlantic states, Risjord found no economic depression. The prices of beef, corn, and flour, the main exports of the Middle Atlantic states, increased over the decade preceding the war, while the price of pork declined only slightly. Risjord maintained that Pennsylvania, which in the House voted 16 to 2 for war with Great Britain, could hardly have been following the dictates of economic interest. "The only unifying factor, present in all sections of the country," he concluded, "was the growing feeling of patriotism, the realization that something must be done to vindicate the national honor."

The swing back to maritime grievances and national honor was given another massive push in 1961 by the appearance of a thick volume by Bradford Perkins entitled *Prologue to War.* Henry Adams, A. L. Burt, and Reginald Horsman had all made use of British as well as American sources. Perkins, however, went beyond any of his predecessors or contemporaries in searching out archival and manuscript collections on both sides of the Atlantic. Though he attempts to deal with the whole problem of causation, the great bulk of Perkins' book is devoted to a re-examination of diplomatic relations with Great Britain. To a greater extent than other American historians, Perkins examines internal politics in England in the decade before the war. His general conclusion is: "While the policy of England was far less rigid than Americans often suggested, the self-righteous spirit of messianism engendered by the Napoleonic wars and a woeful underestimation of the price of American good will combined to prevent a reconciliation Jefferson and Madison eagerly desired." Although he blames British statesmen to a degree, Perkins blames American statesmen even more: ". . . the Republican chieftains must bear primary responsibility for the war. . . . Whereas Washington and Adams kept objectives and means in harmony with one another, their successors often committed the United States to seek absolute right with inadequate weapons. . . . In a state of military and psychological unpreparedness, the United States of America embarked upon a war to recover the self respect destroyed by Republican leaders."

In his *Republic in Peril*, Roger Brown attempts to do for the War of 1812 what Abraham Lincoln did for the Civil War: define the issues on the highest possible ideological plane. He emphasizes the concern for the survival of republican government, or what Madison once called "the last and fairest experiment in favor of the rights of human nature." Making no attempt to follow either the diplomatic developments or the story of internal developments in any detail, Brown makes an exhaustive study of both the public and private utterances of those leaders who supported war and those who opposed it. While not denying that other causes existed, he believes the concern for the republican experiment and the agent of its propagation, the Republican party, were the paramount motives of those advocating war.

Both Brown and Perkins, as well as other historians who question the emphasis on western aims, feel that the sectional character of the vote for war has been overemphasized. While admitting that the South and West gave nearly solid support, they maintain that these sections could not have provided enough votes for war without help that came liberally from the Middle Atlantic states and, to a much less extent, from the northeast. These historians claim that more important than sectional or geographical considerations was the influence of party loyalty. All the Federalists–31 from the Northern and Middle Atlantic states and 9 from the South (and these from the inland rather than the coastal areas)–voted against war. They were joined by 22 Republicans (18 from the northern and middle states) who bolted the party.

What then is the present status of the various explanations that have been advanced? Obviously the war came not as a result of any one cause but the interplay of several. In exploring various avenues historians have not been guilty of hair-splitting. The declaration was carried by a narrow margin and the alteration of even one factor in a complicated equation might have affected the outcome significantly. Historians are justified therefore in investigating the large number of factors entering into the picture, even though it may sometimes seem that their researches complicate rather than clarify the picture. Both sets of causes, the maritime grievances and the internal factors, are necessary to explain the coming of the war, but recent historians are right to give primary weight to the maritime factors.

Though of less importance in the total picture, the internal factors are more difficult to evaluate. Since the land-hunger thesis has not been sustained by recent investigations, it can be dismissed as of little substance. The Indian menace was certainly a factor in the minds of many westerners, but those areas most directly concerned, namely, Mississippi, Indiana, Illinois, and Michigan, were still territories and had no vote in Congress. Economic depression was of more general concern than the Indian problem, but even this factor was operative primarily in the West and South.

Expansionism still has its advocates, but Burt, Horsman, Perkins, and most recently Brown have all rejected the idea of a sectional conspiracy to enlarge the boundaries of the United States. Among these historians there is a consensus that the war hawks were interested in Canada primarily as a means of waging war rather than an object of war. This is not to deny, of course, that what was originally a means could not easily have become an object of war. To use a modern expression, a war to win recognition of maritime rights by seizing a hostage could easily have escalated into a war for maritime rights *and* territorial conquest. It cannot be denied, furthermore, that certain members of Congress wanted both Canada and Florida, and it is possible that they voted for war hoping to get one or both. But Brown maintains, and his conclusions seem borne out by recent research, that "Republicans were willing to give their votes for war even without assurance that either Canada or Florida would ever be annexed. In the face of many obstacles it is doubtful that anyone voted for war primarily on the basis of a future annexation of these areas."

A variety of factors, then, combined to induce a majority of Republicans to vote for war. More than anything else they had become convinced that every alternative had been tried and failed. One often reads in textbooks that the United States "blundered" into war. The declaration may have been a mistake, but certainly the decision was thoroughly debated and few governments have sought alternatives so eagerly and for such a long time. Beginning in 1807, diplomatic negotiation, economic coercion, and military preparations to deter war had all been tried without the slightest success so far as anyone could see at the time. In 1812 Jefferson summed up the views of many when he said: "Every hope from time, patience, and love of peace is exhausted and war or abject submission are the only alternatives left to us." Forced to abandon old policies, the Republicans naturally invoked those symbols that had wide appeal, phrases such as national character, honor, and the world's last and fairest hope of government by the people.

Though some Federalists professed to believe that the Republicans had never genuinely sought peace, others admitted that ample cause for war existed. Daniel Sheffey, a Federalist from the Valley of Virginia, acknowledged that there were ample causes but wanted to know how war would remedy the situation. "I must be persuaded," he said, "that there is a national hope that war will remedy the evil which we experience." Instead of freeing Americans from impressment and liberating trade, war, he feared, was far more likely to bring additional human suffering and greater financial loss. Abstract notions of honor were valuable in private life, but they "ought not to be a rule of action for wise men to whom are committed the affairs of nations—otherwise we might wage perpetual war." According to Sheffey the real cause of trouble lay in the deranged state of the European world. It appeared vain to expect the world to make itself over to conform to what the United States considered proper. There were some things the United States could not change; ". . . we must participate in the evils (in some shape) which have fallen on the community of civilized man," he concluded.

Mr. Sheffey spoke with much wisdom but his words went unheeded. They went unheeded partly because the war hawks had convinced themselves that the state of the European world, far from being hopeless, presented an opportunity for the United States to advance its own interests. Since November, 1811, the war hawks had maintained that although England was one of the most powerful nations in the world, she was doubly vulnerable. Her first vulnerability was the province of Canada. Guarded by only a handful of British regulars, the thin settlements stretched along a single line of communications which for hundreds of miles ran adjacent to the border of the United States. Bending every resource to maintain an army on the Continent, Great Britain could spare little for the reinforcement of Canada and, if the United States acted with proper dispatch, that little would come too late.

Britain's second great vulnerability was her world-wide trade and especially her ships moving men and supplies to the Iberian Peninsula. This vast sea-borne traffic could be harried by privateers, armed merchant vessels, and the navy. To carry out commerce destruction most effectively the United States needed the use of friendly European ports. And here is another important reason why many Republicans opposed a triangular war. William Jones, who later became Secretary of the Navy, said that if the United States declared war on France, "we greatly impair our means of annoying G. Britain by excluding our flag and our prizes of commerce from the continent of Europe from whence we could more effectually annoy commerce & coasting trade than all the maratime [*sic*] forces of combined Europe." Lawrence Kaplan, in a recent article, summarizes Republican thinking as follows: "France, one of the belligerents which caused America so much misery in peacetime, could be the instrument of the United States in redressing the score in wartime. The French diplomatic counterweight, French bases on the Channel and on the Atlantic, French armies in Spain and in Russia were all part of Republican military calculations in 1812. France would thus facilitate the waging of a successful offensive against Britain, with the prospects of a quick and painless victory." This statement does not imply that the United States deliberately timed its declaration to coincide with Napoleon's invasion of Russia or that the United States entered the war as an ally of France. While the administration wished to use France to advantage, they had no wish to make common cause. Federalist charges that Madison and Monroe were sold to France were utterly without foundation. Considering herself morally superior not only to France but to all of Europe, the United States neither sought nor wanted an alliance. In his *Weekly Register* Hezekiah Niles expressed the hope that the war would finally separate the United States "from the strumpet governments of Europe."

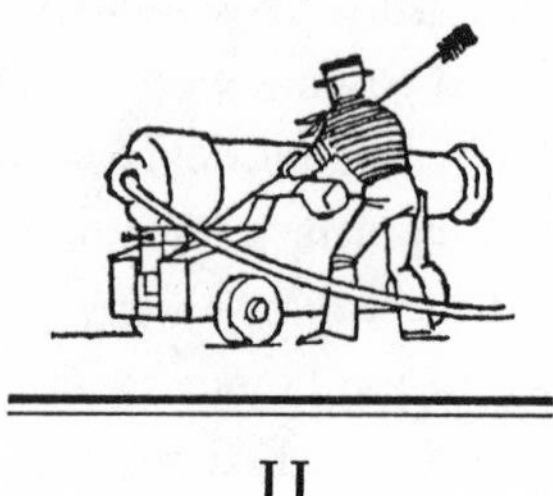

II

Brock and the Defense of Canada

The breezily optimistic statements of some Americans asserting that the taking of Canada would be a mere matter of marching have often been held up to ridicule. Yet there were good reasons for thinking that Canada was vulnerable. At the time war was declared, Napoleon was at or near the zenith of his power and the long struggle with France had drained Britain of men and treasure. Little could be spared for North America. The extensive Canadian provinces were sparsely settled and of uneven loyalty. The United States had a white population of at least six million while Canada had only half a million. By far the most populous section was Lower Canada, which included the cities of Quebec and Montreal. Two-thirds of the people of this province were of French descent and, in the minds of British officials as well as the American war hawks, their willingness to fight for their British king was an uncertain quantity. Upper Canada (now Ontario) had a population of less than one hundred thousand of whom possibly one third were American in origin and sympathies. Strong pro-British sentiments were to be found only in those areas settled by British immigrants and the United Empire Loyalists, that is, along the upper St. Lawrence, the Bay of Quinte, and the Niagara peninsula.

The Canadian frontier stretched 800 or 900 miles between Quebec and the western end of Lake Erie where Fort Malden (Amherstburg) was located. From Amherstburg to St. Joseph's Island, at the lower end of the strait from Lake Superior to Lake Huron, was another 300 miles. To guard this immense area there were four types of forces: the British Regulars, the Canadian Regulars, the militia, and the Indian allies. Four regiments of the line, the 8th, 41st, 49th, the 100th Foot, and the 10th Royal Battalion, totaled about 4,000 troops. Local troops classed as regulars were the Canadian Fencibles, the Canadian Voltigeurs, the Royal Newfoundland Regiment, the New Brunswick Regiment, and the Glengarry Light Infantry. The militia system of Canada, like that of the United States, created a huge army on paper. The Sedentary Militia was simply a manpower pool composed of all able-bodied citizens between sixteen and sixty. From this was drawn the Embodied Militia which was composed of volunteers or men picked by lot. The Embodied Militia, which received some training, could be called into active service in times of emergency. On the eve of conflict the governor of Upper Canada reported that the militia of Upper St. Lawrence Valley was "the most respectable of any in the province," but elsewhere it was weak in numbers and wanting in enthusiasm. The Indians both within the boundaries of Canada and many from the northwestern part of the

United States either remained neutral or were willing to fight for the British. They were by no means a negligible force, but in general the British officers considered them unreliable. Main reliance must be placed on about 7,000 British and Canadian regulars, of whom less than 1,700 were in Upper Canada in 1812.

The governmental organization was reasonably well suited to geographical, religious, and political conditions. British North America was divided into four provinces, New Brunswick, Nova Scotia, Lower Canada, and Upper Canada, each with its own representative assembly and each with its lieutenant governor appointed by the Crown. During most of the war the governor of Lower Canada was Lieutenant General Sir George Prevost, who also held the title of Governor in Chief and Commander in Chief of All Provinces. Sir George's immediate superior in England was the Secretary of State for War and Colonies, Lord Bathurst. In practice the authority of Prevost seems seldom to have extended beyond Lower and Upper Canada. Since the Maritime colonies were geographically remote and sparsely settled, and since they had different local problems the lieutenant governors generally corresponded directly with England. The naval base at Halifax was one of the most important in North America, the Maritimes furnished some reinforcements of regular troops after the first invasions, and they served as a base for the invasion of Maine in 1814. Otherwise these provinces played only a minor role in the war.

General Prevost and the governor of Upper Canada, Major General Isaac Brock, were both men of experience. Entering the British army in 1783 Prevost had served in various posts and with some distinction as civil governor of St. Lucia in the

West Indies. He came to Canada in 1808 as lieutenant governor of Nova Scotia and in 1811 was advanced to Governor in Chief of the Canadas. Of Swiss lineage, he spoke French fluently and his appointment seems to have been motivated by the British government's desire to improve relations with the French-Canadian population. Brock was born on the island of Guernsey in 1769. Coming from a family that had contributed several distinguished men to the army and navy, he had served with the 8th (King's) Regiment and later with the 49th. Ordered to Canada in 1802 he became a major general in 1811 and was appointed administrator of Upper Canada. Concerning the best means of defending Canada, Prevost and Brock had different ideas.

Recognizing the weaknesses of his position Prevost warned Brock on July 10, 1812:

> Our numbers would not justify offensive operations being undertaken, unless these were solely calculated to strengthen a defensive attitude. I consider it prudent and politic to avoid any measure which can in its effect have a tendency to unite the people in the American States. Whilst disunion prevails among them, their attempts on these provinces will be feeble; it is, therefore, our duty carefully to avoid committing any act which may, even by construction, tend to unite the eastern and southern states, unless, by its perpetration, we are to derive a considerable and important advantage.

Prevost issued these words of caution because he knew very well that Brock held different views. Soon after reading President Madison's warlike message of November, 1811, Brock had informed Prevost what should be done to prepare for war with the United States. With the sure instincts of a born soldier, he identified the essential elements of the strategic situation: naval control of the lakes, the role of the Indians ar·

militia, and the problem of supply. The key to these interrelated problems, Brock believed, lay in the district of Amherstburg. Neither the militia nor the Indians were reliable, but by immediately assuming the offensive the energy of both might be aroused. If either got the impression that they would be left to their fate, they would make no effort at defense. With Amherstburg as a base, it was necessary therefore to strike immediately at Detroit and Michilimakinac. From Amherstburg to Fort Erie the chief reliance must be on naval force. "But considering the state to which it is reduced, extraordinary exertions and great expense will be required before it can be rendered efficient." The main attack, Brock predicted, would fall along the strait between Niagara and Fort Erie. "All other attacks will be subordinate, or merely made to divert our attention." Here he recommended a strong defensive. "A protracted resistance upon this Frontier will be sure to embarrass their plans materially. They will not come prepared to meet it, and their troops, or Volunteer Corps, without scarcely any discipline will soon tire under disappointment. The difficulty which they will experience in providing provisions, will involve them into expenses under which their Government will soon become impatient." Finally, Brock pointed out, "The situation at Kingston is so very important in every military point of view, that I cannot be too earnest in drawing Your Excellency's attention to that quarter. . . ." With Prevost advocating strictly defensive measures and Brock anxious to assume limited offensives, divided councils could have led to disaster. But distances were so great and communication so slow that for the first four months of the war Brock was free to put his own ideas into operation. If there was little help from Prevost, there was also little hindrance.

In contrast to the plans worked out by Brock, the American government had only the rudiments of a strategy. The problem of taking Canada has often been compared to the hewing of a tree. The tap roots of this tree were the sea lanes running back to England, the trunk the main settlements along the St. Lawrence Valley, particularly Quebec and Montreal, and the branches the scattered settlements in upper Canada along the lakes and streams running into the lakes. The roots were vulnerable to a degree but Britain's seapower insured her overseas communication. The best strategy would have been to concentrate on severing the trunk as near the roots as possible. Since Canada depended upon a single long line of communications the taking of Montreal or even Kingston would have assured the fall of all that lay above these points.

President Madison favored striking with full force against Montreal and "thus at one stroke have secured the upper province, and cut off the sap that nourished Indian hostilities." But there were practical difficulties that prevented the maximum concentration of effort on a single objective. Despite the fact that Congress had increased the authorized strength of the regular army to 35,000, only about 11,700 men (including 5,000 recent recruits) were actually enlisted when war was declared. These troops were widely scattered throughout the country in various posts. The only way to take Montreal quickly was to employ the New England militia, which was the best in the country. Under the Constitution the militia can be called into the service of the national government to execute the laws of the United States, to suppress insurrection, and to repel invasion. When, on April 15, President Madison called for troops from Massachusetts Caleb Strong replied that he, as governor of the state, rather than the President, had the right to decide when the constitutional exigencies actually existed. Since he apprehended no invasion the governor refused the requisition except for three companies of militia sent to Passamaquoddy on the Canadian border. Connecticut took a similar view and would furnish nothing. With the strength of the nation thus divided something less than an ideal strategy had to be adopted. Not wishing to lose "the unanimity and ardor of Kentucky and Ohio," the President attempted to put into operation a plan suggested by Senior Major General Henry Dearborn which called for a move against Montreal (hopefully still the main thrust) with secondary offensives from Detroit, Niagara, and Sackett's Harbor.

General William Hull, who was governor of the Michigan Territory and who had allowed himself to be appointed commander of the Northwest Army against his better judgment, had ideas on strategy, some of which were quite sound. Like Brock, he was aware of the importance of the role of the Indians and the control of the lakes. In the event of war, he predicted, the British would move against Detroit and Michilimackinac, "with the view to obtain the assistance of the Indians and in the present state of defences in the Northwest country it would be within their power to do it." In fact, Hull estimated British strength in the Detroit area as ten times greater than that of the United States. Concerning control of the lakes he said: "I have always been of the opinion that we ought to have built as many armed vessels on the Lakes as would have commanded them." In spite of this gloomy analysis of British capabilities, Hull came to the amazing conclusion that "a force adequate to the defence of that vulnerable point (Detroit), would prevent a war with the savages and probably induce the enemy to abandon Upper Canada without opposition—and we should obtain the command of the waters without the expense of building such a force."

OPERATIONS IN THE NORTHWEST

Wavering between optimism and pessimism, General Hull arrived in Dayton in April to take command of the army. A month earlier Governor Return Jonathan Meigs had issued a call for twelve hundred volunteers and the response had been most gratifying. The troops, organized into three regiments under Colonels Duncan McArthur, James Findlay, and Lewis Cass, gathered for a grand review and the usual speech-making before plunging into the forest. The governor spoke first and was followed by the general. An eyewitness described General Hull as a "short, corpulent, good natured old gentleman, who bore the marks of good eating and drinking." The delivery of his speech, however, "animated every breast, and great expectations were formed of his prowess and abilities. . . . The frost of time had given him a venerable aspect, and the idea of his revolutionary services inspired the troops with confidence."

In 1812 there was no easy or well-defined route from southwestern Ohio to Detroit. The most direct path would have led into the Black Swamp, a morass formed by the Maumee River and covering extensive parts of the now fertile lands of Sandusky, Henry, and Wood counties. The first thought of the frontier army was to swing westward to avoid the Black Swamp and make maximum use of water transportation. With this idea the army marched first to Staunton, where it was informed that the streams in that part of the country were unnavigable because of drought. The army then shifted east to Urbana where they were joined by the Fourth U.S. Infantry, veterans of the Battle of Tippecanoe, commanded by Lieutenant Colonel James Miller of the Regular Army. The four regiments now under Hull's command marched from Urbana to the Maumee approximately along what is now Route 68. To move through this area of forest and then swamp it was necessary to lay down a trail. Experienced guides went ahead marking out the route by blazing trees with tomahawks. Soldiers of Colonel McArthur's regiment followed with axes, spades, and shovels. They did their work so well that a clean slice through the forest could be detected in some sections as late as the Civil War. By June 16 a trail was opened as far as the present site of Kenton, and a blockhouse named Fort McArthur was constructed.

After the whole army arrived at Fort McArthur, Colonel Findlay's regiment was ordered forward on June 21 to lay down the road. The next day it begain to rain, mildly at first, and then with increasing intensity for several days. Wagons became mired in a sea of mud, and to add to the discomfort of man and beast, black flies and mosquitoes descended. A stockade, not inappropriately called "Fort Necessity," was built. But the chief characteristic of the weather in Ohio is that whatever it is, it will soon change. The rains ceased, the weather improved, and three days after leaving Fort Necessity the army was at Fort Findlay. Colonel Cass was now sent forward to cut a road to the Rapids of the Maumee, which the main army reached by the end of June.

Arriving at the Maumee, Hull found what seemed like a godsend, the schooner "Cuyahoga." Supposing that this was an opportunity to rid himself of impedimenta and hasten his march to Detroit, Hull hired the vessel to carry much of his baggage, medical supplies—and most important—a trunk filled with confidential military papers. Since he knew that the British controlled Lake Erie and that the American vessel would have to pass under the guns of Fort Malden, this was a foolish move. True, he had not been formally notified of the declaration of war of June 18, but having spent several weeks in Washington the previous spring he was familiar with the drift of events and could not have supposed he was leading an army of over two thousand men on a peaceful exercise. It was not until July 2, when he reached Frenchtown on the River Raisin (now the city of Monroe, Michigan), that he received official notice of the declaration of war, four days after the British had been alerted. The Secretary of War had sent the important news by ordinary mail to Cleveland where the postmaster forwarded it by special messenger. On July 2 the British captured the "Cuyahoga" with its valuable supplies and papers.

Reaching Detroit on July 5, Hull prepared to cross over into Canada. McArthur's regiment was sent to Spring Wells to decoy the British from Detroit, while on the morning of July 12 the regiments of James Miller and Lewis Cass crossed the river near Hog Island and occupied Sandwich without opposition. On the same day Hull issued a proclamation promising the people of Canada protection in their persons, property, and rights, and advising them either to remain at home or to come over to the American side. Any white man found fighting beside an Indian, the proclamation warned, would not be treated as a prisoner but would be subject to instant death. Hull's proclamation has often been held up to ridicule by United States historians. Canadian sources show that it was not without considerable effect. The proclamation found its way into the hands of Governor-General Prevost who passed it on to Lord Liverpool in London with the comment that it had "already been productive of considerable effect on the minds of the people." Prevost did not exaggerate: the Canadian militia were deserting in considerable numbers, some to return home and guard their families and crops, others to join the Americans at Sandwich. Four or five hundred Canadians are believed to have joined the Americans.

For several days, in fact, the tide seemed to be running entirely in favor of the Americans. By fortifying his position at Sandwich with breastworks of three sides and artillery along the river, Hull made his position safe from all but a general attack. He improved his supply situation by sending out extensive foraging expeditions which brought in large quantities of flour, blankets, whiskey, and hundreds of sheep and cattle. On July 19 Hull wrote exultantly to the Secretary of War that the Canadian militia were deserting and that preparations were being made for an attack on Malden. This was his last optimistic report.

Already there had occurred an incident that augured ill for the American expedition. On July 16 Colonel Cass, reconnoitering the British position, found a bridge over the river Aux Canards, about four miles above Fort Malden, guarded by only about fifty men. Cass seized the bridge, captured two prisoners, and inflicted ten casualties without the loss of any of his own men. Realizing he had exceeded his orders, Cass asked permission to hold the bridge. Hull would not take a positive stand one way or the other. Maintaining that he must mount his heavy artillery on carriages before he could move in force, Hull pointed out the danger of a small detachment being cut off but left the final decision to Cass. In disgust Cass and his men retreated to Sandwich.

Delay was fatal. Hull's only hope of success was in taking

Major General Isaac Brock. (From Lady Edgar, *General Brock* [Toronto: Morang & Co., Ltd., 1909].)

"Old Ironsides." (Courtesy of U.S. Naval History Division, Office of Chie[f] of Naval Operations.)

Fort Malden by storm as soon as he crossed the river. The fort itself was weak, and on the whole of the Detroit frontier there were only a small detachment of artillery, 100 men of the 41st Regiment, 300 militia of uncertain loyalty, and about 150 Indians. Hull, of course, did not know the particulars of the British position but all of his preliminary probes indicated weakness. As he waited, his position deteriorated. On August 2 he was informed that the Wyandots in the Brownstown area had defected, a development that further endangered his already precarious supply line. On the following day there was an even more frightening piece of news: Fort Michilimackinac had surrendered on July 17. This sent shivers through Hull's elderly frame. Months before he had predicted that the fall of this place would unloose a horde of Indians from the north.

The American fort in the straits between Lakes Huron and Michigan was manned by some sixty officers and men under command of Lieutenant Porter Hanks of the regular artillery. Lieutenant Hanks's opponent was Captain Charles Roberts stationed at St. Joseph Island more than forty miles to the northeast. Captain Roberts received word of the declaration of war on July 8. On July 16 he embarked with a part of the 10th Royal Voltegeurs Battalion, 180 Canadian engagés (employees of the Northwest Company)—half of them without arms—nearly four hundred Indians, and two iron six-pounders. Arriving early on the morning of the seventeenth, by ten o'clock Captain Roberts's troops succeeded in placing one of the unwieldy guns above the American fort. When Captain Roberts sent in his demands, there was nothing Lieutenant Hanks could do but surrender. The British commander no less than the American feared the Indians would run amok, but he reported with relief that "not one drop either of Man's or Animal's blood was spilt."

Hull also began to worry—in fact to become obsessed—about his supply situation. The Americans were at the end of a supply line that ran two hundred miles into Ohio. For sixty miles the route ran along the edge of Lake Erie; on one side it was subject to attack by British gunboats, on the other to raids by hostile Indians. Even as early as July, when things were going relatively well, Hull had sent Governor Meigs a message to send supplies or "the Army will perish." Meigs hastily assembled provisions and on August 4 ordered Captain Henry Brush and seventy militiamen to take them to Detroit. When Brush reached the River Raisin thirty-five miles south of Detroit, he sent word to Hull that he needed protection, whereupon Hull detached Major Thomas Van Horne of Findlay's regiment with two hundred men. When this detachment reached the vicinity of Brownstown, it was attacked by Indians. Suffering seventeen casualties and a number of wounded, Van Horne's detachment abandoned their objective and marched back to Detroit.

Conscious that his men were growing increasingly dissatisfied over his inaction, on August 6 Hull ordered an attack on Malden, only to cancel it the next day when he heard that British regulars were on their way to the threatened fort. He now suggested a retreat to the River Raisin or to the Miami. He was told by the Ohio officers that their men would rebel if ordered to retreat. Hull compromised by leaving a small garrison at Sandwich—now Fort Hope—and crossing the majority of his force to Detroit. With the documents captured on the "Cuyahoga" and with the intercepted mail the British and their Indian allies now possessed extensive information on the size, morale, and condition of the American forces. When Hull sent out a second relief expedition of six hundred soldiers on August 8, the enemy was ready. As the detachment under command of Lieutenant Colonel Miller reached Monguagon, fourteen miles below Detroit, it was attacked by a force of British regulars and about four hundred Indians. The British soon quit the field, but Colonel Miller failed to press on, giving as his excuse "the care of the sick and wounded and a very severe rain storm." After the failure of this second attempt to open the supply lines Hull's officers lost all confidence in him. When he ordered the abandonment and destruction of Fort Hope they circulated a round robin to be sent to Governor Meigs "requesting the arrest and displacement of the General."

While Hull was timidly pulling his forces back, General Brock was hastily strengthening his position on the opposite shore. Since he had arrived in the province ten years before, Brock had given unceasing study to the problems of defending Canada. When the crisis arrived, therefore, he knew what must be done. It was on July 20 that Brock learned that General Hull had crossed into Canada and was making menacing overtures in the direction of Malden. Straightaway he sent Colonel Procter with sixty men of the 41st Regiment as reinforcement and summoned the legislature to a special session on July 27. The parliament voted the needed supplies, but when it refused to suspend the Habeas Corpus Act, Brock dismissed the members on August 5. Having discharged his civil duties Brock turned his attention to the military situation. Satisfied that the Americans were unable to carry out a major attack on the Niagara front and that they intended working on his flanks, he hastened to the relief of Malden. On August 8, the day that Hull retreated to Detroit, he embarked his force consisting of 260 militia and 40 regulars of the 41st at Long Point on Lake Erie. Hugging the treacherous coast, the troops by incessant exertion reached Amherstburg shortly before midnight on August 13. "In no instance," reported Brock, "have I seen troops who would have endured the fatigue of a long journey in boats during extremely bad weather, with greater cheerfulness and constance; and it is but justice to this little band to add that their conduct excited my admiration."

Brock's confidence was heightened by his meeting with Tecumseh and by what he found out about his adversaries. On the day of his arrival, he addressed an assembly said to consist of one thousand warriors. "Among the Indians whom I found at Amherstburg," he reported to Lord Liverpool, "were some extraordinary characters. He who attracted most my attention was the Shawanese chief, Tecumseh, brother to the prophet, who for the last two years had carried on, contrary to our remonstrances, an active warfare against the United States. A more sagacious or more gallant warrior does not exist. He was the admiration of everyone who conversed with him." Brock, who possessed a handsome physique and a quick mind, likewise won the admiration of the Indians. When the British general explained his plan of immediately advancing on Detroit, Tecumseh took a roll of birch bark and spreading it on the ground drew a map of the surrounding country with his hunting knife. Having satisfied himself of the constancy of his allies, Brock made a shrewd appraisal of his adversaries. Reading the numerous documents and letters that had been captured, he quickly came to the conclusion that the Americans were victims of their own apprehensions and despondency.

According to his own report, Brock had 250 troops of the 41st Regiment, 50 Royal Newfoundland Regiment, 400 militia, and about 600 Indians. Crossing the river, the white troops landed at Spring Wells, about three miles below Detroit, and the Indians, who landed about two miles farther below, moved forward and occupied the woods about a mile and a half on the British left. Playing on the American fear of Indian atrocities, Brock wrote Hull on August 15: "The force at my disposal authorizes me to require the immediate surrender of Detroit. It is far from my intention to join in a war of extermination, but you must be aware, that the numerous body of Indians who have attached themselves to my troops, will be beyond controul the moment the contest commences." Hull still had wit enough to reject this demand. But no sooner did Brock receive the refusal than he ordered his shore batteries, recently installed near Sandwich, and the gunboats "Queen Charlotte" and "General Hunter" to bombard Detroit. Making maximum use of psychological warfare, Brock also arranged for a spurious document referring to five thousand Indians ready to descend on Detroit to fall into Hull's hands. The Long Point militia were dressed in the red uniforms of the British regulars and allowed to parade where the Americans could not help seeing them.

Brock's clever moves had their effect. In times of stress, Hull would unconsciously stuff his mouth with quid after quid of tobacco while the dark spittle ran down over his beard and vest. Believing there were vast hordes of British regulars before him and thousands of Indians to his rear, unable to fetch his supplies, concerned about the old people and children who had taken refuge in his fort, and knowing that he had lost the confidence of his men, Hull went into mental and moral paralysis. In a last desperate effort to bring forward his supplies, he detailed Colonels McArthur and Cass on a relief expedition. In order to avoid an ambush that had been the fate of two previous expeditions, the men were ordered to take a roundabout back road. Unable to find such a road, they simply got lost in the woods.

According to Brock's own report, he crossed the river with the intention of waiting the effect of his fire and in the hope of drawing his adversaries into the field. However, when he received information that McArthur and five hundred men were in his rear, he decided on an immediate attack. "Brigadier General Hull however prevented this movement by proposing a cessation of hostilities, for the purpose of preparing terms of capitulation," said Brock. At noon on August 16 the British forces marched into the fort at Detroit and the American forces marched out. Some twenty-five hundred men were surrendered. The British sent the regulars as prisoners to Lower Canada but out of contempt or compassion, or a combination of the two, they allowed the militia to return home on parole. By a proclamation issued on the day of the surrender, General Brock made it known that he considered the whole territory of Michigan reannexed to His Majesty's dominions.

Though it took place in a remote corner of the empire, the taking of Detroit was one of the most glorious victories in British military annals. Writing to his brothers in England, Brock, without the slightest exaggeration, said of his actions:

> Some say that nothing could be more desperate than the measures; but I answer that the state of the province admitted of nothing but desperate remedies. I got possession of the letters my antagonist addressed to the Secretary of War and also of the sentiments which hundreds of his army uttered to their friends. Confidence in the general was gone, and evident despondency prevailed throughout. . . . I crossed the river contrary to the opinions of Colonel Proctor . . . it is therefore, no wonder that envy should

attribute to good fortune what, in justice to my own discernment, I must say, proceeded from a cool calculation of pours and contres.

Hull's surrender was one of the most disgraceful episodes in the military history of the United States. When news of the disaster reached the people, it was treated first with incredulity and then with anger. Cries of traitor went up on every side. Two years after the event, Hull was tried by a court-martial and sentenced to be hanged for cowardice. President Madison, however, taking into consideration his honorable service in the American Revolution, remitted the penalty.

In his own account of the affair, written soon after the event, Hull laid emphasis on the effect of the surrender of Michilimackinac and the hostility of the Indians. He says that "the fort at this time was filled with women, children and the old and decrepid people of the town and country." He might have added that among the civilians were his own daughter and her two children. There seems little doubt that Hull was genuinely concerned for the unfortunate people under his protection and acted partly out of humane considerations. While we may sympathize with Hull, we cannot blame Brock for mobilizing the Indians and playing upon Hull's fears. Brock's situation was desperate and as Henry Adams aptly remarks, "The loss of his province by neglect of any resource at his command might properly have been punished by the utmost penalty his government could inflict."

Hull's claim that he had on hand only a day's supply of powder and "only a few days' provisions" is not borne out by the British who reported the capture of over sixty barrels of powder, thirty-three pieces of brass and iron ordnance and numerous ordnance stores. Though the British never bothered to report in detail the rations captured, it has been estimated that Hull had enough for twenty days which by strict management might have been stretched to thirty days. Had Hull emphasized the poor quality of his troops and the lack of experience in his officers, he would have been on sounder grounds. On both scores, however, he is remarkably restrained. On the quality of his soldiers he merely says, "Being new troops, and unaccustomed to camp life; having performed a laborious march; have been engaged in a number of battles and skirmishes, in which many had fallen . . . are general causes by which the strength of the army was thus reduced." He might have added that before the departure of the army from Urbana, a portion of the militia defied their commander and Hull was able to bring them under control only by using one regiment of regulars to overawe them. When he crossed into Canada, a considerable number refused to leave American soil and "kept constantly firing off their pieces."

Concerning his regimental officers, Hull uttered no word of criticism but expressed his appreciation "for the prompt and judicious manner [in which] they have performed their duties." The only one of these officers who had any significant military experience was the regular army commander, Lieutenant Colonel Miller. Though probably of average ability this officer was unable, as we have seen, with a strong detachment of six hundred men to bring forward the much needed supplies. Of Cass and McArthur, historian Milo Quaife writes: "Ordered to Ypsilanti to meet and convoy Captain Brush, they abandoned the mission, although unopposed; returning to the vicinity of the town they calmly disregarded Hull's order to rejoin him. . . . If either Ohio colonel performed the legendary act of breaking his sword in disgust over the surrender, he had ample cause for doing so; but a greater degree of candor would have fixed the object of the disgust nearer home than the person of Hull."

Admitting that it was hazardous to invade Canada via Detroit without control of the lake and taking into consideration Hull's great problems of supply, transport, and manpower, the fact still remains that the failure was primarily one of leadership. At no time did Hull concentrate his whole force to the accomplishment of any one vital object. Allowing his attention to flit from one problem to another and his fears to become exaggerated, he became demoralized. Some historians, including the influential Henry Adams, have claimed that Hull was made the scapegoat of an inept administration. Such was not the case. Though there were extenuating circumstances, the blame must be put squarely on Hull's shoulders.

The war in the West continued a dreary story in 1812. To protect the frontier settlements from the Indian menace, Governor Isaac Shelby of Kentucky in September called out two thousand volunteers for thirty days and placed them under the command of General Samuel Hopkins, a congressman returned from Washington to fight in the field. This army, which the governor described as the best he had seen "in the western country or anywhere else," was to carry out a punitive expedition against the Kickapoo and Peoria villages in the Illinois country. Following the old trail of George Rogers Clark, the army reached Vincennes and crossed the Wabash early in October. Dissatisfaction among the troops was widespread. As they approached hostile territory, the Indians set the prairie on fire and General Hopkins, unable to discipline his troops, fell back. On November 7 Governor Shelby wrote that the failure of the Hopkins expedition had "ended an enterprise on which the flower of Kentucky enlisted themselves and are now returning home deeply mortified by disappointment."

Something more than disappointment befell the American garrison at Fort Dearborn, on the present site of Chicago. In command of the post was Captain Nathan Held who had fifty-odd regulars under his command. Knowing that the Indians would be emboldened by news of any British success in the east, General Hull, as soon as he heard of the surrender of Mackinac, sent orders that the fort be evacuated. These orders were delivered by Captain William Wells, who arrived at Fort Dearborn on August. 12. As the soldiers were preparing to evacuate, they were warned by a friendly chief, Black Partridge, that "leaden birds had been singing in his ears," and the white men ought to be careful about leaving the protection of the fort. Feeling that he must nevertheless obey orders, Captain Held set out on the morning of August 15. When the party, including women and children, were only a few miles from the fort they were attacked by a band of some five hundred Pottawattomie, who killed over half of the Americans and took the rest prisoners. Among the victims was Captain Wells who had delivered the fatal orders. The Indians first beheaded him, then carved out his heart and proceeded to eat it.

With the disasters at Detroit, Mackinac, and Fort Dearborn, only Fort Wayne remained in American control. The whole northwest lay open to invasion and devastation. A great fear ran throughout the frontier and many settlers in outlying areas began to leave their homes.

OPERATIONS AROUND NIAGARA

The western wing of the four-pronged invasion of Canada had failed miserably. What about the contemplated offensives from Niagara, Sackett's Harbor, and along Lake Champlain? Though Hull had been informed that he could expect no reinforcements or direct aid from Niagara, he had a right to expect—certainly the country had a right to expect—that maximum effort was being exerted all along the line. In charge of Fort Niagara and everything to the east of it was Major General Dearborn, who had laid down the strategy presumably being followed. Hull, it will be recalled, arrived in Cincinnati on May 10 to carry out the invasion from Detroit. About the same time, Dearborn arrived in Albany to establish his headquarters for a campaign against Montreal. In less than two weeks, Dearborn left for Boston, where for two months he occupied his time in strengthening coastal defenses and in useless negotiations with the New England governors. On July 13, when Hull had just crossed into Canada, Dearborn wrote the Secretary of War that "for some time past I have been in a very unpleasant situation, being at a loss to determine whether or not I ought to leave the coast." A week later he inquired: "Who is to have command of the operation in Upper Canada? I take it for granted that my command does not extend to that distant quarter." As Henry Adams aptly remarks, a general-in-chief, who at the beginning of a campaign is unable to decide in what part of his department his services are most needed, or who is ignorant of the geographical limits of his command, is sure to be taught the lessons by the enemy.

In spite of Dearborn's confusion there was a considerable host gathering on the Niagara frontier. Daniel D. Tompkins, the Republican governor of New York, appointed Stephen Van Rensselaer commander-in-chief of the New York militia. Since Van Rensselaer was a leading Federalist, it was thought that his appointment would give a non-partisan aspect to the war effort. Van Rensselaer was wholly without military experience, but it was thought that this deficiency could be compensated by appointing as his aide Colonel Solomon Van Rensselaer, who had considerable experience dating from the American Revolution. By October there were over six thousand troops along the Niagara frontier. Though formidable in sheer numbers, the Americans were plagued by inadequate supplies, improper food, wretched discipline and much illness. Probably the greatest of their ills, however, was divided command.

Brock had predicted a main American effort at Niagara. After receiving the surrender of Detroit, he lost not a moment in hastening back to Fort George which he knew would soon be threatened. While on his way he learned on August 23 of an armistice concluded between Generals Prevost and Dearborn. General Prevost, on learning of the repeal of the Orders-in-Council had sent his adjutant general, Colonel Edward Baynes, to Dearborn's headquarters near Albany. On August 9 Dearborn had agreed to act only on the defensive until he heard further from Washington. Since Hull was directly under the Secretary of War, Dearborn could not include him in the armistice but he hastened a messenger advising him to accept. By the time the message reached Hull, he was a prisoner of war and thus the advice was superfluous. When President Madison learned of the suspension of hostilities, he promptly rejected Dearborn's armistice and advised that general to make haste "in gaining possession of the British posts at Niagara and Kingston, or at least the former."

Canadian historians have criticized Prevost for proposing the armistice; American historians have faulted Dearborn for agreeing to it. On the Canadian side it has been alleged that the armistice prevented Brock from attacking the American naval base at Sackett's Harbor and rendered unavailing the command of the lakes, then held by the British. It is true that Brock did not like the armistice and said so repeatedly. On September 18 he wrote his brother:

> Were the Americans of one mind the opposition I could make would be unavailing, but I am not without hope their divisions may be the saving of this province. A river about 500 yards broad divides the troops. My instructions have made it necessary for me to adopt defensive measures, and I have evidenced greater forebearance than was ever practiced on former occasion. . . . I firmly believe that I could at this moment sweep everything before me from Fort Niagara to Buffalo—but my success would be transient.

In this letter Brock seems to accept Prevost's view that there were good political as well as military reasons for remaining for the time being on the defensive. Furthermore it should be pointed out that in proposing the armistice, Prevost rightly interpreted the wishes of his government. Even after President Madison rejected Prevost's arrangement, the British government instructed Admiral Warren to propose an armistice on the basis of the repeal of the Orders-in-Council. In defending his action, Prevost claimed not only that he had been able to shift men and supplies to the flank attacked (i.e., to Amherstburg), but also that the delay had enabled him to augment his resources against invasion. If this is so, it is equally true that the Americans used the armistice to improve their supply and manpower situation. In other words the armistice seems to have had little practical effect. Neither side was prepared, or wanted, to fight on the Niagara frontier. The Americans, however, were finally pushed into action by the force of events.

In a vague sort of way it was understood that when Van Rensselaer had enough troops he would move. As we have already noted, by October he had well over 6,000 troops to oppose 1,600 men and some 300 Indians under Brock. The only hope of retaining the army was to commit it to action. Furthermore, an unexpected stroke of good fortune provided an extra incentive. On October 8 Lieutenant Jesse Elliott of the U.S. Navy learned that two British brigs, the "Detroit" and the "Caledonia," had anchored near Fort Erie. Elliott and artillery Captain Nathan Towson with about 100 soldiers and sailors crossed the river in two large boats and captured the vessels. The "Detroit," after grounding on a small island, had to be burned, but the "Caledonia" was added to the growing United States naval strength on Lake Erie. Demanding to be led against the enemy, the American militia threatened to go home unless given an opportunity for active service. General Van Rensselaer's original plan called for simultaneous attacks on Fort George and the village of Queenston. General Alexander Smyth, who was at Buffalo with 1,650 regulars, was to embark in boats at the place where Four Mile Creek empties into Lake Ontario, land in the rear of Fort George, and take the place by storm. Van Rensselaer's own force would cross the Niagara at Lewiston and scale the heights of Queenston. General Smyth, not wishing to serve under a militia officer and favoring a crossing above rather than below Niagara Falls, failed to co-operate. Though there may be some question whether Van Rensselaer really wanted Smyth's co-operation, the fact remains that Smyth ignored first a suggestion and later an order that he meet General Van Rensselaer in a conference. At any rate it was decided to cross the river at Queenston, without the attack on Fort George.

The first attempt was made on the morning of October 11 and failed because an officer, either from ignorance or treachery, rowed across the river in a boat containing all the oars and abandoned it on the Canadian side. Unable to resist the clamor of his men, Van Rensselaer made a second attempt on the night of October 12–13. At the point chosen for crossing, the river is about 250 yards wide and though the current is strong a skillful boatman could execute the crossing in about fifteen minutes. The boats used carried about twenty men each. Though plans called for about thirty such boats only twelve were actually available to lift a force of some four thousand men. The gorge through which the river runs at Queenston rises to about 275 feet on the Canadian side. Before daylight some two hundred men landed and were discovered by a Canadian sentry who gave the alarm. The two companies of the 49th Regiment and detachments of militia from York and Lincoln counties–about three hundred in all–rushed to their stations. Colonel Solomon Van Rensselaer's landing party was attacked, and the artillery opened up on the boats of men still crossing the river. The firing was heard at Fort George, six or seven miles lower down the river, where the British army had its headquarters. General Brock had been up late the night before writing instructions to the officers who commanded along the river. Awakened about four o'clock by the sound of the firing and thinking the attack on Queenston might be a feint, he instructed Major General Roger Sheaffe to open fire on Fort Niagara and to be ready for an attack. Setting off alone for Queenston, he was soon joined by his two aides-de-camp, Lieutenant Colonel Macdonnell and Captain Glegg.

As Brock hurried toward the scene of action, things were going rather well for the Americans. Two soldiers, destined for distinguished careers in the U.S. Army, took leading parts in the assault. Lieutenant Colonel Winfield Scott, then only twenty-six years old, was under General Smyth, but hearing of Van Rensselaer's crossing, he hurried to the scene of action without so much as a by-your-leave from his commanding general. Captain John E. Wool, who like Scott was to achieve fame in the Mexican War, assumed command of the beachhead troops when Colonel Solomon Van Rensselaer was wounded in the initial assault. When General Brock arrived on the scene, the troops under Wool had ascended Queenston Heights by a fisherman's path that the British had left unguarded because they considered it impassable. Their position was to the rear and above a gun which was still firing against the Americans crossing the river. Unaware that the Americans had gained the heights above him, Brock stationed himself at the redan battery and was giving directions for correcting its fire when the Americans descended upon him. Hastily retreating to the village, Brock placed himself at the head of a company of the 49th Regiment and charged up the hill to retake the gun. A bullet fired at close quarters hit him in the breast and he died almost instantly. Colonel Macdonnell took over for a brief moment but he too fell in the attempt to retake the position. The battle had begun before daybreak. By two o'clock in the afternoon some seven or eight hundred Americans were on Queenston Heights. By this time, too, Lieutenant Colonel Scott had replaced Captain Wool in charge of the troops on the Canadian side.

Satisfied that the main attack was against Queenston, General Brock had, before he died, ordered General Sheaffe to march from Fort George with every available man. Also the small British garrison at Chippewa joined Sheaffe's command giving him about one thousand men and a party of Indians. If the American position was to be saved from counterattack, it had to be reinforced. General Van Rensselaer tried to hasten the unengaged troops across the river but, he reports, "to my utter astonishment I found that at the very moment when complete victory was in our hands, the ardor of the unengaged troops had entirely subsided. I rode in all directions; urged the men by every consideration to pass over, but in vain."

Abandoned by their comrades, the Americans on Queenston Heights fought bravely but hopelessly. Sheaffe conducted the counterattack skillfully. His main body of troops made a wide detour inland and attacked the American position. With demoniac zeal the Indians led off the charge, a body of British light infantry and Canadian militia fired a volley, and then pressed on with the bayonet. Before the steadily advancing British columns resistance simply melted away. Some of the Americans sought refuge along the steep banks of the river, others tried to swim the river. Many were forced to surrender, including Lieutenant Colonel Scott, who was later exchanged.

From the American point of view, the Battle of Queenston Heights was, both in conception and execution, an example of what not to do. Even if successful it would not have had a decisive effect on the general course of the war. Plans called for a night operation, a difficult thing even for veterans and almost impossible for raw recruits. Available manpower was frittered away or not used at all. General Van Rensselaer, though a devoted patriot himself, was unable to inspire his troops with the will to conquer.

Brock, on the other hand, disposed his inadequate forces along his forty-mile frontier so that they were mutually supporting. No less than Van Rensselaer, Brock had the problem of dealing with ill-trained and, in some cases, ill-disposed militia. But his simple patriotism was infectious and his ability and energy commanded respect—even from his enemies. On the day of his funeral, as he was laid to rest beside his aide, the American forces at the command of General Van Rensselaer fired a salute in honor of a valiant foe. In the history of Canada the battle has a significance quite out of proportion to its military importance. As the British historian, C. P. Lucas, points out: "The crisis was sufficiently grave to give to Upper Canada, in the battle of Queenston Heights and in the death of Brock, the memory of a national achievement and of a special hero. All this was to the good for the making of a nation, widening and enriching its history."

Realizing he could accomplish nothing, General Van Rensselaer asked to be relieved and his request was granted. General Alexander Smyth—he who had sulked in his tent—was put in command. What had occurred under Van Rensselaer might be described as tragedy; what was to follow under Smyth has been rightly described as burlesque. Smyth, born in Ireland and a resident of Virginia for many years, had been an inspector general of the U.S. Army. When the war broke out, he was transferred at his own request to an active command. Concerning the condition of the troops under Smyth, Babcock writes: "After the affair at Queenston the American militia became completely demoralized and had left by platoons and companies. . . . It is not entirely fair to call such men cowards or shirkers in view of the conditions which surrounded them. The fault lay with the government which after six months of war had failed to supply not only a proper system of instruction but also competent officers, essential equipment and stores, and adequate rations." Instead of trying to ameliorate some of these conditions, General Smyth spent his time composing bombastic proclamations designed to bring in more recruits or to overawe the Canadians.

The loss of troops resulting from sickness and desertion after Queenston Heights was partially made up by the arrival at Buffalo, on November 18, of two thousand militia from Pennsylvania. With six thousand troops under his command and with the winter season fast approaching, Smyth felt obliged to make another attempt at invading Canada. Adhering to his preconceived idea of crossing above the falls, Smyth sent over two parties of soldiers before daylight on November 28 who were to clear the way for the main army. One of these detachments, consisting of about two hundred men, did succeed in taking two batteries near Red House, and the other, of about two hundred men, partially destroyed a bridge which blocked the road to Chippewa. Had the main army crossed promptly, they would have stood a good chance of success. Instead of leading his troops forward, General Smyth composed a demand for the surrender of Fort Erie "to spare the effusion of blood." Though the British had suffered relatively heavy casualties during the night—nearly a hundred killed, wounded, or taken as prisoners—they rejected this demand. Furthermore, they proceeded to restore their position by recovering the dismounted batteries and repairing the bridge. General Peter B. Porter in his account of actions on the American side said that the troops were not ready for embarkation until two o'clock in the afternoon.

I have seen no official account of the number of men in the boats. My opinion was that the number exceeded 2,000. Most men of observation who were present, estimated it at 2,600; the men were in fine spirits and desirous of crossing. . . . After remaining in the boats till late in the afternoon, an order was received to disembark. It produced among the officers and men generally great discontent and murmuring, which was, however, in some degree allayed by assurances that the expedition was only postponed for a short time, until our boats could be better prepared.

The soldiers spent November 29 preparing for a crossing, and General Smyth wielded his pen in the composition of another vapid proclamation. "Before 9 the embarkation will take place. The general will be on board. Neither rain, snow, or frost will prevent the embarkation. . . . While embarking the music will play martial airs. Yankee Doodle will be the signal to get under way."

Before "Yankee Doodle" could be sounded, some of Smyth's officers came to him with objections to crossing in broad daylight in the face of batteries which had been remounted. The crossing was therefore postponed again to three o'clock on the morning of December 1 and the place of landing was shifted some miles lower down the river. On the appointed day, according to Smyth's own report, "The embarkation commenced; but was delayed by circumstances, so as not to be completed until after day-light. . . ." General Smyth then called a council of war of his principal officer and put the question: "Shall we proceed?" The answer was unanimously negative. When the men were informed that the invasion of Canada had been abandoned for the season, according to Peter B. Porter, "A scene of confusion ensued, which it is difficult to describe–about 4,000 men, without order or restraint, discharging muskets in every direction." General Smyth returned to Virginia, where he later became a congressman, but his military career was at an end. His permanent office as inspector general was merged into that of adjutant general and, without court-martial or even inquiry, his name was dropped permanently from the rolls of the army.

Brock and the Defense of Canada

THE NORTHEAST

While this tragicomic chapter of the war was being played out in the center, General Dearborn with his headquarters at Greenbush near Albany was presumably preparing the main thrust toward Montreal. As on the other fronts raw recruits gathered in considerable numbers. By the middle of November the Army of the North, variously estimated at six or eight thousand, moved up Lake Champlain to Plattsburg. When the Canadians heard of these movements they sent a strong force of some nineteen hundred from Montreal to guard the frontier. On the night of November 19 a detachment of regulars crossed the border and fought a skirmish on the Lacolle River. Though they captured a blockhouse, the Canadians escaped and in the darkness the Americans became confused and fired on one another, wounding four or five of their own men. The regulars retreated back to their own territory without accomplishing anything, and the militia, standing on its constitutional rights, refused to cross the border. On November 23 the whole army retreated. Three regiments of regulars went into winter quarters at Plattsburg, three went to Burlington, the light artillery and dragoons returned to Greenbush, and the militia went home. With the fizzle on the New York–Canadian border, plans for seizing Canada in 1812 came to an inglorious end.

In assessing the causes of the fiascoes of the first year much has been made of the defects of the militia. That the militia were ill-disciplined and undependable is not to be denied. Yet the regulars, most of whom were raw recruits, were not notably better. Also, it should not be overlooked that the militia however inadequate in quality did turn out in quantity. Kentucky, Ohio, New York, and Pennsylvania sent men forward generously. All told, nearly fifty thousand militia were called into service during 1812. There is much truth in the point often made that the militia merely reflected the unmilitary character and divided sentiments of the nation as a whole. Poor strategy also helps to account for the miserable record of the first year. Yet the fault that dwarfs all others is poor leadership. Though some of the junior officers showed mettle that would improve with time, all the generals were incompetent. Since Dearborn attempted the least he can be accused of the least. Hull was intelligent, but in a crisis he became confused and his fears overcame him. Though the competition was keen, Smyth outdid all the others in sheer folly.

The factor of leadership becomes all the clearer if we imagine the tables turned. In Canada, no less than in the United States, the leaders were faced with internal political dissension, ill-trained militia, inadequate supplies, and a long frontier to defend. Under these conditions it is impossible to imagine any one of the American generals being able to do anything at all to resist the incursions of stronger forces. Brock was able to prevail against the invaders not only because he possessed great personal daring but also because he could draw forth the best efforts of the regulars, the militia, and his Indian allies.

III

The War at Sea

At a gala occasion attended by the highest officials of the United States government in Washington on July 4, 1812, a toast was offered to the U.S. Navy: "An infant Hercules, destined by the presage of early prowess, to extirpate the race of pirates and freebooters." Whatever his destiny or potentialities the infant seemed infinitesimally small beside the fully mature Hercules with whom he was expected to do battle. As Table 1 shows there were only 16 vessels in the U.S. Navy, not counting two or three condemned hulks and upward of 200 gunboats scattered about the country in varying states of disrepair. Opposed to this small fleet was the greatest navy in the world. The British had in active service over 600 vessels, including 120 ships of the line and 116 frigates. Near the coast of the United States, that is, between Halifax and Bermuda, there was only 1 ship of the line, the "Africa" (64), and 7 frigates;

but in the western Atlantic, including squadrons off Newfoundland and in the West Indies, there were about 100 British vessels.

Though the four smallest vessels of the U.S. Navy turned out to be practically worthless, the twelve other vessels were equal to any in the world of their class. The frigates, as the table shows, were built in the 1790's when war with France threatened. During the same period, the Federalists had plans for building ships of the line and they actually acquired six navy yards and timber for that purpose. With the general pacification of Europe in 1800, however, and the accession to power of the Jeffersonian Republicans in the following year these plans were abandoned.

Ships of the line in those days had two or three decks and usually had 74 or more guns though there were some rare types with as few as 50 guns. The frigates had one complete deck, and carried 32 to 44 guns. In Table 1 the rated gun capacity is given, but the guns actually carried might be more or less their rated capacity. The larger American frigates generally carried about 10 more guns than their rated capacity. Two types of guns were used: the long gun and the carronade. The long guns varied in caliber from 2 to 42 pounds but the calibers most generally used were 6, 9, 12, 18, and 24. Except for two long bow-chasers, the American sloops and brigs carried only carronades. The frigates carried their long guns on the main deck and the carronades and two long bow-chasers on the quarter-deck and forecastle, or what the Americans called simply, the spar deck. The carronades—so called because they were first manufactured by the Carron Company of Scotland—were useless at long range but owing to their heavy weight of metal were terribly destructive at short range.

TABLE 1

Name of Ship	Classification	Rate (Guns)	Date of Building	Tonnage
United States	Frigate	44	1797	1,576
Constitution	Frigate	44	1797	1,576
President	Frigate	44	1800	1,576
Constellation	Frigate	38	1797	1,265
Congress	Frigate	38	1799	1,268
Chesapeake	Frigate	38	1799	1,244
Essex	Frigate	32	1799	860
Adams	Corvette	28	1799	560
Hornet	Ship-sloop	18	1805	480
Wasp	Ship-sloop	18	1806	450
Argus	Brig-sloop	16	1803	298
Syren	Brig-sloop	16	1803	250
Nautilus	Brig-sloop	14	1803	185
Vixen	Brig-sloop	14	1803	185
Enterprise	Brig	12	1799	165
Viper	Brig	12	1810	148

The British frigates with which the United States vessels were to come into contact most frequently were rated at 38 guns. The American ships, therefore, were often markedly superior in force to the British. In single-ship duels the British had only one advantage: since their foundries were better than the American, their guns were less liable to accident.

Though small in size the U.S. Navy was well trained and highly efficient. Its officers—there were twelve captains and no one of a higher permanent rank—had seen service in actual battle or were trained by experienced officers. The captains held their rank not because of influence or favoritism but because of demonstrated ability to do their jobs. In qualitative terms the navy itself was all that one could reasonably expect, but the Navy Department was not. The Secretary in 1812 was Paul Hamilton who by the end of the year proved his incompetence to the satisfaction of all concerned. But even the most gifted administrator would have found the job a difficult one. All the duties of the department devolved upon the Secretary himself who was assisted only by clerks without political or professional standing. One of the most time-consuming tasks was corresponding with a number of navy agents scattered throughout the United States and western Europe. The navy agents were civilians whose duties included the purchase of all types of supplies both for the building and equipping of vessels and for feeding and clothing the crews. Supervision of the navy agents was a full-time occupation in itself but the Secretary also corresponded directly with the superintendents of the six navy yards and with the commanders of squadrons or, as was usually the case, with commanders of individual vessels.

Since war had been threatening for a decade, one might suppose that the odds had been considered and some comprehensive plan worked out for the employment of meager naval resources. Such was not the case. A few days before the declaration of war, Secretary Hamilton asked his captains how the navy could be most useful. "The plan which appears to me to be best calculated for our little navy," replied Captain Stephen Decatur, "would be to send them out with as large a supply of provisions as they can carry, distant from our coast and singly, or not more than two frigates in company, without giving them any specific instructions as to place of cruising, but to rely on the enterprise of the officers." Captain John Rodgers, on the other hand, recommended operating in squadrons. In short, though they differed on whether the ships should cruise singly or in squadrons, the navy men wanted to seek out the offensive.

The President as Commander-in-Chief had other advisers, more influential perhaps than naval captains. With an eye to his revenue, Secretary of the Treasury Gallatin wrote in June,

"I believe the weekly arrivals from foreign ports will for the coming four weeks average from one to one and a half million dollars a week. To protect these and our coasting vessels while the British still have an inferior force on our coasts, appears to me of primary importance." Just what the navy was expected to do after the British navy was strengthened in American waters is not clear. It has been alleged that the administration planned to keep the ships safe in port, using them as floating batteries for the protection of harbors. Irving Brant in his recent biography of Madison maintains that the President sided with the naval officers in their desire for offensive action. He concedes, however, that Secretary Hamilton had earlier inclined to the view that in case of war the navy should be laid up. In any case, once war was declared, the naval captains enjoyed considerable freedom of action.

THE SINGLE-SHIP BATTLES

At the beginning of June, 1812, the major part of the United States fleet lay in New York Harbor under command of Commodore John Rodgers (when in command of a group of vessels the temporary rank of commodore was used). The division under Rodgers was divided into two squadrons, that of Rodgers himself and that of Commodore Decatur. In accordance with the President's wishes, Secretary Hamilton, on June 22, ordered the two squadrons to go to sea and separate. Rodgers was to go to the Capes of the Chesapeake and from there cruise eastward while Decatur's squadron cruised southward from New York in order to cross and, if need be, mutually support each other. The plan was not executed because it was not received in time. Within an hour after hearing of the declaration of war, and without waiting to be told what to do,

Rodgers put to sea in pursuit of a British convoy bound from Jamaica to England. He pursued the convoy almost to the English Channel and returned home by way of the Azores. After some two months of cruising, he could report having taken only "seven merchant vessels, and those not valuable." Though the convoy eluded him, Rodgers maintained that his cruise was successful from the defensive point of view. Knowing that a strong American squadron was at sea, but ignorant of its precise whereabouts, the British had to concentrate a considerable proportion of their available strength. Unable, in other words, to station single cruisers before any of the principal ports, the British Navy left American commerce virtually unmolested. Rodgers may have claimed too much for his far-flung cruise, but the fact is that most of the returning shipping did make it safely to port.

As soon as he received the declaration of war, the British admiral at Halifax sent out a strong squadron to American waters. This fleet, which consisted of a line of battleship and four frigates under command of Captain Philip Bowes Vere Broke, on July 16 scooped up the brig "Nautilus." The next day the British flushed a more promising quarry. When the war broke out, Captain Isaac Hull, in command of the "Constitution," was in Annapolis assembling a new crew. His orders told him to proceed to New York when ready, there to await further orders. Having completed his work, Hull set sail on July 12 and five days out he encountered the British squadron under Broke.

On the morning of July 18 there began what Henry Adams was to call "one of the most exciting and sustained chases recorded in naval history." Four British frigates bore down upon the "Constitution" (the line of battleship "Africa" was with the fleet but she was too slow to take part in the chase). Preparing for a fight, Hull cut away part of the rail across the stern and mounted a 24-pounder and a long 18. Two more 24-pounders were pointed through his cabin portholes after they had been widened. There was so little wind that Hull put out boats to tow the "Constitution." The British did likewise, all the small boats of the fleet coming to the aid of the "Shannon" (38 guns). Ascertaining that he was in a mere 150 feet of water, Hull abandoned the tow boats and resorted to kedging. This laborious method of propelling (more accurately, pulling) a ship consisted of sending a small anchor forward in a cutter, dropping it, and then heaving away with all hands at the cable until abreast. Another anchor was taken forward and so on. The "Belvidera" (36), working with two kedge anchors gained on the Americans, but her cutters dared not come within range of the stern guns of the "Constitution." In the afternoon a slight breeze came up and the tired crews left off one form of exhausting labor to take up another. Since a wet sail will hold more wind than a dry one, Captain Hull ordered his men aloft to dash water over the sails. Hull also calculated that by ridding himself of ten tons of drinking water, he could lessen the draft of his ship by one inch. Though the loss of supplies might circumscribe future operations Hull did not hesitate; he ordered the water started. Seeking every expedient for increasing their speed the British and American ships continued the chase for two days. Finally, on the evening of the third day, a rain squall broke the calm and by skillfully taking advantage of it Hull pulled away and left the British far astern. The "Constitution" entered harbor on July 26 and her story quickly spread from Boston to the entire east coast.

As soon as he had the necessary supplies aboard Hull sailed

on August 2, still without orders. To the gratification of even the Federalists, the escape of the "Constitution" had shown that American seamanship was not inferior to that of the British. Would American fighting qualities be equal to that of the mistress of the seas? British officers, having established a record of something like two hundred victories with only five defeats during the struggle with France and her allies, thought they knew the answer. So anxious were the British captains for a fight that they sometimes published challenges in American newspapers. Captain James R. Dacres, of the "Guerrière," issued a challenge in a somewhat different form. Hailing the "John Adams" from Liverpool, he endorsed the register as follows: "Captain Dacres . . . presents his complements to Commodore Rodgers . . . and will be very happy to meet him, or any American frigate of equal force as the 'President,' off Sandy Hook, for the purpose of having a few minutes tête à tête." It was not long before the captain's wishes were to be gratified without the necessity of going to Sandy Hook.

The handling of a sailing ship in an actual battle situation was so complicated a matter that any description of naval tactics is likely to result in vast oversimplification. Nevertheless it may be worthwhile to readers unfamiliar with sailing ships to have some elementary points. Ships had some guns in both bow and stern and these were sometimes pivot guns, but the main batteries were on the port and starboard sides. The object then was to maneuver the ship so that the full weight of either battery could be brought to bear without the enemy's being able to reply with a broadside. In other words, the ideal position was to be able to rake the enemy fore and aft. Since the wind was the only propellant, it played an important role in every commander's calculations. Though no ship can sail directly into the wind, a ship was said to have the weather gauge, or "advantage of the wind," or "to be to windward" when the wind allowed her to steer for her opponent and did not allow the opponent to head straight for her. Lee is the opposite of weather. A commander would seek the lee or weather gauge according to his intentions, his fire power, and the velocity of the wind. Since the weather gauge conferred the advantages of the offensive, an aggressive commander usually tried to get a position to windward. In a strong wind, however, the lee gauge might be preferable because a strong wind made the ship heel over so that some of the low guns could not be used.

Captain Isaac Hull, who had gone to sea when he was only fourteen, served in the U.S. Navy during the quasi-war with France and as commander of the "Enterprise" during the Tripolitan war. He was only thirty-nine years old when he sailed from Boston in 1812. At about 3:00 P.M. on August 19, when he was about 750 miles east of Boston, Hull sighted a ship that turned out to be H.M.S. "Guerrière" commanded by Captain Dacres–he who was so eager for a tête à tête. The wind blew fresh from the northwest. Hull ran down before the wind while Dacres waited. Both ships maneuvered for position. At 5:00 Dacres opened up with a fire from his starboard battery that fell short. He then wore ship (turned round, making a half circle) and fired the port broadside but this time the shot was too high. As the two ships maneuvered at some distance Hull had the "Constitution" under "fighting sails"–top sails and jib. As she made her near approach at about 6:00 P.M., however, the "Constitution" set her main-top gallant and foresail and closed so quickly that Dacres seems to have been taken by surprise. Holding his fire until he was within fifty yards of the "Guerrière," Hull gave his order in typical American fashion: "Now boys, pour it into them."

The guns of the "Constitution," double shotted with round and grape, were so well handled that after fifteen minutes the mizzenmast of the "Guerrière" had fallen over the starboard quarter, the main yard was in the slings, and the hull, rigging, and sails were badly cut up. The British crew fought bravely, but they were faced with considerable odds. Hull's broadside was heavier than Dacres' by about the proportion of 7 to 5 and his crew numbered 468 compared to 263 aboard the "Guerrière." Hull gave his adversary no rest: he raked her with his starboard guns and then wore to rake her again with the port battery. The "Guerrière's" bowsprit fouled the mizzen rigging of the "Constitution" and for a while the two were locked in combat. It was at this time of close contact that the heaviest casualties on both sides occurred. The British poured volleys of deadly musket fire into the crowded deck of the "Constitution," and the American marines took a heavy toll from the deck of the "Guerrière." Both captains gave the order, "Boarders away." An American marine lieutenant leapt to the rail to lead his fifty men, but was struck in the head and fell dead to the deck. Just at this moment the "Guerrière" lurched away in a heavy sea and the two ships parted. As they did so the weakened fore and main masts fell leaving the "Guerrière" rolling and dipping like a log. The "Constitution" ran off some distance to repair her rigging and then returned for the *coup de grace*. But there was no need. Realizing that his ship was a helpless, leaking hulk, Captain Dacres surrendered. Throughout most of the night, the crew of the "Constitution" worked removing prisoners and caring for the wounded. Too badly

The "Essex" and her prizes in the bay at Nuku Hiva, in the Marquesas. (From a drawing by Captain Porter reproduced from Benson J. Lossing, *The Pictorial Field-Book of the War of 1812* [New York: Harper & Bros., 1868].)

Perry changing ships on Lake Erie. (Courtesy of Library of Congress.)

damaged to be taken to port as a prize, the "Guerrière" was set afire and she soon blew up.

After reaching Boston safely, Captain Dacres spoke warmly of the courtesy shown him and his crew by a "brave and generous enemy." When the news reached London *The Times* was unable to share this view of the enemy. Pointing out that "never before in the history of the world did an English frigate strike to an American," it predicted that such triumphs were likely to render the Americans "insolent and confident."

Though one might choose other words, essentially *The Times* was right: the victory at sea did encourage the Americans to feel they could win. Only a few days after the "Constitution" sailed into Boston with its prisoners, news of General William Hull's ignominious surrender of Detroit reached the east coast. Without Captain Isaac Hull's victory to sustain them the whole country might have turned defeatist. Henry Adams writes: "Isaac Hull was nephew to the unhappy General and perhaps the shattered hulk of the *Guerrière*, which the nephew left at the bottom of the Atlantic Ocean, eight hundred miles east of Boston was worth for the moment the whole province which the uncle had lost, eight hundred miles to the westward; it was at least the only equivalent the people could find and they made the most of it."

Besides helping morale at a time when it needed a boost, Hull's victory had another important result: it laid to rest any lingering notion that the U.S. Navy might be kept in American harbors as floating batteries. By September 7 most of the navy was again back in port and new orders were issued. The vessels were to be divided into three squadrons, each consisting of one 44, one light frigate, and one sloop. These three squadrons commanded by Rodgers, Bainbridge, and Decatur were to spread fanwise over the central Atlantic trade routes. The three commanders were given wide latitude: they were to pursue "that course which to your best judgment may appear best calculated to enable you to accomplish these objects [annoying the enemy and protecting U.S. commerce]."

Captain Decatur in the "United States" left harbor in company with the "Argus" but, preferring single-ship actions, he sent the "Argus" on her way to operate alone. On October 25 about six hundred miles west of the Canaries the "United States" encountered the "Macedonian." Unlike the "Guerrière," which was an old ship captured from the French, the "Macedonian" was fresh from overhaul and her crew was reputed to be in peak condition. Captain John S. Carden and his first lieutenant, David Hope, enforced a rigid discipline by an unsparing use of the lash. As the ships closed for action, Captain Carden ordered his midshipmen to shoot instantly any crewman who ran from his quarters. He is also reported to have quoted Nelson's famous words: "England expects every man to do his duty."

It is easy enough to parrot the words or to ape the mannerisms of a great captain, but to capture the essence of his genius is quite another thing. Captain Carden entered the fight with grave handicaps: though his ship was superior in speed she was inferior in force. The heaviest long guns on the "Macedonian" were only 18-pounders while the "United States" mounted a battery of 24-pounders. The "United States" therefore enjoyed an advantage not only of range but also of broadside which was about 50 per cent heavier. In these circumstances the best plan would have been to bring on a close action. Carden attempted to do this, but only after it was too late. The movements and countermovements of this battle were extremely complicated. In summary what happened was this: When the two ships sighted each other, Carden had the advantage of the weather gauge and by continuing his original course he could have closed quickly. However, overanxiety to retain the weather gauge and concern for the danger of being raked caused him to alter his course and to stay at some distance. Then, according to Theodore Roosevelt, "he tried to remedy one error by another, and made a foolishly rash approach."

Captain Decatur exploited these errors to the maximum. In the previous battle between the "Constitution" and the "Guerrière," Captain Hull won partly by taking advantage of the weather gauge. In his engagement with the "Macedonian" Decatur made skillful use of the lee gauge. By prolonging Carden's approach, he was able to utilize fully his long-range guns, which inflicted mortal damage. Not only did Decatur maneuver his ship skillfully, his broadsides were delivered with such rapidity that the British crews thought the "United States" was on fire. By the time the "Macedonian" got the closest she ever came–about one hundred yards–she was already beaten. Having shot away the spars and rigging and having killed or wounded one-third of the crew, Decatur took up a raking position to finish the job. But realizing that further resistance could only lead to useless slaughter, Carden surrendered.

When this action took place Captain Decatur was only thirty-three years old. Brilliant, daring, and fiery-tempered, he had established an enviable reputation in the war with Tripoli. Contrary to what one might have expected from some of his previous actions, in his capture of the "Macedonian" he showed coolness, calculation, and restraint. Maneuvering with consummate skill he fought the battle in such a way as to sustain a minimum of damage to his own ship. Cognizant of the immense advantages in morale and prestige of bringing in a British frigate, he put a prize crew aboard the "Macedonian" and headed straight for New England.

Other victories followed. On December 29, 1812, Captain Bainbridge, who had taken command of the "Constitution," met and defeated the "Java" off the coast of South America near Bahia. Some of the smaller American ships also gained glory. On October 17 the "Wasp," a sloop of 18 guns, defeated the "Frolic," 19 guns, some five hundred miles east of the Chesapeake. In February, 1813, the "Hornet," the sister ship of the "Wasp," defeated the "Peacock," 16 guns, off the coast of British Guiana. During the war there were eight sloop and brig actions and in all but one the American ship gained the advantage.

Though these single-ship victories hardly created a dent in the vast resources of the British navy, they were greeted in England first with incredulity and then with gloom. "What is wrong with British seapower?", *The Times* wanted to know. It is now clear that at least two things were wrong: British gunnery was not so good as American and the ships were not so good. Noting the superior force of the American ships, the British press charged in outrage that they were not frigates at all but battleships in disguise. The Admiralty was shaken but was not panicked by the American victories. After appraising the court-martial proceedings which followed these early surrenders, they ordered frigates equal to the American to be built, and until such should become available captains were not to challenge larger American ships. Where possible, frigates were to cruise in pairs or small squadrons.

That these were sensible measures and that the British could win when evenly matched, subsequent events were to show. As late as the spring of 1813 the commercial blockade had not been extended to New England, but British ships of war stood off the coast to seize American shipping. Watching Boston was Captain Philip Broke in the "Shannon," 38 guns, and another frigate, the "Tenedos." If other captains in the Royal Navy neglected training in gunnery, Captain Broke did not. He had personally superintended the mounting of the ordnance on the "Shannon" and, circumstances permitting, he daily drilled the crew in the use of their arms, heavy and light. Inside Boston harbor was Captain James Lawrence trying to gather supplies and a crew for the "Chesapeake," the same ship that six years before had been so roughly handled by the "Leopard." Captain Lawrence was given command of the ship as a reward for past services. As commander of the sloop "Hornet," he had captured a brig with $20,000 aboard, and shortly after he had defeated the sloop "Peacock" in a bloody battle. Toward the end of May, Captain Broke received intelligence that the "Chesapeake" was about ready to sail. Anxious to prove that the British were still the masters of the sea, Broke sent Lawrence a challenge. Saying that he was sending off the "Tenedos," he asked for a meeting "ship to ship, to try the fortune of our respective flags."

Lawrence never received the challenge, but he needed no goading. On June 1 he sailed out of Boston determined, despite the rawness of his crew, to fight. The "Shannon" took its position well out to sea between Cape Cod and Cape Ann. There were no intricate maneuvers: the ships simply came within fifty yards of one another and proceeded to exchange broadsides. Broke's emphasis on gunnery paid off: in less than fifteen minutes the "Chesapeake" was out of control, most of her officers were casualties, and her captain was mortally wounded.

But while Lawrence went down to defeat, the manner of his going was an inspiration. As he was carried below he gave the famous command that became a motto of the American navy: "Don't give up the ship. Fight her till she sinks." The order was obeyed literally; in this battle no American ever did haul down the flag. The British came aboard and by determined hand-to-hand fighting took possession of the ship. Lawrence, taken aboard the "Shannon," died before he reached Halifax. His body was eventually returned to the United States and was buried in the yard of Trinity Church in New York.

The American captains, as we have already seen, were allowed considerable latitude in carrying out their missions. None exceeded Captain David Porter, of the "Essex" (32 guns), in the exercise of individual initiative. Captain Porter left the east coast of the United States in the autumn of 1812 with orders to join the "Constitution" and the "Hornet" in the South Atlantic. Missing these ships he decided in December, 1812, to double Cape Horn and attack British whaling vessels in the South Pacific. Even if the whaling industry was not of major economic importance to the British, Porter could create annoyance, he could arouse apprehension about where the American navy might strike next, and he could count on making the British disperse at least some of their naval forces to this far-off scene of action. After a stormy passage round the Horn on half rations, Porter entered Valparaiso, Chile, in March, 1813. Never before had an American ship of war entered the Pacific. Cruising northward toward the Galapagos Islands, Porter hunted for months like a wolf in a pasture of unguarded sheep. The harvest was so rich that Porter's foster son, David Glasgow Farragut, a midshipman only thirteen years old, was put in charge of one prize. After five months Porter's ship needed refitting. He therefore headed westward to the Marquesas. In this tropical paradise the American sailors enjoyed a romantic interlude with episodes long since made hackneyed by Hollywood—native tribal warfare in which Porter's men helped the good guys chase off the bad guys, fabulous oriental feasts served by Polynesian beauties with swaying palms in the background, etc. When the time finally came for departure, Porter recorded in his *Journal:* "The girls lined the beach from morning until night, and every moment importuned me to take the taboos off the men, and laughingly expressed their grief by dipping their fingers into the sea and touching their eyes, so as to let the salt water trickle down their cheeks." But Porter claimed more than mere exotic adventure for his expedition. "The valuable whale fishing there [in the South Pacific] is entirely destroyed," he reported, "and the actual injury we have done them may be estimated at two and one half million dollars, independent of the expenses of vessels sent in search of me. They have supplied me amply with sails, cordage, cable, anchors, provisions, medicines and stores of every description—and the slops aboard them have furnished clothing for the seamen. We have in fact lived on the enemy since I have been in that sea; every prize having proved a well-found store for me. . . ."

It was not to be expected that the British government would permit this marauding to go on indefinitely. The "Phoebe," 44 guns and the "Cherub," 28 guns, were sent in pursuit. The British ships found the "Essex" and one of its prizes, "Essex Junior," at Valparaiso in February, 1814. For over a month the

British blockaded the harbor. Toward the end of March, Porter attempted to escape and almost succeeded when a sudden heavy squall brought the topmast down. Crippled, Porter anchored his ship about one-quarter mile off shore. Ignoring neutral waters, Captain Hillyar of the "Phoebe" moved in and there ensued a bitter fight. Before her colors were struck, the "Essex" was battered to splinters and of the 255 men on board, 58 were killed, 66 wounded, and 31 drowned. In the words of the victorious captain: "The defence of the 'Essex,' taking into consideration our superiority of force, and the very discouraging circumstances of her having lost her main topmast, and being twice on fire, did honour to her brave defenders, and fully evinced the courage of Captain Porter and those under his command." The defeat of one ship meant the end of American seapower in the Pacific. Having disposed of the "Essex," Captain Hillyar proceeded northward to destroy the American fur posts on the Columbia River, and later the American whaling industry in the South Seas.

THE BLOCKADE

By the time the "Essex" was put out of action in March, 1814, Britain was in effective control of both the Pacific and Atlantic oceans. Though the American frigates could win glory they did not and could not effectively alter the course of the war. The blockade of the coast had the effect eventually not only of ruining American trade but also of reducing the blue water navy to a minor role.

British seapower was applied to the American scene of operations only gradually as the interests and resources of the empire dictated. Early in the war Britain left American trade practically untouched for several reasons: she hoped the repeal of the Orders-in-Council would bring peace; there was need also for American foodstuffs on the Iberian Peninsula and in the British West Indies, and the extensive naval building activities of Napoleon on the Continent made the withdrawal of cruisers from other stations inexpedient. When hopes of reconciliation faded, orders were issued on December 26, 1812, proclaiming a rigorous blockade of the exits of the Delaware and Chesapeake. Later the license trade brought the needed supplies to the Iberian Peninsula and the West Indies and the loss of Napoleon's divisions in the snow-covered wastes of Russia produced a favorable turn in the military situation. In May, 1813, the blockade was extended from Long Island to the Mississippi. New England was still excluded with the purpose of encouraging the peace movement in that part of the country. The downfall of Napoleon brought the third and final stage. The treaty with the restored Bourbon government of France was signed on May 30, 1814, and the following day an order placed all "ports, harbors . . . and seacoasts" of the United States under strict blockade.

The effects of these measures were of crucial importance for both the external and internal trade of the United States. Exports, which had risen to $130 million in 1807, fell to $45 million in 1811, a year of peace but restricted trade. In 1813 exports fell to $25 million and in 1814 to $7 million. Needless to say, the blockade was a blow to the revenue. Import duties, which had yielded over $13 million in 1811, fell to less than half that amount in 1814.

The coastal trade also suffered greatly. The British stationed a large portion of their ships in the central section of the country. This meant that a runner, to get from one end of the country to another, had to break the blockade in starting, make a wide sweep out to sea, and then break through the cordon of ships again at the place he wished to land. Few were willing to take such risks. Land transportation was a poor alternative, for it was still slow, difficult, and expensive. It took forty-six days for a wagon load of goods to move from South Carolina to Philadelphia, and to go on to Boston required seventeen days more. By creating a glut of products in some sections and a famine in others, the blockade deprived the various sections of the country of mutual support. Sugar quoted at $9 a hundredweight in New Orleans sold for $21 in New York in August, 1813, and by December had risen to $40. Rice which at Charleston or Savannah sold for $3 a hundredweight brought $12 in Philadelphia.

The accomplishments of the blockade were impressive, but they were achieved only with considerable diversion of seapower. As early as August, 1812, the British naval forces in the American theater were united under the command of Admiral Sir John Borlase Warren. The government steadily augmented Warren's strength until by February, 1813, he had scattered through his extensive command some seventeen ships of the line, two 50-gun ships, twenty-seven frigates and about fifty smaller vessels. Concerned about the unexpected success of the American navy and under pressure of public clamor for more positive action, the Admiralty repeatedly urged Admiral Warren to do something to bring the war home to the Americans.

The Delaware and Chesapeake bays with their numerous tributaries, their extensive coastal trade, and their rich tidewater farms offered tempting targets. Leaving his headquarters in Bermuda, Admiral Warren appeared in the Chesapeake in February, 1813, in company with his second in command, Rear Admiral Sir George Cockburn. The background and abilities of these two men complemented each other. Warren, who as a youth had hesitated between the navy and religious orders, was an able administrator and organizer but was somewhat shy on fighting qualities. Cockburn, on the other hand, having gone to sea when he was nine years old, was a hard-bitten sea dog ready to carry out any assignment, however unpleasant. After the war he escorted Napoleon on his voyage to St. Helena and acted for a while as his jailer. Though Napoleon certainly cannot be considered an objective critic, he was not very wide of the mark when he described Cockburn as "rough, overbearing, vain, choleric and capricious." After an unsuccessful chase of the United States frigate "Constellation," Warren sent Cockburn to Lynnhaven Bay, Virginia, to pillage the countryside. Captain John Poo Beresford, commanding the "Poictiers," 74 guns, was sent to Delaware Bay.

Arriving at the town of Lewes early in April, Captain Beresford sent in a demand for meat and vegetables for his crew. When it was refused, Beresford opened up a bombardment. The town was so far back, however, that little harm was done. In fact, the townspeople found that the cannon balls from the "Poictiers" exactly fitted their own guns. With the aid of powder brought down by the DuPont brothers, the balls were sent back to the place they came from. After an unsuccessful attempt to land to fill his water casks, Beresford sailed off to Bermuda.

Admiral Cockburn was a more accomplished marauder. After cleaning out the chicken coops and pig sties around Lynnhaven he headed north, reaching Frenchtown, Maryland, on the Elk River on April 29. Besides taking five small vessels, Cockburn's men destroyed government property consisting of a great quantity of flour, a large amount of army clothing, and saddles, bridles, and other equipment. Havre de Grace, near the mouth of the Susquehanna, fell next under the torch and sword. Some forty of the sixty dwellings comprising the town were burned, according to Cockburn's own report "to cause the proprietors (who had deserted them and formed part of the militia who had fled to the woods) to understand and feel what they were liable to bring upon themselves by building batteries and acting toward us with so much useless rancor." This work done, Cockburn ascended the Susquehanna for sixty miles to destroy a cannon foundry. On May 5 he entered the Sassafras River on the Eastern Shore of Maryland and destroyed Fredericktown and Georgetown.

This marauding of the upper Chesapeake was carried out with a small flotilla and perhaps four hundred marines and seamen. By June Admiral Warren had at his disposal a reinforcement of some three thousand troops under General Sir Sydney Beckwith, a force sufficient to undertake more ambitious projects. With little hesitation, Admiral Warren decided on an amphibious operation against Norfolk. Two objects beckoned: the frigate "Constellation," which earlier in the war had reached safe anchor near the town, and the Portsmouth navy yard. To reach Norfolk the British had to pass Craney Island, which guards the mouth of the Elisabeth River and which the Americans had fortified. The British planned to take Craney Island by sending one group of men to land and march on the island from the flank, while another group attacked from barges in front. The landing party under General Beckwith got under way, but for reasons still obscure it abandoned the flanking operation. The frontal assault was made, according to some accounts, by fifteen hundred marines and sailors in fifty barges. As soon as the British came within range, the

Americans opened up a well-directed fire that sank three of the barges and threw the others into confusion. Admiral Warren reported that he decided that "persevering in the attempt would cost more men than the number with us would permit."

Frustrated in their attack against Norfolk but determined to make some use of their forces, the British turned to the little town of Hampton which stood on the north shore of the James about ten miles away. Though there were four or five hundred raw militia near Hampton, the military and commercial importance of the town was negligible. On June 25 Admiral Cockburn made a demonstration in front, while soldiers were landed on beaches about two miles above. Thus the land forces marched on the town from the rear. The militiamen stood their ground for a while–long enough to inflict fifty casualties–and then broke and ran. The night was spent in relative quiet, but the next day the soldiers looted, pillaged, and–so it was alleged–raped several women. Among the miscreants were troops variously known as the Independent Foreigners, the Canadian Chausseurs, or Chausseurs Britanniques. They were not Canadians at all but French prisoners who preferred serving in the British army to languishing in prison. Perhaps they were not the only guilty ones, but they were blamed for the affair and dismissed from His Majesty's service.

After the exploit at Hampton, a part of the British fleet continued in the Chesapeake until the end of the year, to the discomfort of the people of Virginia and Maryland. Another detachment under Admiral Cockburn sailed southward to harry the coasts of the Carolinas and Georgia. Lieutenant Colonel Napier, of the 102d Regiment, recorded in his diary: "Strong is my dislike to what is perhaps a necessary part of our job; namely, plundering and ruining the peasantry."

The British blockade not only stifled trade and brought the weight of war directly to bear upon the people of the coastal areas, it gradually put an end to the careers of the frigates which played such a glamorous role early in the war. The "Constellation," bottled up near Norfolk, was never able to get to sea. The "United States," which had successfully taken her prize, the "Macedonian," into New York was unable to escape for further operations. The "President" lay bottled up in New York also. Only that lucky ship, the "Constitution," was able to escape, once in January, 1814, and again in the final stages of the war.

The very success of the British blockade inspired American inventors to find a means of breaking it. Robert Fulton, who had produced various submarine inventions and who had proved the practicability of steam propulsion, designed a heavy steam man-of-war which he called the "Demologos." An Edinburgh newspaper gave a graphic, if not altogether accurate, description of this vessel and its strange devices:

> Her length on deck is 300 feet, thickness, 13 feet of alternate oak and planks and cork wood, carries 44 guns, 4 of which are 100-pounders, and further to annoy an enemy attempting to board, can discharge 100 gallons of boiling water a minute, and by mechanism, brandishes 300 cutlasses with the utmost regularity over the gunwales, works also an equal number of heavy iron pikes of great length, darting them from her sides with prodigious force and withdrawing them every quarter of a minute.

The "Demologos" was launched October, 1814, but lack of money and Fulton's death delayed her first trial run until June 1, 1815, nearly six months after the war ended. Hearing of the potentialities of the new ship, the Admiralty in 1815 ordered the construction of a steam sloop named the "Congo" to match the "Demologos."

The War at Sea

PRIVATEERING

While the frigates decreased in effectiveness, the number and effectiveness of the privateers increased to the end of the war. No sooner was war declared than a large number of small vessels of every description took to sea to prey upon British commerce. There were over 500 registered privateers but most of these were small vessels that made only a single cruise. Only about 200 were large enough to carry a crew of 50 men or more, and probably there were no more than 50 seagoing vessels on the ocean at any one time. Through a process of trial and error the size and design of the ship best suited to privateering was brought to near perfection. The most efficient vessels were of 400 or 500 tons, carried a crew of 150 to 160 men, and were armed according to the varying ideas of owners or captains, but usually included one "long Tom," or pivot gun. Since the main purpose of the privateer was not to fight but to escape, the designers sought speed, ease of handling, and economy. Concerning the results achieved, Henry Adams has written some of his most lyrical prose:

> Americans were proud of their privateers, as they well might be; for this was the first time when in competition with the world, on an element open to all, they proved their capacity to excel and produced a creation as beautiful as it was practical. . . . In truth the schooner was a wonderful invention. Not her battles, but her escapes won for her the open-mouthed admiration of the British captains, who saw their prize double like a hare and slip through their fingers at the moment when capture was sure. Under any ordinary condition of wind and weather, with an open sea, the schooner, if only she could get to windward, laughed at a frigate.

To protect themselves the British merchantmen sailed under convoy or as armed "running ships." The convoy regulations were strict, but there were always laggards and strays that fell easy victims to the privateers. Sometimes the privateers would draw off the watchdogs and double back to cut out ships. Operating at night they would sometimes run directly into the fleet and cut out vessels. Generally, however, the privateers concentrated their efforts against the "running ships" because these constituted the richest prizes. The West Indies were a favorite hunting ground but the privateers attacked British commerce the world over.

And it was not commerce alone that became an object of pursuit. The British war effort on the Peninsula suffered losses that were annoying, if not critical. Early in the war, while one portion of the American shipping interest through the license system was raking in gold by supplying food for Wellington's forces, another sector was attacking his lines of supply. Repeatedly the duke told the Admiralty that they were doing a poor job of keeping his communications open. On one occasion he informed their lordships of the "capture and ransom of the 'Canada,' horse transport, by an American privateer, with a detachment of the 19th Light Dragoons and other troops aboard." On another he complained that "unfortunately some vessels were taken on the coast of Portugal, which had on board equipment for troops."

The careers of individual ships cannot be followed in any detail but one or two examples may be noted. An American living in Paris bought a small vessel, said to have been in both the French and British navies, refitted her and christened her the "True-Blooded Yankee." Though the United States was not allied to France, the ports of either could be used as a base of operations against a common enemy. The "True-Blooded Yankee," sailing on March 1, 1813, cruised for thirty-seven days along the coasts of Ireland and Scotland, took twenty-seven vessels as prizes, captured and held for six days an island off the coast of Ireland, and took a town in Scotland, where seven vessels were burned in the harbor.

The "Chausseur," built in Baltimore, took more than thirty prizes during the war. While cruising off the coast of Great Britain and Ireland in the summer of 1814, Captain Boyle sent a mock "Proclamation of Blockade" to be posted in Lloyd's. Returning to the United States the "Chausseur," after refitting, embarked on a winter cruise in the West Indies. On February 26, 1814, she sighted near the coast of Cuba what she believed to be a merchant vessel. Not until she was within pistol shot did she realize that her adversary was the British schooner "St. Lawrence." After a sharp contest lasting about ten minutes the "St. Lawrence" struck her colors. "I should not willingly, perhaps, have sought a contest with a King's vessel, knowing it is not our object," Captain Boyle reported to the owners, "but my expectations at first were a valuable vessel, and a valuable cargo. When I found myself deceived, the honor of the flag intrusted to my care was not to be disgraced by flight."

Another instance of a privateer engaging in hard fighting was the "General Armstrong," which on September 14, 1814, found itself pinned down by three British men-of-war in the harbor of Fayal in the Azores. First the British sent in two hundred men in boats to board. When these were fought off with hideous losses, the British, disregarding the neutrality of the port, opened with a long-range bombardment. Scuttling the "General Armstrong," Captain Reid led his men ashore. The destruction of one privateer cost the British thirty-four killed and eighty-six wounded.

Altogether the American privateers cost the British hundreds of lives and millions of dollars. Of a total of some 1,300 prizes taken, about 1,000 were captured during the last eighteen months of the war. With an average of two ships being lost every day, the merchants of Glasgow, Liverpool, and Bristol complained loud and long to the government. To the direct losses must be added the indirect costs of higher insurance rates and general frustration and weariness among the merchants and seafaring people.

Commerce destruction is of course a two-way street: American shipping with only a small navy to protect it was if anything more vulnerable than the British. And though the Royal Navy was principally responsible for the ruination of American trade, its efforts were ably supplemented by privateers and letters of marque. The Maritime Provinces of Canada, with their position overlooking the American seaboard, enjoyed particular advantages, and their privateers have an interesting if little-known history. In all some thirty-seven privateers and twelve letters of marque were commissioned in Halifax and New Brunswick. One of the most successful of these was the "Liverpool Packet," whose commander, Joseph Barss of Liverpool, Nova Scotia, had an intimate knowledge of the ways of New England shipping. Cape Cod juts out, like a sickle of sand, into the Atlantic. The tip of the Cape was a favorite landfall for ships returning from Europe and, of course, all traffic along the coast had to pass around the Cape. In order to shorten the voyage, it was the habit of mariners to bring the tip of the Cape as close aboard as possible. Barss, who was one of the first of the maritime privateers on the scene, brought in a large number of prizes by simply pouncing on the traffic as it came around the corner. The activities of the

"Liverpool Packet" were so successful in the autumn of 1812 that some of the Boston and Salem newspapers suggested the cutting of a canal through Cape Cod. Just how many seizures the "Liverpool Packet" made is a matter of some dispute but it is definitely known that forty-four of her victims were condemned by the prize courts with a value conservatively estimated at $262,000. Besides the "Liverpool Packet," the "Matilda," the "Shannon," the "Sherbrooke," the "Dart," and others had interesting careers. In all there were 207 captures brought to Halifax, St. John, Liverpool, Digby, and Yarmouth.

The Canadian privateers seem to have operated under more restrictions than their American counterparts. Since officers of the Royal Navy supplemented their meager incomes with seizures of enemy shipping, they regarded captures made by privateers as so much money out of pocket. Owners and commanders had to post bonds of from 1,500 to 3,000 pounds to ensure compliance with the terms of their commissions. Not only were the privateers forbidden to take ransom for either goods or prisoners of war, they had to bring all their seizures to port for final disposition by a prize court. Refusing to allow the privateers to wear the naval ensign or pendant, the British government required them to fly a red jack. A Canadian historian remarks that this "was somewhat in the nature of duck-hunting with a brass band."

STRATEGIC LESSONS

Among the generation of historians that came to maturity around the turn of the century, the War of 1812 was studied and analyzed with as much intensity as historians today study World Wars I and II. Theodore Roosevelt, Alfred Thayer

Mahan, and Henry Adams, all men of first-rate ability in military history, wrote long books on this early struggle. On the issue of the strategy of the naval phase of the war they came to different conclusions. Roosevelt and Mahan held views that, while not identical, were closely related. Briefly, they maintained that the United States should have built a strong navy including ships of the line that could have cruised far from American shores and kept the sea lanes open. This navy by its very existence would have prevented war, or at least have prevented the crippling blockade. Though their knowledge of both the strategy and tactics of the war was profound, Roosevelt and Mahan being advocates of a strong navy were apt to read into history needs of their own time. Theirs was essentially a military point of view. Adams, on the other hand, though not without prejudices of his own, expressed a civilian point of view in his famous *History of the United States in the Administrations of Jefferson and Madison.* After surveying the various alternatives open to the young republic, he concluded that the United States should have concentrated on commerce-destroying sloops of war. Let us examine these points of view in more detail.

Maintaining that what was needed was "a great fighting fleet," Roosevelt asserts that "twenty ships of the line, as good of their kind as were the frigates and sloops, would have rendered the blockade impossible even if they had not prevented war. . . ." Mahan put the case more subtly. In fact, Mahan is so subtle and prolix that his position can only be summarized with some difficulty. He concedes that "the lesson to be deduced is not that the country at that time should have sought to maintain a navy approaching equality to the British." Rather, in the decade preceding the war the United States should have placed the navy on such a footing "in numbers and constitution, as would have made persistence in the course Great Britain was following impolitic to the verge of madness." Reviving the naval argument used by Hamilton in *Federalist* No. 11, Mahan points out that the British were vulnerable in the West Indies and the United States was not without potential allies in Europe. War could have been avoided "had there been a dozen sail of the line, and frigates to match."

Perhaps the first thing to be noted is the bland assumption that a mighty navy would have prevented war. Then, as now, military men talked confidently of deterring war as if they were in possession of some magic formula. Actually they knew little about the relation between force and diplomacy and we have until this day progressed little beyond their deplorable state of ignorance. Another weakness of the thesis is the assumption that Great Britain would have sat idly by while the United States built a large battle fleet that could only have been used against her. Far from preventing conflict, such a fleet might have provoked war sooner. Though a fleet of twenty ships of the line was not beyond the financial and physical capacities of the country, it would certainly have strained those resources. The construction of such a fleet would have sacrificed one of the natural advantages of the country demonstrated during the Revolutionary War—the fact that the elements of power and control in the United States were so diffused that the enemy could find no fatal spot against which to direct his blow. A fleet would have constituted a center of power the British could have defeated with relative ease. Having but few harbors to service such ships, the fleet would be forced to place itself at a certain time, in a certain place, both of which could be foreseen by a strong naval power. All the British needed to do would be to gather a decisive fraction of their seapower at that place at the appointed time and destroy the incoming or outgoing ships. The assumption that Britain would have regarded a strong United States fleet a menace is strengthened by what actually occurred. The early successes of the United States frigates gave rise to a hue and cry that the navy must be utterly destroyed. *The Times*, for example, after the defeat of the "Guerrière," stated that "there is one object, to which our most strenuous efforts must be directed—the entire annihilation of the American navy."

A final objection to statements like "twenty ships of the line would have prevented war" is the assumption that it is possible to change one element in a complex social-political structure and allow all others to remain the same. The military and naval forces of any country represent or reflect the social and economic policies, prejudices, and predilections of the country—or its ruling elements—at a given time. More specifically, the only body in the United States that could build a navy was the Congress. The Jeffersonian Republicans, who governed the country after 1801, came to power on a program of antimilitarism and economy. After war broke out in Europe in 1803, and both the British and the French began to trample on neutral rights, perhaps the Jeffersonians should have changed their policies and prepared either to build up armaments or simply to forego their rights for the duration. In justice to the Republicans it must be said that it is doubtful that either alternative would have received widespread popular support. At any rate they chose to adhere to their doctrines and to seek earnestly, if unrealistically, for alternatives to military preparedness. Furthermore, the Federalists, though they had built up the navy during the 1790's when there was trouble with France, never during the decade before 1812 advocated a mighty fleet of ships of the line. The reason is obvious. The Federalists were, generally speaking, pro-British. After Trafalgar American ships of the line could only have been used against Great Britain and a building program could only have tipped the scales of world power in favor of Napoleon. In order therefore to have had Roosevelt's navy, it would have been necessary for both ruling factions to have altered their principles drastically. This is asking a good deal of history. One is forced to the conclusion that the Roosevelt navy was a dream.

Mahan, as already noted, was more subtle than Roosevelt; he prepared his big navy case in depth. He argued not only for the line of battleships but also for more of the heavy frigates. There is certainly a case for the frigates: though the single-ship victories did not alter the over-all balance of naval power, they saved American morale at a time when it was in great danger of being lost. Practically ignoring this factor, Mahan claims that the heavy frigates forced the British to divert a disproportionate number of their battleships and cruisers to the American theater of operations. In arguing this thesis he points out that the Admiralty's problem was to cover a wide sweep of ocean and to cover at certain strategic points through which streams of commerce flowed or converged. For this purpose, His Majesty's naval strength from Newfoundland to the West Indies was united as early as September, 1812, under Admiral Sir John Warren in a single command. It was the Admiralty's wish that a ship of the line should form the backbone of the blockade before each of the principal American harbors. For this purpose Admiral Warren was reinforced so that by early 1813 he had several ships of the line under his command. "It has not been without interfering for the moment with other very important services that my Lords have been able to send you this re-inforcement," Warren was informed, "and they most anxiously hope that the vigorous and successful use you will make of it will enable you shortly to return some of the line of battle ships to England, which if the heavy American frigates should be taken or destroyed, you will immediately do, retaining four line of battle ships." Mahan points out that in this dispatch it was not the light cruisers and privateers but chiefly the heavy vessels that counted in the estimate of the Admiralty. Doubtless this is true, but one might point out that in a country that had ships of the line by the score, the diversion of half a dozen counted for relatively little—unless of course England were hard pressed by a strong European naval power. No such power existed.

It matters not whether the United States had concentrated on ships of the line or heavy frigates, or a combination of the two. The fact remains that it simply was not within American capabilities to make a serious dent in British seapower, or even to cause a diversion of crucial proportions. Nor was total victory desired or desirable. British seapower as such was not a menace to the United States. The leaders of both the Federalists and Republicans realized that the abuses of which the United States complained were incident to the European war and that once the war was over they would disappear. Since the Orders-in-Council were withdrawn before the fighting even started; there remained only impressment as a cause of war. An issue involving national pride on both sides, impressment was certainly a difficult problem but not beyond the wit of man to resolve. It was not necessary to defeat the British but only to convince them that the few sailors they were getting by impressment were not worth a war. By causing harassment to trade and embarrassment to the navy, such a situation might have been brought about.

At any rate, as Adams maintained, the only course open to the Americans was destruction of commerce, and it would have been the part of wisdom to have brought this method of war to the highest possible degree of efficiency. The privateers, as we have already seen, though they accomplished much, operated under serious handicaps. One disadvantage was getting prizes to port. It has been estimated that one-half of the prizes taken were recaptured by the British navy. Another objection was that the privateers competed with the ships of war for seamen. For example, before the last sailing of the "Chesapeake" Lawrence had a very difficult time scraping together a crew. Probably the greatest weakness, however, was that the government could exercise little or no control. The privateers came and went as they pleased and their activities were stepped up or curtailed only according to whim or chance.

After the spectacular success of the frigates, Congress in January, 1813, voted funds for the construction of six additional frigates and four ships of the line (74's). In March of the same year funds for six new sloops were voted. The original cost of a frigate varied between $200,000 and $300,000 and the construction required especially heavy timbers. Four or five sloops could be built for the price of one frigate and of ordinary material. Of the vessels voted in 1813, all the sloops were launched within eleven months; none of the larger vessels saw service. Though their activities are less well known, the sloops were spectacularly successful both in destroying commerce and in encounters with ships of their own class. Unlike the privateers, the government sloops did not have to get their prizes to port; they could burn them at sea. By prohibiting privateering the government could have eliminated the competition for seamen. Most important of all, had it concentrated its efforts on the sloops of war, the United States would have had a tremendously powerful instrument which it could wield according to its plans and wishes. By conducting an aggressive guerrilla-type warfare upon the sea the United States might have created that disposition for peace so ardently desired by both sides.

Though the United States could not hope to overcome Britain's supremacy on the high seas, the situation on the lakes was very different. When the war broke out, the British had control of both Lake Erie and Lake Ontario, but here the United States possessed advantages that made it possible to challenge that control. After Hull's surrender the administration finally accepted the fact that they must make the effort to get control of the water if they were to succeed on land. The story of naval warfare on the lakes properly belongs, however, with a discussion of the land campaigns on the northern frontier.

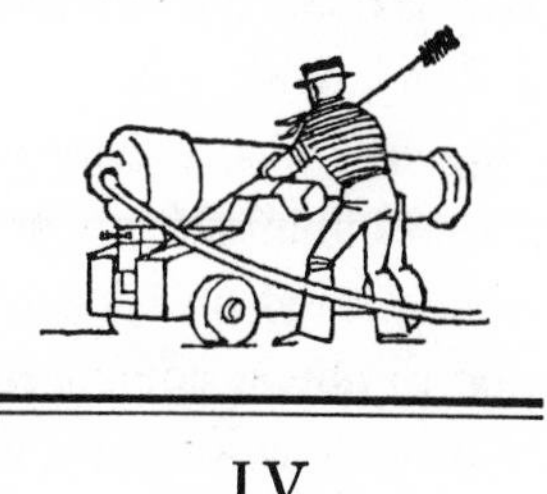

IV

American Redemption of the Northwest

Hull's surrender and the fiascoes along the northern border in the half-year of war in 1812 drove home at least three lessons: to succeed on land the Americans must first control the water; better leaders, civilian and military, must be found; and a strategy which concentrated effort on crucial objectives must be adopted. During 1813 the administration made considerable progress on the first of these goals, some progress on the second, but little or none on the third.

No one in a responsible position on either the American or Canadian side ever seriously questioned the importance of naval control of the lakes. By all—Brock and Prevost in Canada and Hull and Harrison in the United States—it was recognized as the key to success. Nevertheless in a fit of over-optimism the administration persuaded first itself and then General Hull that taking Canada was a mere matter of marching. When General Brock with a handful of British regulars and an uncertain band of Indians shattered that delusion, on September 3, 1812, the administration ordered Captain Isaac Chauncey to assume command on lakes Erie and Ontario and to "use every exertion to obtain control of them this fall." At about the same time President Madison wrote General Dearborn emphatically, if somewhat belatedly, that "the command of the lake by a superior force on the water ought to have been a fundamental part in the national policy." Arriving at Sackett's Harbor on October 6, Chauncey found only the 18-gun "Oneida" but he soon acquired a half-dozen merchant schooners and armed them with one or more long guns. On November 26 he launched the "Madison," a 24-gun corvette, and before the lake froze over for the season he claimed to have control. In March of 1813 Chauncey sent Oliver Hazard Perry to hasten the building of a fleet on Lake Erie.

The administration was slow to act on the need for better leadership at the top. Devotion to one's friends was a virtue that President Madison took to excess. Nearly everyone was aware of the inadequacies of Secretary of War William Eustis and Secretary of the Navy Paul Hamilton, even in time of peace. A few months of war were sufficient to demonstrate their utter incapacity even to the satisfaction of the president. Nothing in Hamilton's background as a South Carolina planter prepared him for the Navy Department and he seems to have learned little on the job. According to gossip he was frequently intoxicated by mid-day. Ironically enough, however, it was not so much his drinking as the very success of the little navy that got Hamilton into serious trouble. The early victories made the navy very popular and brought a demand that it be increased. Then questions began to be asked whether ships of the line, frigates, or sloops should be built and in what proportions. Though he knew nothing of naval strategy, Hamilton, influenced by the opinions of certain of his captains, allowed himself to become an advocate of 74-gun ships. When his scheme was defeated and when Madison informed him that Congress had lost all confidence in his judgment, Hamilton resigned on December 29, 1812. His successor was William Jones of Philadelphia. As a veteran of the Revolution, Jones knew something of fighting; as a merchant engaged in the China trade he had acquired considerable knowledge of ships; and as a former congressman, he knew the ways of politics and politicians. With great energy and ability, Jones set about improving the organization of his department, pushing the building program, and hastening the efforts to secure control of the inland waters.

The problem of finding a better Secretary of War was not so easily solved. Penny-pinching William Eustis of Boston wasted his time with trivial matters to the utter neglect of more important things. According to Gallatin, "His incapacity and total want of confidence in him were felt through every ramification of the service." Under increasing pressure he resigned on December 3 and Secretary of State Monroe took over the War Department temporarily. Monroe was such an improvement over Eustis that he was asked to take over permanently. When he refused, President Madison asked General Dearborn and William H. Crawford, but no one, said Gallatin, was anxious to accept the War Department "with all its horrors and perils." Since it was desirable to maintain the Virginia–New York political alliance, the choice finally fell upon

John Armstrong, a leading Republican politician in New York. Armstrong had served as minister to France, he had supported Madison against Dewitt Clinton in New York, and since August, 1812, he had been charged with the defense of New York as a brigadier general in the U.S. Army. Taking over from Monroe on February 5, Armstrong resolved to rid the army of its superannuated generals, to introduce a strategy that called for concentration of effort, and to develop a new manpower policy.

British strategy in the American war remained defensive. As long as Napoleon remained the arch enemy, Britain simply expected the Canadians to hold their own. As late as September, 1813, Prevost wrote Lord Bathurst, "Your Lordship must ere this be well aware that I have not been honoured with a single instruction from His Majesty's Government upon the mode of conducting the campaign. . . ." In reply Lord Bathurst expressed something akin to amazement that Prevost should wish a strategic plan. "His Majesty's Government felt that to present you a specific plan of campaign . . . was a measure only to add to your embarrassments and to fetter your judgment . . . more especially as the correct view which you expressed on the two points most essential to the Defence of the Canadas, the maintenance of naval superiority on the Lakes and the uninterrupted communication with our Indian allies."

Though the regular army in Canada received only small reinforcements, the British did take advantage of Napoleon's retreat from Moscow to strengthen the blockade—as we saw in the preceding chapter—and they also made an effort to prevent the Americans from seizing naval control of the lakes. Early in the war the naval forces on lakes Ontario and Erie were known as the Provincial Marine of Upper Canada. This force was not a proper fighting navy but primarily a transport service administered by the quartermaster general's department of the army. When the Americans began extensive building on their side of the border Prevost pleaded with the home government to send supplies and men from the Royal Navy to maintain control of water communication—which was the only practical line of communication with Upper Canada. Not until May, 1813, did Commodore Sir James Yeo arrive at Kingston. Taking personal command on Lake Ontario, Yeo sent Captain Robert Heriot Barclay to be Perry's opposite number on Lake Erie. The Royal Navy finally arrived but too late and with too little. Failure to maintain original British naval control of the lakes was probably the greatest mistake of British military policy in North America in 1812–13. From this fundamental error flowed the principal American gains of the year: Perry's victory on Lake Erie, the defeat of the British at the Battle of the Thames, and the collapse of the Indian confederacy.

Though the redemption of American territory in the Northwest was an impressive accomplishment it should be noted that it only restored the situation existing before the outbreak of hostilities. Canada more than held her own in 1813. Harrison was unable to follow up his victory on Canadian soil. In the center the Americans got control of the Niagara peninsula only to lose it, and to end the year with the frontier in desolation and partial occupation. So far as taking Montreal or carrying out any significant operation in the northeastern theater was concerned, the Americans accomplished nothing whatever. The federal government could properly take credit for building naval forces on the lakes but so far as raising an army to exploit that control Washington was more a hindrance than a help.

THE SECOND NORTHWESTERN ARMY

Nowhere were the overlapping jurisdictions of state and federal authority and the confused military system of the United States better illustrated than in the efforts to raise a second Northwestern Army. After news of Hull's surrender spread over the country, the administration in Washington and the people of the western states were agreed on one thing: Detroit must be retaken and the West freed of the Indian menace. With the elections coming up in November, it was desirable to have a victory in the West and soon. For a while President Madison toyed with the idea of making James Monroe a lieutenant general and giving him command of all troops along the Canadian border. But the western people had their own ideas. Ever since the days of Tippecanoe the Kentuckians looked to William Henry Harrison as the man best qualified to lead them to victory. A technical obstacle—the fact that Harrison was not a citizen of Kentucky—was overcome on August 25, 1812, by the simple expedient of having a caucus elect Harrison a major general of the Kentucky militia.

Harrison hurried to the relief of Fort Wayne, then under siege by the Indians. When he reached Piqua, Ohio, Harrison received a letter from the Secretary of War informing him that he had been appointed a brigadier general in the regular army as of August 22. If Harrison accepted this appointment he would be under command of James Winchester who had been commissioned as brigadier general in March. The sixty-one-year-old Winchester, a planter of aris-

Tecumseh saving American prisoners during the Battle for Fort Meigs.
(Courtesy of Indiana Historical Society Library.)

"Those are regulars, by God!" Battle of Chippewa, July 5, 1814. (Courtesy of U.S. Army Photographic Agency.)

tocratic bearing from Tennessee, was not popular in the West and Harrison knew it. The people of that area would "never perform anything brilliant under a stranger," he informed Washington. President Madison, impressed with the action of the Kentucky caucus, on September 17 appointed Harrison commander-in-chief of the Northwestern Army which was to consist of all the regulars, rangers, volunteers, and the Kentucky, Ohio, and Indiana militia, and all troops coming from Pennsylvania and Virginia. With this force—expected to reach ten thousand—the thirty-nine-year-old Harrison was to defend the frontiers and retake Detroit.

Harrison's hopes of a successful autumn campaign soon faded. He was frustrated not so much by the Indians and the British as by nature. The big swamp that stretched from the Sandusky River on his right to the Auglaize River on his left barred the passage of supplies "as effectually as though it had been the Andes," says Adams. True, Hull's army had passed through this area the previous spring by laying down a road, but Hull marched with a small army in May and June. With the heavy rains that came in the autumn, it became impossible to transport the heavy guns, matériel, and rations for an army of ten thousand men.

Convinced that an autumn campaign was impossible, Harrison's next idea was to wait until the winter freeze enabled the army to use the rivers and margins of lakes for the transportation of baggage and artillery on the ice. While the main army gathered its strength, expeditions were sent out against the Indians. One of these was led by Lieutenant Colonel John B. Campbell, who with six hundred men, set out from Franklinton (now Columbus), Ohio, on November 25. Marching by way of Dayton and Greenville, this force attacked the Miami and Delaware towns on the Mississiniwa River, a tributary of the Wabash.

Harrison's general plan was that the army would assemble in three main columns, which would converge at the Maumee Rapids and then march on Detroit. Early in December, General Simon Perkins, with an Ohio brigade from the Western Reserve, arrived on the Sandusky, where they were joined by the units from Pennsylvania and Virginia. These forces, which constituted the right wing, built a series of blockhouses along the Sandusky (Forts Stephenson, Ball, Seneca) and undertook the construction of a fifteen-mile causeway across the Black Swamp towards the Maumee Rapids. The central column under Brigadier General Edward Tupper consisted of about twelve hundred troops who were trying to stockpile provisions at McArthur's Blockhouse on Hull's old road and forward them to the rapids. The left wing, based at Fort Defiance, was under General Winchester.

Though all the soldiers of the Northwestern Army suffered during the winter, none underwent greater privations than those under Winchester. Shivering in crudely made huts, the Kentuckians were on half rations exept when they had no food at all. Nowhere within one hundred miles was there a human habitation that offered a warm fire, a clean bed, or a decent meal. With isolation breeding despair, the wonder is not that the men were sometimes mutinous but that there was any army at all. In spite of all these difficulties, Harrison probably had a total of sixty-five hundred men in his three columns by the middle of December. At any rate he decided that he must now set in motion the concentration of his troops, and on December 20 he ordered Winchester to the rapids.

American Redemption of the Northwest

THE RIVER RAISIN MASSACRE

Though snow fell to a depth of two feet, Winchester's force of some twelve hundred men reached the rapids on January 10 and began to lay out a fortified camp on the north bank of the Maumee. About thirty-five miles northeast of the rapids and only eighteen miles southwest of Malden was the small settlement known as Frenchtown (later Monroe, Michigan) on the River Raisin. Soon messages began to be received from Frenchtown that the American settlers and a considerable quantity of food supplies were in need of rescue. The town was supposed to be garrisoned only by fifty Canadian militia and one hundred Indians. After months of waiting, the chance to strike at the enemy was all the Kentuckians wanted. Winchester summoned a council of officers and though the only regular army man, Colonel Samuel Wells, dissented, the majority voted in favor of sending a relief expedition.

On January 17 Colonel William Lewis, who was particularly anxious to carry out the enterprise, advanced with 550 men and Colonel John Allen soon followed with 110. On the following day, the British garrison fought long enough to kill 12 Americans and wound 55 but by nightfall Colonel Lewis was in possession of the town. With half of his force at the rapids and half within 18 miles of a strong British force at Malden, Winchester suddenly realized how perilous his position was. He therefore decided to march to Allen's help with 300 additional men.

As soon as he had news of the American advance, Colonel Procter also realized that the Americans had overextended themselves. On January 21, with from 1,200 to 1,400 men, he crossed the river on the ice and halted his advance only about six miles north of Frenchtown. About half of Procter's force were Indians led by Roundhead and Walk-in-the-Water. Tecumseh was still on the Wabash collecting warriors. During the night Procter moved three or four pieces of artillery into position, placed his regulars in the center behind the artillery, and Indians and militia on the right and left flanks.

Outnumbered and without artillery, Winchester should have deployed his men so that the River Raisin was to his front instead of his rear. Taking up his own abode on the southern bank, Winchester placed his men on the northern bank. On the American left the men were partially protected by a heavy picket fence but on the right there was only a crude rail fence. Winchester admitted afterward that "neither night patrol nor night pickets were ordered by me, from a belief that both were matters of routine."

These derelictions enabled Procter, when he attacked about four o'clock on the twenty-first, to overwhelm quickly the American right. Hurrying from his headquarters half a mile distant from the main camp, Winchester tried in vain to rally his men. Before anything could be done, however, the Indians got to the rear and literally hacked the Americans to pieces. At least one hundred Kentuckians were scalped within a few minutes. The rest were captured, including General Winchester, who was taken to Roundhead.

Meanwhile on the American left nearly four hundred men under command of Major George Madison held off several attacks and were under the impression they had gained a victory when a white flag appeared. Actually this was a message from Winchester saying that he, a prisoner, had surrendered on behalf of the entire army. Madison replied that he would not agree to any capitulation unless the safety and protection of all prisoners were provided for. At first Procter refused any conditions. When, however, Madison assured him that the Americans would sell their lives as dearly as possible, the British general promised protection to the prisoners.

With the prisoners that were able to march, Procter recrossed the Detroit River on the day of the battle. A number of wounded were left in Frenchtown under the care of American doctors. Just how many wounded prisoners there were is uncertain—maybe as few as thirty, possibly as many as a hundred. When the regular army left, the Indians began to loot and to consume the liquor they found. Drunk with whiskey and with the desire for revenge, the Indians hunted down the wounded and scalped them. Coming across one house with several prisoners, they set it afire and as the wounded tried to escape through doors and windows the Indians beat them back with tomahawks. There were several eyewitnesses and their stories of the night's horrors lost nothing in the telling. "Remember the River Raisin" soon became the rallying cry of the soldiers of the Northwestern Army.

Most Americans, and some Canadians for that matter, blamed Procter for the massacre. It is easy to blame him, for he was an overbearing, supercilious, and rather mediocre soldier. But in justice we must remember his circumstances: he had on his hands as many prisoners as he had soldiers, and he had every reason to suppose that a large American force might soon appear from the south. It would have been taking a chance, to say the least, to have risked the displeasure, or possibly open hostility, of his Indian allies.

THE BRITISH OFFENSIVES

Informed that Winchester had marched off into the snows of Michigan, General Harrison hastened to the rapids where he was informed of the disaster on January 22. Without men to replace those lost at the River Raisin and with the terms of enlistment of many of his militia drawing to a close, there was nothing for Harrison to do but to call off his winter campaign. As an alternative he decided to establish a strong defensive position on the Maumee. With the aid of Captain Eleazer Wood, an engineer trained at West Point, he chose an excellent site just below the rapids on the south bank and began building a well-planned fortification which he named Fort Meigs.

With the coming of spring the offensive passed over for a while to the British. Harrison's force having been reduced to about one thousand men, he appealed to Governor Shelby of Kentucky, who sent forward about twelve hundred men under General Green Clay. Marching by way of Cincinnati, this force reached Fort Defiance and began moving down the Maumee early in May. At about the same time General Procter, hoping to wipe out Fort Meigs before it could be reinforced, marched from Amherstburg with a force consisting of about five hundred regulars, about five hundred militia, and twelve hundred Indians under Tecumseh and Roundhead. Bebetween May 1 and 3, Procter established three batteries, two on the north and one on the south side of the river and laid siege to Fort Meigs. Using hot shot in the hope of blowing up the powder magazine, the British pounded at the fort for four days. Just before midnight on May 4 Harrison received a message from General Clay saying that he was within two hours of the fort.

Harrison immediately determined upon a plan for raising the siege: the troops under Clay would be used for capturing the batteries on the north side of the river while his own troops destroyed the battery on the south side. About eight hundred of Clay's men were to pass the rapids, land on the left bank, spike the cannon, and destroy the carriages. They were then to retreat immediately to their boats, hopefully before the main body of British troops could get into action. The remainder of Clay's forces were to land on the right bank and cut their way through the besieging Indians to the fort.

The Kentuckians under Lieutenant Colonel William Dudley landed on the left bank and spiked the guns as planned. But instead of returning to their boats, the men advanced toward the main British camp. In doing so they walked into a trap: they were counterattacked by British regulars in their front, while the Indians closed in on their flanks. About six hundred men were either killed or captured. Again, as at the River Raisin, the Indians began to massacre the prisoners. This time, however, Tecumseh was present and attempted to restrain his warriors. One British regular of the 41st was murdered while trying to protect some prisoners. Tecumseh, observing Procter's indifference, is reported to have said: "Begone, you are not fit to command, go and put on petticoats."

On the right bank things went somewhat better for the Americans. The British battery was taken and General Clay with about four hundred men reached Fort Meigs without great loss. Though the fighting of May 5 was extensive it was not immediately decisive. Procter got his guns back into working order (they had been ineffectively spiked) and resumed the siege. But not for long. Many of his Indian allies, having captured boats and supplies, stole off with their plunder and prisoners toward their towns. Eight militia captains from the Kent and Essex regiments informed their commander that they must go home soon and plant their crops or face starvation. On May 9 Procter lifted the siege and returned to Canada.

The next few weeks were spent by both sides in gathering men and supplies. By July Procter had about four hundred regulars, mostly of the 41st Regiment, a few artillerymen, and about one thousand Indians. With this force he again ascended the Maumee on July 20 and laid siege to Fort Meigs. With nothing heavier than 6-pounders it was useless to attempt to bombard the fort into surrender. Tecumseh suggested a stratagem of enticing the defenders out of their stronghold; when this failed, Procter had to find employment elsewhere for his Indians. Dropping down the river, he coasted along the lake until he came to the Sandusky River, which he entered with the intention of attacking Fort Stephenson. Defended by only 160 soldiers under the command of Major George Croghan, the fort was extremely vulnerable. So much so that when General Harrison, at Seneca Town, received word on July 29 of the British movement, he sent orders that the fort be evacuated. Croghan, a Kentuckian twenty-three years of age, replied: "We have determined to maintain this place, and by Heaven, we will." Incensed at this willful disobedience, Harrison at first planned to relieve Croghan. But when Croghan hastened to headquarters and explained his position in person, Harrison relented.

Returning to his post Croghan prepared for the attack, which came on August 1. The fort was bombarded from gunboats in the river and three 6-pounders on the shore. Failing to make a breach, Procter ordered the regulars of the 41st to make an assault because, he explained, "unless the fort was stormed we should never be able to bring an Indian warrior into the field with us."

Croghan had but one piece of artillery, affectionately called "Old Betsy," which was brought to bear on the northwest angle. As the British marched forward, they were mowed down by the Kentucky sharpshooters and by Old Betsy belching grape and nails. According to Procter's own account: "The fort, from which the severest fire I ever saw was maintained . . . was well defended. The troops displayed the greatest bravery . . . and made every effort to enter; but the Indians who had proposed the assault . . . scarcely came into fire before they ran. . . . A more than adequate sacrifice having been made to Indian opinion, I drew off the brave assailants." Croghan's gallant stand put an end to the British offensive. An American fleet was nearing completion at Presque Isle, which if allowed to escape, would deprive the British of freedom of movement in the Detroit area.

THE BATTLE OF LAKE ERIE

In September, 1812, Daniel Dobbins, a lake trader, turned up in Washington and persuaded President Madison and his cabinet that Presque Isle (or Erie, Pennsylvania) was a good place to construct a lake flotilla. Beginning work in October, Dobbins laid the keels of two fifty-foot gunboats. In December Commodore Chauncey visited Presque Isle and ordered Dobbins to start the construction of two brigs. Anxious to expedite the work and to put the vessels under command of a regular naval officer, Chauncey was delighted to receive a letter of application from a young naval officer then commanding a small group of gunboats off the Rhode Island coast. "You are just the man I have been looking for," Chauncey wrote Master Commandant Oliver Hazard Perry.

Son of a Newport captain, Perry had gone to sea at the age

of eleven and had fought in the war with the Barbary pirates. Only twenty-eight years old, he arrived at Erie with his brother Alexander, aged thirteen, and 150 seamen, on March 27, 1813. Though Perry had able assistants in Dobbins and in Noah Brown, a New York shipwright, there were innumerable details to which he gave his personal attention. Of timber there was an ample supply locally but most of the equipment had to come from the east coast or from Pittsburgh. In April Perry went to Pittsburgh to hurry his suppliers; two months later he was cursing them for failure to deliver on time. Though no one moved fast enough to satisfy Perry, he was nevertheless much in debt to the growing industries of the West. Pittsburgh, which doubled its population between 1810 and 1815, furnished Perry's fleet with its galley stoves, cables, anchors, and shot.

It was, indeed, the logistical advantages enjoyed by the Americans and the tardiness of the Royal Navy that enabled Perry to lay the foundations of victory. The British held a precarious control of Lake Erie with some six small vessels but these, as we have already noted, were in the hands of the notoriously inadequate Canadian Provincial Marine. In spite of Prevost's many pleas for reinforcement it was not until late spring of 1813 that Commodore Yeo, of the Royal Navy, arrived at Kingston and Captain Barclay took up his duties on Lake Erie.

Though Yeo undertook an extensive building program on Lake Ontario and Barclay tried to expedite the completion of the "Detroit," a 20-gun vessel being built at Amherstburg, British efforts to maintain their supremacy were not successful. By the end of April, 1813, the American fleet on Lake Ontario was strong enough to carry out a raid against York (Toronto), the details of which will be described later. It need only be said here that though the operation has often been dismissed as a futile waste of effort, the Canadian historian C. P. Stacey points out that the raid had important consequences. For one thing, the British were forced to burn the 30-gun frigate "Sir Isaac Brock," which was being built at York and which would have tipped the balance in favor of the British on Lake Ontario for 1813. Secondly, the naval and ordnance stores intended to equip the squadron on Lake Erie were captured by the Americans or destroyed to prevent capture. Lastly, the raid on York set into motion a series of events that eventually enabled Perry to assemble his flotilla.

Perry's fleet was to consist not only of the four ships being built at Presque Isle but also five vessels at Black Rock. These vessels could not be moved into Lake Erie as long as the enemy held Fort Erie because the British could easily shell them from their side of the river. The raid on York was followed a month later by the capture of Fort George, which in turn forced General Vincent to order the evacuation of Fort Erie. Perry was now free to move his vessels provided he could overcome the physical obstacles. The largest of the vessels was the brig "Caledonia" (180 tons), captured from the British. The others were trading vessels purchased by the navy. They had been strengthened to support guns but were without bulwarks. All these vessels had to be warped up the swift waters of the Niagara in order to reach the open lake. With great difficulty this was accomplished, but once in the lake a constant watch for the British fleet had to be maintained. By taking advantage of thick weather and by clinging to the shallows, the American vessels made it safely to harbor. Soon after, however, the British fleet reappeared and maintained strict vigilance.

By July 10 the process of building and rigging the Presque Isle fleet was completed. News of the "Don't give up the ship" episode had reached Perry as his ships were nearing completion. Much impressed, Perry named one of his 480-ton brigs the "Lawrence," and christened its twin the "Niagara." Perry now faced the problem of getting over a bar that obstructed the mouth of the harbor. Though the bar had served to protect the vessels while they were being built, it now imposed a danger because in order to get over it the brigs had to be stripped of their guns and lifted on floats. While this operation was being carried out, the brigs could easily be destroyed by the British.

For reasons that have never been satisfactorily explained, Barclay relaxed his blockade on August 1. The depth of the water over the bar was ordinarily about six feet. Since they could cross without great difficulty, five of the smaller vessels were ordered out on August 2 to take up their positions outside the channel. The devices employed to lift the brigs were known as "camels." Developed by the Dutch, the camels, or floats, were filled with water and attached to the sides of the vessels. As the water was pumped out, the camels would rise and lift the vessel. The devices were attached to the "Lawrence" in an attempt to get her over first. The operation became even more time-consuming and difficult when it was discovered that the water level over the bar had fallen to four feet. Finally, by dint of great exertion the "Lawrence" was put over on August 4 and the "Niagara" came over on the following day.

Safely over the bar, Perry drew a sigh of relief only to face another difficulty: the lack of seamen. For months he had been begging Chauncey for men. In one of several complaining letters he said: "Conceive my feelings: an enemy within striking distance, my vessels ready, and not men enough to man them." The situation was partially alleviated on August 10 by the arrival of Jesse D. Elliott—the young officer who had captured the "Caledonia"—with about one hundred prime seamen including about a half-dozen officers. Though still short of men Perry placed Elliott in command of the "Niagara" and sailed westward on August 12. Putting into Sandusky Bay, Perry held a conference with General Harrison and his principal subordinates. In an effort to ease the manpower problem, Harrison lent Perry a hundred Kentucky marksmen. Though most of these had never seen anything but a flat boat or a raft, Perry patiently explained what was expected and the Kentuckians turned out to be pretty good sailors. Perry and Harrison also agreed on a general plan of campaign and fixed Put-in-Bay in the Bass Islands as their headquarters. A good harbor there afforded an excellent position for watching Barclay, should he attempt to sail out of Amherstburg.

Meanwhile, Barclay too was struggling with manpower and supply problems. According to his own account, he had approximately 450 men for his six vessels. Of these only about 50 were regular seamen and the rest were Canadian boatmen and regular soldiers from General Procter's command. Though the "Detroit," a slightly larger ship than any under Perry's command, was now completed, the armament intended for her had been captured or destroyed, as we have already seen. As a result Barclay stripped the ramparts of Fort Malden to mount a curiously composite battery. The matches and tubes of these pieces were so deficient that pistols had to be fired into the vents to produce a discharge.

Unable to use the lake for transportation, the British commanders at Amherstburg had a supply problem that grew steadily worse. They were attempting to feed a large number of Indians—fourteen thousand, according to some accounts—and little could be obtained locally. "So perfectly destitute of provisions was the port, that there was not a day's flour in store," wrote Barclay, "and the crews of the squadron under my command were on half allowances of many things, and when that was done there was no more." In this desperate situation Barclay and Procter decided that an attempt must be made to bring supplies. Accordingly, without waiting for the additional seamen, said to be on their way, Barclay sailed out on September 9 to face his enemy.

Much has been written concerning the relative strength of the two squadrons, comparing the tonnages of the ships involved, the number and caliber of guns, weight of broadside, the crews, etc. There are so many variables that comparison is difficult. Two facts stand out. One is that Perry, with nine vessels to Barclay's six, had the greater force at both long and short range but he had marked superiority only at short range, where he could utilize his carronades. Barclay, on the other hand, had thirty-five long guns to Perry's fifteen, and they were better concentrated. Seventeen of the long guns were in the "Detroit" and three each were in the "Queen Charlotte" and the "Lady Prevost." Perry's twin ships, the "Lawrence" and the "Niagara," had only two long 12's each, but each had eighteen short 32's. Perry, who was well informed on the size and character of Barclay's squadron, planned his dispositions so as to bring superior firepower against each of the British ships. Barclay, on the other hand, hoped to be able to choose his distance and to defeat the enemy ships in detail, a hope he nearly fulfilled.

The British fleet was first sighted by the Americans at 5:00 A.M. on September 10, and by 7:00 the entire fleet was visible.

At first the wind favored the British but about 10:00 it shifted so as to give the Americans the weather gauge. Where, as in the case of the Americans, the vessels were armed principally with short-range but large-caliber carronades the windward position was particularly advantageous. The careful planning that had marked all Perry's actions was evident in his last-minute preparations. The decks were strewn with sand to prevent the men from slipping on any blood that might be spilled, and at 10:30 food was served so that the men could go into battle with full stomachs. At 11:45 the British opened fire with their long guns. Finding this very destructive, Perry reported that he made sail and "directed the other vessels to follow for the purpose of closing with the enemy." The schooners "Scorpion" and "Ariel," who were in line ahead of the "Lawrence," kept their places and fought valiantly throughout the action.

The rest of the American fleet lagged behind. The "Caledonia" was a slow sailer and Captain Elliott of the "Niagara," kept at a distance, using only his long-range guns. Years after the war Perry censured Elliott's conduct but the matter never received thorough investigation. Hence, to this day many questions are unanswered and unanswerable. In Elliott's behalf it has been said that his orders assigned him a place in the line behind the "Caledonia" which he could not leave without signal. Mahan says that this type of reasoning applies "the dry-rot system of fleet tactics of the middle of the eighteenth century to the days after Rodney and Nelson, and is further effectually disposed of by the consentient statement of several of the American captains, that their commander'd dispositions were made with reference to the enemy's order: that is, that he assigned a special enemy's ship to a special American, and particularly . . . the 'Queen Charlotte' to the 'Niagara.' "

However all this may be, the "Queen Charlotte," failing to find other suitable employment, made sail ahead and joined the "Detroit" in battering the "Lawrence." For two hours the "Lawrence" sustained a galling fire without any assistance from the "Niagara." When every brace and bowline was shot away, when every gun was made useless, Perry might have surrendered. But having given as well as taken punishment, he realized that with a fresh ship he might still win the day. Hauling down his broad banner with Lawrence's famous words on it, Perry leapt into a boat—miraculously there was a boat left—with his brother and four seamen and rowed toward the "Niagara." Shot fell around Perry like hailstones but on this day he seemed to lead a charmed life.

On reaching the "Niagara" Perry took command and ordered Elliott to bring up the three schooners that had lagged behind. Soon afterward the "Lawrence," now drifting out of control and without a single gun that could be fired, hauled down her flag. But before the British could take possession, Perry set into motion the last act of the drama. In the swift-sailing, well-manned "Niagara" he broke through the British line. On the port side the "Niagara" fired her battery into the "Chippewa," "Little Belt," and "Lady Prevost," and on the starboard side the "Detroit," "Queen Charlotte," and "Hunter" received a raking fire. In attempting to wear the "Detroit" fouled the "Queen Charlotte" and while the two ships were locked together Perry shot both to pieces. By this time the first and second in command of each of the six vessels had been either killed or wounded. Barclay, who had fought at Trafalgar and who had lost an arm in the service, had his remaining arm badly shattered. Having fought to the last extremity, he surrendered at about 3:00 P.M. and soon all but two of the British ships followed suit. The "Chippewa" and the "Little Belt" tried to escape but were overtaken by the "Scorpion" and the "Trippe."

In certain of his preliminary actions, particularly in allowing Perry's fleet to escape from Presque Isle, Barclay may have been culpable. But once the battle was joined he fought superbly. His defeat resulted from want neither of bravery nor judgment but from well-directed superior force. In the early part of the battle, the American captains, failing to support each other, nearly went down to defeat. Though literally battered out of his ship, Perry transferred his flag to another ship and crushed the last remnant of British power on Lake Erie. On the back of an old letter Perry wrote in pencil his famous dispatch to General Harrison: "We have met the enemy and they are ours: two ships, two brigs, one schooner, and one sloop." The victory was complete; the way was now open for redeeming the American position in the Northwest.

BATTLE OF THE THAMES

The significance of Perry's victory was not lost upon British officials in Canada, least of all upon the man directly in charge. "The loss of the fleet is a most calamitous circumstance," wrote General Procter. "I do not see the least chance of occupying to advantage my present position, which can be so easily turned by means of the entire command of the waters here which the enemy now has, a circumstance that would render my Indian force very inefficient. It is my opinion that I should retire on the Thames without delay. . . ."

General Procter did retire but only after considerable delay. Not until September 18 did he summon his Indian allies and propose a retreat toward Niagara. Tecumseh in the best style of Indian eloquence denounced such an idea as cowardly, and his warriors backed him up with a menacing demonstration. Whereupon Procter suggested that they retreat northward to the Thames and there make a life-or-death stand against the enemy. Moving, according to his own account, "by easy marches," he did not reach the Thames until the twenty-ninth.

Meanwhile, on the American shore there had been feverish activity. Although the "Lawrence" had to be sent to Erie for extensive repairs, Perry within a week had most of his squadron and four of his prizes ready to transport the army. In addition to Perry's fleet there were some seventy transports of the type known as Schenectady boats built near Cleveland at the order of the War Department.

That there was an army of forty-five hundred men ready to invade Canada was not the result of the exertions of the federal government. Armstrong's plan to rely upon regulars rather than militia, though fine in theory, was ineffective in practice. To raise the men needed, Harrison had again to appeal to Kentucky. Writing to his old friend Governor Shelby, Harrison made an interesting proposal: "To make this last effort, why not, dear sir, come in person—you would not object to a command that would be nominal only; I have such confidence in your wisdom, that you in fact should be the guiding head, and I the hand. The situation you would be placed in is not without parallel: Scipio, the conqueror of Carthage, did not disdain to act as the lieutenant of his younger and less experienced brother Lucius." This appeal to personal vanity and ancient history had the desired effect. The sixty-three-year-old Shelby, a hero of the Battle of King's Mountain in the American Revolution, raised over three thousand volunteers, placed himself at their head, and by the middle of September marched into Harrison's camp near the shores of Lake Erie. In addition to the forces under Shelby, Harrison had also the services of a mounted regiment of one thousand volunteers raised by Congressman Richard M. Johnson.

Harrison's plan was to send the mounted men by road to Detroit while the rest of the army made a landing at Hartley's Point, some four miles below Malden. The troops assembled at their rendezvous, Middle Sister Island, and on September 27 were transported to the landing beaches. Marching into Amherstburg the Americans found the town in smoking ruins. Procter's rear guard, whose duty it was to destroy the navy buildings and the government storehouses, had finished their business only a short time before.

Two days later the army reached Sandwich, General McArthur and seven hundred regulars were sent across the river to occupy Detroit. On the following day Colonel Johnson's regiment, which had been advancing by road, also arrived at Detroit. As the horses and men were being ferried across the river on October 1, Harrison called a council of his general officers and consulted them on the question of the best route to pursue. There were two possibilities: by land in the rear of the British, or by water to Long Point, where a march across country might be made. The decision was in favor of the land route.

Once under way the pursuit was rapid. As the American army skirted the shore of Lake St. Clair and then advanced up the banks of the Thames, it met few impediments and no organized resistance until near the town of Chatham. Here the Indians drew up as if to challenge the American advance but scattered after a brief skirmish. As the Americans continued to gain on the British they picked up hastily abandoned supplies.

On the morning of October 5 they captured two gunboats and the soldiers who had been left to guard them. These boats contained all the ammunition that had not already been abandoned or issued to the British troops.

Though Procter's intentions are difficult to fathom, he probably planned to make his stand at Moraviantown, which offered an excellent defensive position, especially against mounted troops. This place, however, had not been cleared of civilians and wounded troops. With the Americans on his heels Procter ordered his men to make their stand in a wooded area about two miles west of Moraviantown. The position chosen, though far from ideal, had advantages: on the left was the river and on the right a large swamp. The Americans had therefore to make a frontal assault along a narrow front. Along the road running parallel to the river the British regulars were drawn up in two lines to a small swamp which was in the center. On the road also a single six-pound brass piece was placed but there was not a single round of ammunition with which to fire it. On the right flank, between the small and large swamps, the Indians were deployed. The exact strength of each side is difficult to determine, but the Americans were certainly more numerous. Since Harrison had left a considerable number of troops on garrison duty at Detroit and at Sandwich and since he had detailed men to guard supply transports along the route of advance, he probably had between twenty-five hundred and three thousand troops. Procter had also lost men along the way, and so he had only about four hundred regular troops and possibly one thousand Indians. "But unfortunately," writes Sir John Fortescue, historian of the British army, "numerical inferiority was not the only defect . . . for the men were also thoroughly demoralized. During the retreat they had formed the conviction, which unhappily appears to have been justified, that their commander was more anxious for the safety of his family and his private property than of his troops."

Harrison's first thought was to use the infantry against the British regulars, but when he was informed that the British, contrary to their usual custom, had drawn up in open order he changed his mind and ordered Colonel Johnson's mounted riflemen to charge the regulars and to get to their rear. This method of attack, General Harrison admitted, "was not sanctioned by anything I had seen or heard of, but I was fully convinced that it would succeed. The American backwoodsmen ride better in woods than any other people. . . . I was persuaded, too, that the enemy would be quite unprepared for the shock, and that they could not resist it." Just before the attack Colonel Johnson found that the space along the river was too small for the whole regiment of one thousand men. Without consulting Harrison he left his brother, Lieutenant Colonel James Johnson, with one battalion while he himself crossed the swamp with the other battalion of five hundred men.

When the bugle sounded, the mounted riflemen charged the two lines of British regulars and scattered them in utter confusion. Only one officer and about fifty men of the 41st Regiment escaped. On the right the battle was over in about ten minutes.

On the American left the Indians under Tecumseh waited until the charging Americans were within a few paces and then poured in a withering fire. Unable because of the thick undergrowth to accomplish much, Johnson's men dismounted and engaged in severe hand-to-hand combat. In the melee

Tecumseh was killed. Deprived of their leader, short of ammunition, and faced with overwhelming odds, the Indians fled into the swamps. The Battle of the Thames, fought mostly by Johnson's mounted regiment, was over.

General Procter and his personal staff, who were well to the rear when the action started, were out of sight when it was over. A small detachment of American troops gave hot pursuit and they captured Procter's carriage, his sword, and many of his personal and official papers. The general himself escaped. Several days later the remnants of the right wing of the British army in Canada made a rendezvous in Ancaster. Besides a good deal of Procter's personal baggage, the Americans captured equipment of all sorts estimated to be worth $1 million. At least eight field pieces were taken, including three cannon captured from Burgoyne in 1777, then lost by Hull at Detroit in 1812.

Who killed Tecumseh is a historical riddle that will probably never be solved. Several participants, in both the American and the British armies, believed that Colonel Richard M. Johnson was responsible. And though the claim was revived when Johnson became a candidate for Vice-President in 1836, Johnson himself said that he did not know who killed the Shawnee chieftain. A story—very likely true—is that a group of frontiersmen right after the battle found the body of a gaily clad Indian. Thinking he was Tecumseh, they cut long pieces of skin from the thighs and back to be used as razor strops. This revolting act of mutilation was probably performed on some other fallen chief. Tecumseh's latest biographer says simply, "The weight of evidence is that Tecumseh's body never came into the possession of the whites, but was recovered by his followers as darkness settled over the field." Whatever happened to Tecumseh's body, there is no question that his courageous spirit lived on among his own people and that he became a folk hero even to his former enemies.

Procter fled to safety and disgrace, and Harrison, having burned Moraviantown to prevent its reoccupation, returned to Detroit. There he attempted to organize a force to send against British-held Mackinac. The expedition was first delayed by a severe storm which drove off the supply vessels and then was canceled because of the lateness of the season. Brigadier General Lewis Cass was left with some four hundred regulars and thirteen hundred Ohio militia to garrison Detroit and occupy Sandwich and Malden in Upper Canada. The Kentucky militia, which had marched with Governor Shelby, went home. When the expedition against Mackinac was canceled, McArthur's men crossed the lake with Harrison and landed at Buffalo.

After making contact with the Army of the Center, Harrison hoped to invade Canada again and to attack the British in the vicinity of Burlington Heights. But Secretary Armstrong had other ideas. First, he saw to it that Harrison had nothing of importance to do on the northern frontier and then assigned him to the inactive Cincinnati area. After several slights and provocations Harrison resigned on May 11, 1814. Though Governor Shelby hurried a protest to Washington, Madison was at Montpelier and Armstrong accepted the resignation in the absence of the President.

DEARBORN MOVES WEST

The main accomplishments of 1813—establishing naval superiority on Lake Erie, retaking Detroit, and breaking up the Indian confederacy—were subsidiary actions, outside the grand strategy, at least as conceived by John Armstrong. A year before he became Secretary of War, Armstrong wrote that the proper strategy was to close the St. Lawrence River as near its mouth as possible. Since the capture of Quebec was beyond the capabilities of the United States, the main effort should be against Montreal, the capture of which would give control over all that portion of Canada lying westward. But this was Armstrong out of power; in power he wavered and compromised.

Soon after assuming office Armstrong explained his ideas to the cabinet. The main attack should be against Montreal, but effective operations against it could not begin before May 1. In order to save time—six weeks according to the Secretary's calculations—the campaign should begin with an attack on Kingston. In approving the plan the President, who favored concentration on Montreal, probably thought he was hastening the main effort. Historians have often made it appear that a sound strategy worked out by Armstrong was defeated by incompetent commanders in the field. Incompetent commanders contributed to the fragmentation of effort, but they were not solely responsible. It is apparent that the plan faced westward from the beginning. Without so much as a mention of Montreal, the orders to Dearborn described the first object as Kingston, the second alternative as York, and the third as Forts George and Erie and their dependencies.

In the hands of weak and timid commanders such orders invited revision. General Dearborn and his naval opposite, Commodore Isaac Chauncey, soon reported, in error, that Prevost's Kingston garrison had been increased to six thousand men. Fearing that the four thousand men at Sackett's Harbor would be insufficient to carry out the original plan they suggested an inversion of Armstrong's system of targets. Control of Lake Ontario, they argued, necessitated the destruction of the shipping at York, reduction of the forts on the Niagara, and lastly an attack on Kingston. On March 29 Armstrong wrote that the alteration of plan "would appear to be necessary or at least proper."

The attack on York was carried out on April 27. Chauncey's squadron landed, under the protection of naval bombardment, sixteen hundred men commanded by Brigadier General Zebulon M. Pike, an able soldier and explorer. Pike's troops stormed ashore west of the town and pushed aside a scratch force of British regulars and local militia. They then seized the batteries and magazines guarding the harbor. After burning one ship and some supplies, the British commander, Major General Sheaffe, withdrew his regulars east along the lake. At the moment of triumph, however, a magazine explosion pushed American casualties for the raid over three hundred and killed General Pike, who was crushed by a falling stone.

Soon after the explosion American soldiers and sailors looted a number of unoccupied houses and took a royal standard and the mace from the parliament buildings. Also books were taken from the subscription library (and later returned by order of General Dearborn). On April 30, two parliament buildings were burned. Concerning these facts historians are generally in agreement. But on the question of whether Americans or Canadians were responsible for burning the capitol buildings and on the problem of who did the major part of the looting, they disagree. W. B. Kerr, a Canadian, and Milo Quaife, an American, have both contended that contemporary accounts are noncommittal and that unscrupulous Canadians may have burned the buildings. However, recent accounts by C. W. Humphries and C. P. Stacey suggest that the Americans were responsible both for the incendiarism and the major part of the looting, although certain Canadians shared in the plunder. In any case the incident left a reservoir of Canadian ill will toward the Americans.

While York was still in turmoil Dearborn's army was preparing for the next target on its agenda: Fort George. The troops from York and Sackett's Harbor assembled slowly near the American border post of Fort Niagara during May. With Dearborn ill the management of the assault fell to the chief of staff, Colonel Winfield Scott, assisted by Oliver Hazard Perry (whose ships at Black Rock could reach Lake Erie only if the British hold on the river loosened). Scott revived and put into execution Van Rensselaer's plan of the previous year for an attack in the rear from the lake. The real object of the assault was the fourteen-hundred-man garrison rather than the fort itself. Fort George, with most of its guns pointed across the river, and its ramparts crumbling, was not a formidable bastion. Its guns, further, were restricted by the hamlet of Newark, which rested between the fort and the lake.

On May 27 Brigadier General John Vincent, the British commandant, watched the morning mist burn away to unmask the American flotilla. Under intensive sea and cross-river bombardment, the United States forces rowed ashore in a high surf with Scott and Forsythe's Rifle Corps in the first wave, Boyd's brigade in the second. Chandler's and Winder's brigades were in reserve. Momentarily checked at the beach by a handful of defenders, the Americans advanced on Vincent's battleline formed west of the fort. After a sharp fight dominated by American numbers and artillery fire, the sorely wounded garrison abandoned the fort and limped off to the southwest. Scott's pursuit was hampered by the delay of a dragoon column from Fort Niagara, his own wounding, and the vacillation of Generals Dearborn and Morgan Lewis. Vincent, joined by his garrisons from Queenston, Chippewa, and Fort Erie, retreated unmolested to Burlington Heights at the western end of Lake Ontario. While the Americans had indeed retaken the Niagara, freed Perry's ships, and momentarily panicked the British commanders in Canada, their efforts were again indecisive.

Dearborn's campaign along the Niagara had left only a few hundred American regulars at Sackett's Harbor, and Prevost at his most cautious could hardly have avoided this opportunity to strike at his enemy's key naval base on Ontario. Moreover, the British lake flotilla, enlarged and reinforced with experienced seamen, was ready for action under a new commander. Commodore Sir James Yeo, who at thirty had twenty years' service in the Royal Navy, arrived in Kingston on May 15. On May 26 he embarked with eight hundred regulars and sailed the thirty-five miles to Sackett's Harbor.

Though almost denuded of troops, Sackett's Harbor presented formidable defenses. The post boasted well-fortified barracks, blockhouses, and redoubts and had ample artillery. It also had Jacob Brown, a brigadier of the New York militia, whose energy and pugnaciousness were ample substitutes for his lack of military training. Given twenty-four hours' grace when the British were becalmed, Brown hurriedly organized his forces in a manner reminiscent of Dan Morgan at the Battle of the Cowpens in the Revolution. Expecting little from his five hundred militia, he placed them in the front line at the beaches where the British were expected to land. Six hundred regulars formed a second line near the fort, and then there were the supporting batteries.

Before dawn, May 29, the British land forces, under Colonel Edward Baynes, went into the boats and, spearheaded by the grenadiers of the 100th Regiment, forced their way ashore on Horse Island, a spit in the harbor. Darkness and confusion took their toll. The British landed in the wrong place and without artillery. Still they routed the militia and soon tangled with Brown's regulars in a sharp exchange of gunfire. Whether becalmed or reluctant to pit wooden ships against entrenched batteries, the Royal Navy did not sufficiently cover the infantry's advance. When he came ashore Prevost found the situation desperate. After a charge at the walls of the fort was battered back, Prevost, fearing an American flanking movement by the rallied militia, ordered a withdrawal. Outnumbered and with 25 per cent casualties, the British did not tarry. Jacob Brown was exultant: "Had not General Prevost retired *most rapidly* under the guns of his vessels, he would never have returned to Kingston."

But as a raid on American naval supplies, the sally on Sackett's Harbor was not totally unsuccessful, for in the heat of battle a navy lieutenant mistakenly burned his own stores and endangered the "General Pike," a new, heavily gunned United States ship in the stocks. Brown was outraged: "The Navy alone are responsible for what happened on Navy Point, and it is fortunate for them that they have reputations sufficient to sustain the shock."

Even without the attack on Sackett's Harbor, Henry Dearborn found sufficient embarrassment and frustration west of the Niagara. On June 1 he ordered Winder's brigade, some thousand men, to pursue Vincent's force of sixteen hundred.

Winder had sufficient wisdom to request reinforcements four days later. Chandler's brigade came up, giving the pursuers about three thousand men. Chandler, "a tavern keeper and Revolutionary War veteran . . . with neither sense nor discretion," took command.

On Stoney Creek, ten miles from Vincent's camp, Chandler, Winder, and two thousand men made a careless bivouac. In the early morning of June 6 a force of seven hundred and fifty British regulars commanded by Lieutenant Colonel John Harvey overwhelmed the sleeping outguards and stormed the camp. Only some shouting and premature shooting prevented complete surprise as the thin red line swept forward in the dark. In the scuffle and close musketry the British suffered severely, but the Americans broke first. Among the American prisoners were Generals Winder and Chandler, who stumbled into the attacker's lines. The Americans, harassed further by Yeo's fleet which arrived on June 7, hurried back to Fort George.

The debacle at Stoney Creek and Vincent's subsequent march toward Fort George broke Dearborn's fragile health. He requested relief "to a place where my mind may be more at ease" and appointed Morgan Lewis temporary commander of his whole military district. With Lewis at Sackett's Harbor, command at Fort George fell to John Boyd, the last of the brigadiers.

Boyd, anxious to restore his army's lost reputation and to end the annoying raids by the swarm of Indians and partisans in front of Vincent's army, ordered Lieutenant Colonel Charles G. Boerstler, 14th Infantry, to take a force of regulars, artillery, and dragoons and attack a British outpost at Decau's Farm, sixteen miles distant. Boerstler's column, eventually reinforced to six hundred men, set out from Queenston at daylight on June 24. At Beaver Dams, four hundred Indians, led by a French-Canadian, Captain Dominique Ducharme, ambushed the Americans and after three hours of fighting drove Boerstler to bay. The Americans fired back staunchly enough but without much success. A British lieutenant, James FitzGibbon, and fifty troops from the 49th Infantry appeared on the field to lend moral support to the Indians. Playing on Boerstler's fear of a massacre, FitzGibbon persuaded the wounded colonel to surrender his command.

Though FitzGibbon deserves credit for his courage and presence of mind in bluffing Boerstler into surrender, it is clear that the Battle of the Beaver Dams, which did so much to improve British morale, was fought by the Indians. John Norton, who called himself a Mohawk chief, put the matter succinctly—and probably truthfully—when he said: "The Cognauga Indians fought the battle, the Mohawks got the plunder, and FitzGibbon got the credit."

Another person who gets a great deal of credit is Laura Secord, who warned FitzGibbon of the coming of the Americans. Laura was the wife of James Secord, a United Empire Loyalist who was wounded fighting with Brock at Queenston Heights. The story is that when she went out to milk her cows early on the morning of the twenty-second or twenty-third (accounts disagree on chronology) she heard some American soldiers talking of the surprise in store for FitzGibbon the next day. Dropping her milk pail, Mrs. Secord is supposed to have walked over twelve miles on a hot day by rough and little-known back paths to warn FitzGibbon. For her intense patriotism and her desire to help, even in the face of grave danger, Laura Secord of course deserves to be remembered. But that her information saved any lives or affected the outcome of the battle is doubtful.

Dearborn called Boerstler's defeat "an unfortunate and unaccountable event." It certainly ended any pretense of Dearborn's generalship and he was relieved on July 6.

CHATEAUGUAY AND CHRYSLER'S FARM

Even before Dearborn's failures along the Niagara, Secretary Armstrong had moved to improve the army's uncertain leadership on the border. The Secretary's novel solution was to transfer to Sackett's Harbor in March, 1813, Major General James Wilkinson, commander at New Orleans. Thus, though he did not reach the army until August, Wilkinson became Dearborn's successor. He brought with him an unsavory reputation, a talent for conspiratorial mischief, and a new invasion plan.

Armstrong, faced with stalemate ashore and afloat, proposed a new move on Kingston or Montreal. In the meantime on Lake Ontario Yeo and Chauncey sparred indecisively; naval superiority seemed a question of ship-building rather than combat. Dearborn's army was demoralized and inactive. To get the war moving again, Armstrong ordered a new concentration at Sackett's Harbor and a fresh attack on Kingston. The alternate plan was for a joint offensive down the St. Lawrence with two columns from Sackett's Harbor and Plattsburg converging on Montreal to block the river. By letter and conversations with Wilkinson through the summer, however, Armstrong was again persuaded to avoid Kingston. First, Wilkinson, who had favored the attack on Kingston, declared it too hazardous and favored an offensive on Montreal (which, incidentally, was far stronger in men and resources than

Kingston) or in the Niagara country. Armstrong wisely vetoed a westward move; an offensive there "but wounds the tail of the lion." The Secretary agreed, however, to a most indirect approach to taking Kingston: Wilkinson's army could go down river, join the Plattsburg column, capture Montreal, *then* return and take Kingston.

Armstrong, in his shifting of generals, gave the Plattsburg command to Major General Wade Hampton, a South Carolinian who had learned war as Francis Marion's lieutenant. To Hampton, Armstrong implied that the Plattsburg command was distinct from Wilkinson's though it was by organization in Wilkinson's district. Wilkinson, who bombarded Hampton with harassing letters, clearly considered him a subordinate. Relations between the three men became so strained that Armstrong wrote Wilkinson in September that "General Hampton will go through with the campaign cordially and vigorously, but will resign at the end of it."

Preparations for the campaign stretched into the early fall. Wilkinson assembled seven thousand men at Sackett's Harbor and Hampton four thousand at Plattsburg. Secretary Armstrong, whose urge to direct field operations dated back to April, moved the War Department to Sackett's Harbor in early September, allegedly to co-ordinate the activities of his two feuding generals. His presence only further complicated an excruciatingly tangled situation and allowed Wilkinson, a sick man in several senses, to force the Secretary to issue him a written order directing him against Montreal: "Before I abandon this attack (on Kingston), which by my instructions I am ordered to make, it is necessary for my justification that you . . . direct the operations of the army . . . particularly against

Sir George Prevost. (Courtesy of Dominion Archives.)

Plan of the naval action on Lake Champlain. (From Benson J. Lossing, *The Pictorial Field-Book of the War of 1812* [New York: Harper & Bros., 1868].)

Montreal." Wilkinson also sought authorization to surrender his army if disaster threatened.

The impossible campaign under reluctant and querulous leaders began in bad weather in October. British confusion after the disasters in the West gave the Americans a short period of grace, but resistance soon hardened. Hampton's first move westward to Four Corners (New York) on Chateauguay River put his army in a position where it could either advance on Montreal or join Wilkinson on the river. Sir George Prevost appreciated the threat and rushed regulars and French-Canadian militiamen to block the American advance. Hampton's column, moving slowly through wooded and difficult terrain, was nearing the Canadian town of Spears when, on October 25, it ran into the barricades of Lieutenant Colonel Charles M. DeSalaberry's troops, numbering fifteen hundred. That night, Hampton ordered Colonel Purdy to cross the Chateauguay and flank the Canadians. Purdy's misfortunes were numerous: his column was led astray by guides; it was fired on both by Canadians and Americans; the swampy forest was cloying and disheartening. Both Purdy and Hampton's main body recoiled on October 26 without serious loss before the enthusiastic French-Canadians. No doubt Hampton's retreat was speeded by the knowledge that Armstrong had already ordered winter quarters for ten thousand constructed far south of Montreal. "This paper sank my hopes," said Hampton, "and raised serious doubts of receiving that . . . support which had been anticipated." Prevost, on the other hand, found hope in the French-Canadians' stout defense, for their loyalty had been an uncertain quantity.

Wilkinson's main effort down the St. Lawrence set sail in mid-October and ran into rough weather. Chauncey's vessels needed two weeks to get the army's four infantry brigades (Boyd, Brown, Swarthout, Covington), reserve (Macomb), and artillery (Moses Porter) into the river. Meanwhile, American gunboats bottled up the British in Kingston. Then the expedition was obliged to run past the fortified Canadian river towns for another two weeks. The campaign's chances became so dimmed that on November 8 Wilkinson held a council-of-war to discuss further advance. Though his generals voted to continue, their sentiments were best voiced by Covington and Porter: "We proceed from this place under great danger . . . but . . . we know of no other alternative."

Two further developments proved ill omens for Wilkinson's army. First, Secretary Armstrong started back to Washington. He left behind an unco-ordinated campaign, two unfriendly generals, and a stockpile of mistrust. He told Wilkinson that Hampton was under his command, but continued to issue orders directly to the South Carolinian. Secondly, Captain Mulcaster of the Royal Navy slipped out of Kingston with eight hundred regulars commanded by Colonel Morrison. This force followed closely on Wilkinson's heels awaiting an opportunity to strike. It did not have to wait long.

On November 10 Wilkinson's army was halted by a long stretch of rapids and, while Brown's brigade disembarked to clean out British snipers and cannon from the shore, Morrison's small band closed on the American rear. With Wilkinson and Morgan Lewis sick abed, Boyd took the rest of the army and turned to crush Morrison at Chrysler's Farm. The next afternoon, November 11, the American infantry charged repeatedly across Chrysler's muddy, snow-flecked fields only to be repulsed with loss. Boyd's attacks were delivered as the troops arrived on the field; the attacker's lines were enfiladed; the Americans never mounted the fire or momentum their numbers (around two thousand) should have provided. Around four o'clock Covington's brigade broke when its commander was killed. Apparently without orders, the American infantry, who had fought stubbornly and suffered nearly four hundred casualties, re-embarked and the flotilla shot down the Long Sault, cleared by Brown.

On November 12, Wilkinson, with the enemy still harassing him front and rear, learned of Hampton's retreat. The next day he issued a general order canceling the campaign. Hampton, predictably, was blamed for its failure. The army then moved into winter quarters at French Mills, just south of the border.

The British, with the U.S. Army moving forlornly away from the St. Lawrence, seized the opportunity to raze the unguarded Niagara frontier. An energetic new commander, Lieutenant General Gordon Drummond, a Canadian-born officer with international military experience in the British Army, directed most of the campaign, but Vincent made the first move. Vincent's troops ran militia General Samuel McClure's weak garrison out of Fort George on December 10. As he was leaving McClure burned the helpless village of Newark, allegedly to deprive the British of shelter.

On December 18 Colonel Murray and a party of six hundred stormed Fort Niagara on the American side of the river in an early morning bayonet charge, killing sixty-five and capturing three hundred. The fall of Niagara freed Drummond's counterstroke, and between December 19 and January 1 his British, Canadians, and Indians destroyed Lewiston, Fort Schlosser, Black Rock, and Buffalo. The militia was routed; ships and supplies burned; civilians killed and discomforted. In one month Drummond more than canceled out the American successes of the summer and brought "hard war" to American soil. It was an inauspicious beginning for the new year.

Along Lake Ontario and the St. Lawrence the cold new year of 1814 ended a long twelve months of frustration and waste for the American cause. There was much in the year past to justify the complaint of a nameless American: "Our soldiers can beat their soldiers in fighting, but their generals beat ours in management."

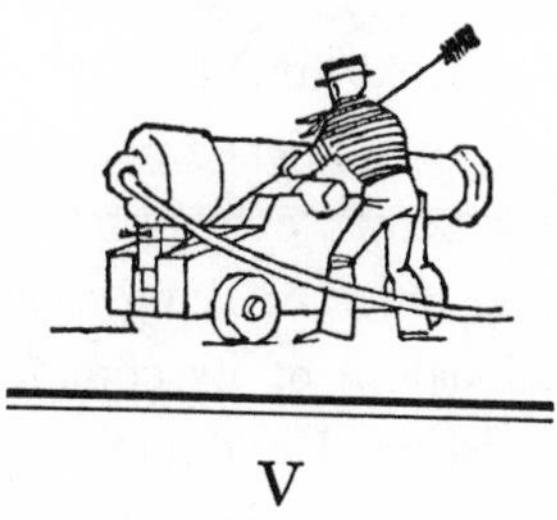

V

1814: The British Offensive in the North and in the East

At the beginning of 1814 the American navy and army were stalemated along Lake Ontario and the St. Lawrence. Fort Niagara remained in British hands while the settlers of the Niagara frontier buried their neighbors and poked in the ashes left by Drummond's December blitzkrieg. Along the coast from Maine to Georgia, the defenseless towns anticipated with fear the end of the Atlantic storms and the return of the Royal Navy. Spring would bring more devastating raids and further strengthening of the blockade. Along the southern frontier the backwoodsmen of Tennessee and Georgia, many of them commanded by the hardest soldier in America, Andrew Jackson, marshaled their forces for another campaign against the Creeks.

The new year promised, however, that the American army on the Canadian border would fight and be directed with improved ability. Driven by Winfield Scott's thirst for military perfection, the American soldiers underwent long, grinding hours of drill. Though Scott's own brigade was uniformed in militia-gray (regulation blue not being available), it mirrored the confident professionalism of its commander. The militia, on the other hand, remained a dubious quantity. Certainly some of the citizen-soldiers, particularly those from the frontier communities, had had a surfeit of experience. Whether they had learned anything of soldiering in the British-Indian school of practical application remained to be seen. In any case, they would be better led. The Madison administration, though it neglected William Henry Harrison, managed to replace its elderly combat commanders with promising younger men. By the summer of 1814, Jacob Brown, George Izard, and Andrew Jackson were major-generals and Daniel Bissell, Edmund P. Gaines, Alexander Macomb, Winfield Scott, T. A. Smith, and E. W. Ripley became brigadiers. In 1812 the eight generals of the regular army averaged sixty years in age; in 1814 the nine new appointees averaged an athletic thirty-six. The youth movement—for which Madison and Armstrong share credit—injected new vigor into the army.

For both nations the dominating development of 1814 was the end of the war in Europe. Spring brought the surrender of Bayonne and the occupation of Paris. The implications of Napoleon's fall on the war in America were far-reaching and touched the core of the causes of conflict. Peace in Europe would end the need for impressed seamen and the blockade, and it was doubtful that the welfare of the American Indians would prove a cause worth continuing the war. The most immediate effect of the peace was to release fourteen British regiments for use against the United States. The former colonies had struck Mother England in her hour of greatest trial, assaulted her while she struggled to save Europe from despotism. America must be chastised for "her perfidy and ingratitude." Not so well advertised was the fact that the demands of European reconstruction and a growing distaste for war on any continent might be the guiding influences on British strategy. In the popular imagination, however, Wellington's Peninsular veterans became the instrument to salve British pride and properly punish their rude American cousins.

The British strategy, as it emerged, was geared to force a quick, decisive, and advantageous settlement. Essentially, it was designed to foster disunion, disillusionment, and political turmoil in the United States. The Madison government would be forced to sue for a hasty peace. The Royal Navy would tighten the blockade and liquidate privateering. The army would invade New York at Lake Champlain and blackmail the northern states into clamoring for peace. The British army-navy team, the ultimate weapon of 1814, would bring hard war to the coastal cities, then seize New Orleans at the mouth of the Mississippi. The torch and the sledge would aid the sword in bringing the Americans to terms.

There were built-in limitations to the War Office's plans. First, any advance from Canada was likely to be commanded by Sir George Prevost, who though an able administrator and astute politician in his office as governor-general, was an indifferent strategist and fumbling commander. Hard-pressed for eighteen months to defend his vast domain, he might not be able to surmount his monumental caution when he switched to the offensive. Secondly, the political and geographical obstacles to waging war on the United States were awesome. In February, 1814, Britain's greatest soldier, the Marquis of Wellington, was anything but optimistic about the coming campaign's prospects. He wrote Bathurst that America was no place to wage a war with large bodies of troops, because the lack of transportation and communications facilities was appalling. Furthermore, the United States was a political jellyfish; it could not be hurt in one spot:

> I do not know where you could carry on . . . an operation which would be so injurious to the Americans as to force them to sue for peace, which is what one would wish to see. . . . the prospect in regard to America is not consoling.

Wars, like depressions, are difficult to stop. For both the United States and Great Britain, the investment of gold, national honor, and lives cried for some return, though the chance for profit had long since passed. Nevertheless, ahead was a full year of war in which armies would fight harder and better, more men would die, and towns from Lake Ontario to Chesapeake Bay would collapse in smoking ruins.

THE CANADIAN BORDER

The active campaigning west of the Niagara was all but ended by 1814. Though raids and skirmishes marked the whole year, neither side hurt its enemy. In March American regulars and rangers won a sharp fight on French River, but in August failed in an attack on Mackinac. In May an American expedition looted and burned Dover on the Canadian side of Lake Erie, an act of dubious military value. The British in turn captured an insignificant American outpost at Prairie du Chien, Wisconsin, in July. Both sides were limited by a lack of men and supplies and expended much of their resources feeding their Indian charges.

The British high command in Canada eyed Lake Erie and Detroit hoping to blunt American control in the West, but their scanty manpower was tied to the defenses along the Niagara, Lake Ontario, and the St. Lawrence. Major reinforcements did not reach Prevost until June, and so his subordinates on Ontario, Drummond and Riall, had to fight with the troops on hand. The inconstant weather and the manpower shortage forced Prevost to restrain Drummond, who wanted to move on Detroit, Put-in-Bay, and Sackett's Harbor. Prevost waited to see where the Americans might strike next.

On the American side, General James Wilkinson, his time in command about at an end, made a stab at La Colle Mill south of Montreal in March. His purpose, he said, was to prevent the flow of British troops west. At the time there was no such movement. A small garrison of British and Canadians in a stone mill outlasted his bombardment and shot up the infantry enough to discourage the project. Wilkinson withdrew and soon was on his way to Washingon for one of his periodic courts-martial.

In the meantime Secretary Armstrong was planning to get some action out of his new fighting general at Sackett's Harbor. On February 28 Armstrong wrote Jacob Brown two orders. One sent Brown's division (two thousand men) and Chauncey's squadron against Kingston. The other seemed to be an alternative measure, a campaign on the Niagara frontier to retake Fort Niagara and block an anticipated British move on Lake Erie. It seems that Armstrong intended the Niagara plan as a ruse; the dispatch was intended for British eyes. Since Chauncey and Brown both believed their force too weak to attack Kingston, Brown put his soldiers on the road for Niagara. Armstrong wrote Brown on March 20: "You have mistaken my meaning." The second order was "merely a mask for the operations against Kingston" but "go on and prosper. Good consequences are sometimes the result of mistakes." Confused by the Secretary's strategy, Brown put his force into camp at Buffalo where they received some much needed training from Winfield Scott.

There was much about the strategy and command situation to puzzle Brown. He was subordinated to Wilkinson and after May 4 to George Izard at Plattsburg, yet he sometimes received orders directly from Armstrong. Chauncey, apparently, acted by order of the Navy Department and only when he personally believed his fleet fit to sally out on the lake. The future promised more confusion and frustration.

At Kingston, Captain Sir James Yeo's fresh-water branch of the Royal Navy gained strength while the Americans temporized. On April 14 two ships, of 58 and 40 guns, were launched while another of 102 guns was still a-building. The new vessels gave Yeo temporary control of Lake Ontario. He sought to use his superiority by damaging Chauncey's active building program and denying naval support to any American invasion at Niagara. At Drummond's urging, Prevost sent Yeo's fleet and a landing force of a thousand to destroy the American depot at Oswego. Oswego was a key link in Chauncey's vulnerable supply line. There the guns and stores for the American squadron were accumulated for water transport to Sackett's Harbor. But much of the naval armament destined or Chauncey's new ships had been moved inland before Yeo struck on May 5–7. Though the American garrison resisted staunchly and retreated in order, the British captured the town with all the supplies, and burned the fort.

Yeo moved on to blockade Sackett's Harbor, but Chauncey's stubborn sailors kept the supplies coming. The lighter equipment could, and did, come overland, but the heaviest guns had to come by boat. One such convoy of barges, which had slipped along the coast at night, was overtaken by seven British vessels. The Americans fled up Big Sandy Creek and, on May 30, the British followed. Their commander, Captain Popham, landed troops on both banks to protect his flanks. At mid-morning American riflemen and Indians ambushed Popham and captured the entire British force. Chauncey eventually got the guns, and the naval arms race on Ontario continued.

In June the Americans appeared ready to move. At a cabinet meeting on the seventh Armstrong proposed, and received approval for, another invasion across the Niagara. Jacob Brown's army—a projected eight thousand regulars and militia—would capture Burlington Heights at the head of Lake Ontario, a move which would sever most of Upper Canada from Prevost's dominion. With Chauncey's co-operation, the invasion could then advance to York and Kingston. The move would have to be made quickly, for British troops from Europe were nearing the lakes.

General Gordon Drummond's problems in defending Upper Canada were staggering. He had to guard Niagara and also look for an attack from Detroit or across Lake Erie. At York he kept a thousand men to rush to any threatened point. Another twenty-six hundred, most of them commanded by Major General Phineas Riall, were scattered in garrisons from Burlington Heights to Fort Erie, opposite Buffalo. To meet an

American invasion the British would have to march hard and fast. Lacking high regard for the American soldiery, they were confident of being able to do more than hold their own.

Little did the British suspect that Brown's army, poised at Buffalo, had developed some new qualities: training, discipline, leadership, and *esprit.* Its men saluted smartly, policed their camp, handled a bayonet like something other than a chicken spit, and did not desert. The two regular brigades (Scott's and Ripley's) set the pace, but Peter B. Porter's militia-Indian brigade possessed good morale. The four artillery companies were veterans. As game as it was, Brown's army numbered only around thirty-five hundred effectives.

On July 3 Brown, finally freed from his harrowing correspondence with Armstrong, launched the army against Fort Erie. That afternoon the undermanned garrison surrendered. The same day Phineas Riall began to march south from Fort George to meet Brown. Gathering in the other garrisons, his force—three regiments of regulars and six hundred militia and Indians—assembled at Chippewa. Brown's army, on July 4, advanced north along the Niagara, skirmishing throughout the hot day with Riall's advance outposts. At Street's Creek, sixteen miles from Fort Erie and a mile below Chippewa, Scott's brigade halted. The rest of the army encamped and waited the morrow. The skirmishing, militia against militia, continued.

Before Brown could carry out a planned flanking movement, Riall launched his force of two thousand against the American camp. The ground between the two forces was level and open, bordered by a forest. In front of Riall's line of march, screened from Scott's camp by a thin line of trees, Porter's militia and Indians had driven back their Canadian counterparts. Riall's regulars routed them in turn. Seeing Porter's hasty withdrawal, Brown ordered Scott's brigade, conveniently drawn up for an evening parade, to give battle. Already Towson's battery and three British guns were pounding each other and the infantry. Scott's men crossed Street's Creek and deployed quickly. The 25th Infantry took to the woods to guard the left flank and the other regiments (11th, 9th, and 22d) formed on line. Riall's force was in column, two regiments abreast. Scott extended his ranks to form a concave line, for this maneuver allowed his men to put converging fire on the British.

Behaving in the best tradition of regulars, the Americans closed ranks around their fallen and kept up a steady fire. The British, too, though severely punished by Towson's guns, advanced without falter. Seventy yards apart, the two forces halted and fired. British officers toppled, a Royal Artillery caisson exploded, and the two leading regiments started to melt away from the firing line. Scott then ordered a bayonet charge, and Riall's force collapsed. Using the 8th Regiment, his reserve, to cover his retreat, Riall disengaged. His losses were near five hundred, the Americans, three hundred.

It was a stunning victory for the Americans, more important for its psychological impact than for its strategic value. The battle is still remembered in the gray cadet uniforms at the United States Military Academy; Riall's surprise—"Those are Regulars, by God"—is army tradition.

Exhilarated by his good fortune, Brown marched his army around Riall's flank at Chippewa and forced the British to withdraw to Fort George and to Burlington Heights. Brown encamped at Queenston and from "the mountain" surveyed both Fort George and the blue waters of Lake Ontario, eight miles distant. To reduce Riall's garrison he would need heavy guns and supplies to support a siege. Despite the fact that Yeo had lifted his blockade of Sackett's Harbor on June 6, Chauncey's fleet was nowhere in sight. Pleading for naval assistance, Brown wrote:

> I have looked for your fleet with the greatest anxiety since the 10th. I do not doubt my ability to meet the enemy in the field and to march in any direction over his country—your fleet is carrying the necessary supplies. . . . For God's sake, let me see you! . . .

Chauncey, however, was ill and reluctant for anyone to use his ships to fight, let alone ferry supplies. He simply replied that his business was to engage enemy ships, not to serve as an "agreeable appendage" to Brown's army. The navy stayed at Sackett's Harbor. Brown, convinced by reconnaissance that it was beyond his means to assault the British forts at the mouth of the Niagara, led his army back to Chippewa on July 24.

The British regrouped during Brown's idleness. While Brown longed for Chauncey's fleet, Gordon Drummond left Kingston to direct his army personally. He ordered his scattered troops to concentrate; Riall had already been reinforced at Fort George. In the last week of July, the British force, elements of eight regular regiments, and the steadfast Canadian militia numbered three thousand.

With Riall following Brown's withdrawal, on July 25 Drummond sent another force to the New York side of the Niagara to menace the depot at Fort Schlosser. Drummond himself, with more troops, started after Riall.

Brown fully realized his desperate situation. Hoping to draw the British away from Schlosser, he ordered Scott to attack Riall's position at Lundy's Lane immediately. Lundy's Lane was simply a low hill split by a country road which joined the river road at right angles. The hill, no more than twenty-five feet in elevation, ran a mile to the west into a wooded area. Near the river, across the Portage Road, was a low meadow and a forest; beyond that, Niagara Falls. Most of the terrain was open fields.

Scott's advance surprised Riall. Outnumbered and now fully aware of his enemy's skill, Riall began to retire. Before the British completely cleared the hill, Drummond's force appeared. The lieutenant general commanding reoccupied the position, placing his guns on the hill and the infantry on line slightly to their rear. Already Drummond had recalled his cross-river detachment, and they were on the way to his aid.

It was five o'clock when Scott's brigade deployed in the field south of Lundy's Lane. Scott sent Jesup's 25th Infantry in a flanking attack against the British left on Portage Road and took his other three regiments against the hill. Though Jesup temporarily turned the British flank (and, incidentally, captured the wounded Riall), Scott's soldiers were blasted back each time they charged. At nightfall the First Brigade was shattered, and the Canadian militia had driven Jesup back. At that moment the rest of Brown's army reached the field, as did the remainder of Drummond's command.

Brown would not be denied: he ordered another attack. The battle continued into the night, but the hill was not taken. Finally, around nine o'clock, James Miller's 21st Infantry, concealed by the darkness, rushed the British battery after firing a close volley and in a melee of bayonets seized the crest and seven guns. Brown advanced his entire force to the hill, and the British backed off.

Drummond counterattacked. Three times the British regulars pressed the American line, taking severe punishment from cannon and musket. Volleys were exchanged almost muzzle to muzzle. Both Brown and Scott were hit and both evacuated. Around midnight Brown ordered Ripley, now commanding the dazed and bleeding American defenders, to withdraw for ammunition and water. In making his withdrawal, Ripley inadvertently left several guns, and Drummond reoccupied the hill. At daylight, the two armies, each diminished by nine hundred casualties, eyed each other from their positions of the day before.

Lundy's Lane—the sharpest fight of the war on the Canadian border—was a tactical stand-off, but strategically a victory for Drummond. That fiery night near Niagara Falls, the will of Brown's invasion disappeared. Though Brown ordered Ripley to attack the next morning, the army was exhausted. Ripley mustered a scant eighteen hundred effectives and wisely resisted his wounded superior's demands. That night, July 26, with Riply in command, the army retreated to Fort Erie.

Thanks to the Army Engineers, Fort Erie was a much more formidable post than it was when captured July 3. It had become a two-sided complex of batteries, abatis, trenches, blockhouses, and earthworks backed by the waters of Lake Erie. Ripley put his men to work and daily the fortifications were improved. On August 5 General Edmund P. Gaines from Sackett's Harbor took command of the garrison. Inside the works he found eighteen guns and about two thousand men.

His command stunned by two battles, Drummond paused after Lundy's Lane to draw reinforcements to his army. The arrival of De Watteville's regiment (German, Polish, and Spanish mercenaries), and the 41st Foot made up for the loss at Lundy's Lane. Cautiously, Drummond marched on Fort Erie. He had probably somewhat revised his thinking on the Americans' military abilities; earlier in the year he had told Riall that a professional soldier could take liberties with the Americans. Now he moved south, slowly, probing for a weakness in the American defenses. On August 2 he jabbed at Black Rock across the river. Entrenched riflemen drove off the raiders, which led Drummond to comment: "Crouching, ducking, or laying down when advancing under fire are bad habits and must be corrected." With Prevost's approval, Drummond then invested Fort Erie and the entire war in Canada became focused on a single 700-by-250-yard fortress.

On August 13 the British guns began pounding Fort Erie as Drummond planned a three-pronged assault. He believed the Americans "much spirited" and fewer than they were. One of his officers, Colonel Hercules Scott of the 103d Regiment, was not optimistic about the assault, writing his brother: "I expect we shall be ordered to storm tomorrow. I have little hope of success from this manoeuvre." Storm they would–in three columns under Colonels Drummond, Fischer, and Scott. It would be at night, and to preserve surprise, only one-third of the most reliable men would be trusted with musket flints.

In the dark, damp morning hours of August 15, the British columns plunged against the batteries at Snake Hill, Battery Douglas, and Fort Erie itself. The sentries were alert, and the Americans soon opened fire. Fischer's column–primarily De Watteville's regiment–was smashed back by the Snake Hill guns on Lake Erie's banks. Scott's column veered off from Battery Douglas (Scott was dead) and joined Colonel William Drummond's assault on the main fort. The merged columns breached the walls and overran an American battery. Though Gaines's artillery blocked off reinforcements, his infantry could not dislodge the staunch British. The fighting was bitter, close, and bloody. At five o'clock the Fort Erie blockhouse, the center of British resistance, exploded when a powder cache was touched off by a fire. The survivors, stunned and demoralized, fled the works. General Drummond's assault cost him nine hundred men, nearly one-third of his force. Gaines's casualties were nearly a hundred.

The siege dragged on until September 21, when Drummond broke off and returned to Chippewa. Jacob Brown, who had resumed command when Gaines was wounded in a bombardment, helped Drummond make this decision by sallying from the fort and temporarily capturing the British siege works. On September 17 a party of a thousand militia and six hundred regulars, concealed by a heavy afternoon rain, rushed two British positions, spiked some guns, and, after a sharp battle in the trenches, returned to the fort. Brown's audacity was vindicated by his troops, for the battle was no skirmish of irregulars. Over five hundred men fell on both sides. When Drummond finally retired, his army and Brown's were mere skeletons of the confident regiments of early July.

By the time the autumn frosts began to gild the yellowing maples of Ontario, the war had forgotten Niagara. Prevost and the crack brigades from Spain were on Lake Champlain, and Drummond reported to Sir George that his army was too weak for anything but defense. On Lake Ontario, however, James Yeo put to sea in October with the 102-gun "St. Lawrence" and locked Chauncey's squadron in Sackett's Harbor for the rest of the war.

Niagara continued to be a lodestone for American troops. On October 5 General George Izard, commander of the 9th Military District, arrived with four thousand reinforcements. His movement, ordered by Armstrong and begun in August, stripped Plattsburg and did not change the Niagara situation.

Without naval support and faced by a still determined British army, Izard restricted his operations to raiding. Finally, with winter coming on and the war limping to a close, Izard pulled all his troops back to American soil. Fort Erie was blown up on November 5, and the invasion ended with both a bang and a whimper.

Brown's army, which never mustered more than four thousand men, added bright names to America's young military tradition: Chippewa, Lundy's Lane, Fort Erie. The tradition was expensively bought. General James Miller, the hero of Lundy's Lane, wrote a friend: "Since I came into Canada this time every major save one, every lieutenant-colonel, every colonel that was here when I came and has remained here has been killed or wounded and I am now the only general officer out of seven that has escaped."

The harsh truth was that history had been made, but for all the bravery of the Americans, British, and Canadians, the outcome of the war was not altered. While Brown and Drummond punished each other along the Niagara, the British high command had long since launched the two offensive operations further east with which it hoped to end the war.

PLATTSBURG

After Napoleon's abdication in April, 1814, the battle-tested regiments of the Peninsula army tramped into Bordeaux and into various Mediterranean ports to board Royal Navy transports. The red-coated, gray-trousered infantry were proud men of proud regiments—the 4th, the 44th, the 85th, and the 21st. Their flags carried bloody names: Torres Vedras, Talavera, Badajoz, Vitoria, Bayonne. There could have been other names on the colors—Quebec, Lexington, Concord, and Bunker Hill—for some of these regiments had seen America before. Though twenty-five hundred men and eleven ships weighed anchor for Bermuda, their ultimate destination Washington and New Orleans, the bulk of Wellington's fifteen thousand veterans sailed to join Prevost in Canada.

Of all the areas where a campaign along the Canadian frontier might have been expected, Lake Champlain was the most likely. Poised like a dagger pointed at lower Canada and the Hudson Valley, its waters offered the easiest approach from either Canada or the United States. Traditionally it was the road of armies; in the French and Indian War and in the Revolution it was bitterly contested. Yet until 1814 Lake Champlain was little more than a backwash theater, potentially active but neglected by both sides.

In 1813 the British had nosed across the border with a small flotilla to challenge an equally tiny American fleet. Their aim apparently was to discourage invasion and they succeeded. In June, two American sloops, fighting at the lake's north end, were captured. Repaired and renamed "Chub" and "Finch," the two vessels gave the British temporary control of the lake. They then raided the American base at Plattsburg, New York. This experience convinced the navy's commander on Champlain, Thomas Macdonough, that safer quarters were needed for his shipbuilding program. He set up quarters at Vergennes, Vermont and, with local material, began building a fleet.

Macdonough, a veteran of the Barbary Wars and a dedicated student of naval warfare, was not the only able American officer on Lake Champlain. At Plattsburg, located at the juncture of the lake and the Saranac River, Major General George Izard commanded six thousand men. As the summer of 1814 wore on and he received reports of the British build-up at

Montreal, Izard fortified Plattsburg. For his principal defenses he selected a peninsula formed by the Saranac and the lake across from Plattsburg. With water and difficult terrain protecting three-quarters of his front, Izard constructed three forts (Moreau, Brown, and Scott), and numerous blockhouses, batteries, and trenches.

At Montreal, Sir George Prevost received instructions in June to take the initiative and invade the United States. The new regiments, said Lord Bathurst, should be used to make Canada more secure by seizing either Sackett's Harbor or Plattsburg, the two American bases of invasion. Any victory on American soil, too, could lead to the territorial rectification and the sole control of the border waters that the British wanted from any peace settlement. But there was to be no hazardous forward movement. In reply, Prevost decided against Sackett's Harbor (Yeo's fleet was not ready) and pointed out that any land invasion demanded naval supremacy on Ontario and Champlain. He doubted that such control could be gained before September.

The choice of Plattsburg was doubly fortunate for Prevost. Since his army had been fed by enterprising New York and Vermont drovers throughout the war, he might expect his supply problem to be lessened. He reported that he would not enter Vermont for fear of antagonizing his commissariat. Furthermore, though Prevost could not have predicted he would be so lucky, Secretary Armstrong in Washington decided to dispatch Izard and four thousand men to Brown's assistance on the Niagara frontier. Izard, when he received the order on August 10, protested, predicting a British invasion at Lake Champlain. At the time probably ten thousand British regulars were marshaled some thirty miles from Plattsburg. Armstrong's reply was adamant: "It has become good policy on our part to carry the war as far to the westward as possible." Though Izard moved slowly (perhaps he hoped to be recalled to Plattsburg), he nonetheless marched west on August 29. Behind, General Alexander Macomb manned Plattsburg with a motley force of recruits, convalescents, and militia. He reported his effectives at fifteen hundred men.

Meanwhile, the naval force on which Prevost pinned his hopes of success prepared for the campaign. Captain George Downie assumed command on September 2, and found that one brig, "Linnet," and two sloops, "Chub" and "Finch," and twelve gunboats and row galleys constituted his force. His best hope, the 36-gun ship "Confiance," was not yet completed. He had other problems, as well. He was short of men, and the sailors he had were castoffs, draftees, latecomers, and Canadian militiamen. Not only was their state of training low, but many of the officers and men were unfamiliar with one another. Downie, who was prodded by Prevost almost daily to get under way, must have had some second thoughts as he ascended the lake with his flagship's rigging incomplete and the carpenters' hammers still banging on her deck.

The American fleet was better manned, but no more formidable. Macdonough's squadron consisted of the 26-gun "Saratoga," the brig "Eagle," the schooner "Ticonderoga," the sloop "Preble," and ten gunboats. When all the heads were counted, guns tallied, and broadsides weighed, the two fleets were approximately evenly matched. The Americans were on the whole better trained. Downie's longer-range guns, however, might have given his fleet an advantage in an open-water fight.

Such an equality of forces, however, did not exist between

the opposing armies. At the time Prevost crossed the border on September 3, he was leading the finest army ever to campaign on American soil. In four brigades (Major Generals Robinson, Brisbane, Powers, and Kempt) his fifteen regular regiments, Canadian militia, and artillery numbered around fifteen thousand men. On the American side, Macomb called in his scattered detachments and, with eight hundred New York militiamen, mustered some four thousand defenders at Plattsburg. He was cheered, however, by the news that twenty-five hundred Vermont volunteers (their governor would not order the militia to serve beyond his state's borders) were on their way to help.

Prevost's column of hard-muscled regulars made their way south irresistibly. Though Macomb sent troops forward to harass the advance, the British never deployed. Their advance guard and flankers repeatedly drove off their annoyers. Reaching the banks of the Saranac on September 6, Prevost briefly probed Macomb's cannon-studded works, saw Macdonough's fleet anchored at Plattsburg Bay, and decided to wait for the Royal Navy.

As the British advanced, Thomas Macdonough won the battle he had not yet fought. Bringing his squadron into Plattsburg Bay, he hoped to lure Downie into a close-range gunnery duel with both fleets at anchor. Under such conditions he could engage the Royal Navy at the place in the manner of his choosing. He chose well. First, he arranged his four larger vessels in an echeloned line across the bay (north to south: "Eagle," "Saratoga," "Ticonderoga," and "Preble") in such a way as to force Downie to approach him with the wind in the Briton's face. This would prevent Macdonough's line from being turned. Then Macdonough rigged his vessels with anchors, kedges, and hawsers so that they might be turned around during the battle. This would bring fresh broadsides to bear when the starboard batteries were damaged. The "springs" were rigged to port to prevent their injury by gunfire. The gunboats were placed at intervals in Macdonough's line.

After an exchange of messages in which Prevost became increasingly insistent on an immediate, joint attack, the governor-general and Captain Downie agreed on a full assault on September 11. The infantry and naval attack were supposed to be simultaneous.

Driven by a northeast wind, Downie's fleet sailed for Plattsburg Bay in the early morning of September 11. Making ready for the attack, Downie "scaled" his guns (fired them to clear them of dirt and rust) about 5:00 A.M. The fleet hove to briefly and Downie reconnoitered Macdonough's position. Downie's plan, simply, was to bring his fleet as close to Macdonough as possible and knock out "Saratoga" and "Eagle" with (from north to south) "Chub," "Linnet," and "Confiance." "Finch" and the gunboats, he believed, could take "Ticonderoga" and "Preble."

The British squadron rounded Cumberland Head a little after eight o'clock. As they swung on line and headed for their anchorages, the wind turned foul—as Macdonough had hoped—and with limp, flapping sails, the four vessels struggled to within three hundred yards and there had to anchor. The Americans opened fire as the British approached, and their shot tore rigging and sails.

"Linnet" and "Confiance" anchored without firing. His vessel steady, Downie ordered the first broadside from "Confiance," and her iron tore into "Saratoga," downing one-fifth of Macdonough's crew. The firing quickly became general and severe. The British suffered an important loss when Captain Downie was killed some fifteen minutes after the first shot. Struck in the groin by a dismounted gun, he died of internal injuries. "Eagle," the northernmost American vessel, traded broadsides with "Linnet" alone; "Chub," damaged and unmanageable, drifted past its anchorage into the hovering American gunboats and struck its colors.

Aboard "Saratoga," Macdonough directed his crew with vigor and ability. Often sighting a gun himself, he urged its crew on despite the pounding "Confiance" was giving them. His guns, better handled than those of the "Confiance," tore the British ship's hull and gundecks apart. As the destruction to both fleets mounted, the American squadron moved. The first American vessel to change position was "Eagle" which at about 10:30 A.M. ran down the line, anchoring south and to the rear of "Saratoga" with her fresh battery to bear on "Confiance." Though "Linnet" was thus freed to engage Macdonough, many of its guns were dismounted. "Confiance," on the other hand, soon suffered even greater damage from "Eagle" and "Saratoga." In response to Macdonough's orders, "Saratoga" was turned at its anchorage. The new guns raked "Confiance," though the British vessel, now commanded by its first lieutenant, desperately sought to turn also. With her equipment destroyed and most of her crew wounded, she was able to complete only half a turn. Receiving even worse punishment in this position, "Confiance" surrendered. Fifteen more minutes of battle made a wreck of "Linnet" also and she struck her colors.

The battle between "Ticonderoga" and "Preble" against "Finch" and the gunboats also ended in American victory.

The gunboats closed on the two American vessels, but "Finch" lost headway in a baffling wind and, damaged by a broadside from "Ticonderoga," eventually ran aground on Crab Island, south of the battleline. About half the British gunboats drove in on "Ticonderoga" and "Preble"; the latter was forced from its anchorage and ran aground under the protecting guns of Fort Scott. "Ticonderoga" so pounded the attacking gunboats that several had hardly an oarsman left. The majority of the gunboats, apparently manned by militiamen, fled shortly after the action began. They went unpursued because Macdonough did not have a single mast on which to spread a sail.

The American victory, determined primarily by Macdonough's ability to bring new batteries to bear, cost the British over two hundred casualties and their Lake Champlain squadron. Macdonough gave his losses as fifty-two killed, fifty-eight wounded. One of the American vessels, "Saratoga," and all of Downie's were so damaged that they were later scuttled.

Ashore, Prevost's grand assault quickly fizzled. The attack got off to a bad start when Robinson's and Powers' brigades became lost swinging west of Plattsburg to cross the Saranac at a ford. Brisbane's brigade, directed to cross the bridge at Plattsburg, never reached the river. Disheartened by these incidents and convinced that the loss of Downie's fleet ended any hope of adequately supplying and protecting his land forces, Prevost decided that Plattsburg was not worth the losses his army would suffer taking it. Though combat losses were only 250, Prevost was faced with a growing number of desertions as he led his dispirited army back along the lake.

The Canada George Prevost returned to was not a haven for a defeated general. Prices were high; both the army and the Indians, parasitic in their feeding habits, were disliked. Prevost was ridiculed and slandered by civilians and soldiers alike. One of his subordinates, General Robinson, scored Prevost for his indecisiveness and timidity and mourned the hasty, wasteful retreat of his army: "I am sick at heart, everything I see and hear is discouraging, this is no field for a military man above the rank of a Colonel of riflemen."

In retrospect, Prevost seems mistaken in his insistence on a simultaneous land and sea assault on Plattsburg. Had the American works been seized, Macdonough would have had to risk open water eventually, whether shore fire reached his squadron or not. By sacrificing the element in his offensive he could least afford to lose—Downie's ships—Prevost ruined his campaign. In a sense he was enslaved by the idea that a naval engagement was absolutely necessary.

Plattsburg was to the War of 1812 what Saratoga was to the American Revolution. In both cases a major attempt at invasion was foiled and a change in diplomacy resulted. After Saratoga, France signed a treaty of alliance that led ultimately to victory. No such dramatic event followed Plattsburg but when this victory was complemented three days later by Cochrane's repulse at Baltimore, the American negotiators at Ghent were encouraged to resist the more extreme demands of their British opponents.

WASHINGTON AND BALTIMORE

The twenty-five hundred men who sailed from Bordeaux for Bermuda early in June, 1814, were commanded by Major General Robert Ross. An Irishman best remembered for his taste for discipline, his courage, and his diffident urbanity, Robert Ross was a thoroughly professional commander. In late July his force picked up more men in Bermuda, putting the army's strength above four thousand. At Tangier Island in Chesapeake Bay, the soldiers joined the rest of Vice-Admiral Sir Alexander Cochrane's warships. It was an imposing fleet: four ships-of-the-line, twenty frigates and sloops, and more than twenty transports.

The British force in the Chesapeake in August, 1814, was part of a larger, ambitious plan. Though the main effort against the United States would come from Canada, the Royal Navy, with its army landing forces, was to blockade and raid along the entire Atlantic Coast. There were other squadrons out, but Cochrane, who commanded all naval forces in America exclusive of Yeo's border fleets, led the largest. Though the aims of the Royal Navy's operations varied by locale and time, they were principally diversionary and punitive. Strikes against the long, populated, and vulnerable coastline of the United States would prevent any large invasion of Canada. The year 1814 saw British ships raiding Connecticut, Massachusetts, and the coast of Maine. Soldiers went ashore at Castine, Maine, and raided inland to Bangor. Contemplating a territorial annexation that would open an overland route from Quebec to Halifax, Nova Scotia, the British remained in Maine until April, 1815. The Americans, it is said, were unhappy to see the affluent invaders leave.

Chesapeake Bay, nonetheless, was the center of the Royal Navy's attention. From its hundreds of bays and rivers came much of America's export shipping and many privateers. Along its coastline lived a large portion of America's people. Best of all, it was relatively undefended; despite the naval strikes of 1813, the Madison administration, its eyes fixed on faraway Canada, had neglected to guard the nation's front door.

Armstrong's inconsistent management of the War Department, the Secretary's strong notions on the conduct of the war, and his feud with the Virginians all contributed to Washington's defenselessness. He did not have a staff worth mentioning, and the department was slipshod in operations. The Secretary dictated strategy and made policy. Though Madison, communicating the alarm of the Chesapeake settlements, pressed Armstrong for defense plans, none was forthcoming until July. The area was almost devoid of regulars. While the neighboring states had thousands of soldiers on paper, the militia was unprepared, physically and emotionally, for hard fighting. Armstrong himself was convinced that Washington had no strategic value and would not be attacked. There is little doubt that Madison had had enough of Armstrong by the summer of 1814, but the President could not muster the courage to demand his fractious Secretary's resignation.

The appearance of Cochrane's fleet forced the cabinet on July 1 to consider seriously the problems of defense. Perhaps a thousand regulars could be mustered, Armstrong thought. Secretary of the Navy Jones had a hundred and fifty marines handy and the sailors from the Chesapeake Bay gunboat flotilla. The five hundred flotillamen were veterans; their commander, Commodore Joshua Barney, a deep-water captain and Revolutionary privateer, was as aggressive a sailor as the United States had. The bulk of the defenders, however, would have to be militiamen. The three neighboring states and the District of Columbia were then carrying ninety-three thousand men on their militia rosters.

On July 2 the 10th Military District was created and given to Brigadier General William H. Winder. Winder was Madison's choice. The general's claims to military distinction were his capture at Stoney Creek, his comfortable captivity in Canada, and his efforts to arrange a truce and prisoner exchange earlier in 1814. He was, however, related to Levin Winder, Federalist governor of Maryland, and it was hoped that his appointment would enlist Maryland's full support. To Winder's immediate command were assigned the regulars in the district and fifteen thousand unmobilized militia.

From early July until he arrived at Bladensburg on August 24, Winder was a study in unproductive motion. He was busy, compulsively so, without accomplishing much beyond driving himself to the brink of mental and physical collapse. He spent much of his time on personal reconnaissance, for he had no staff. He did not receive much help from Armstrong and little more from Madison and Monroe. Of three thousand militia called to active service, perhaps three hundred appeared. Winder asked for more, but Armstrong refused to approve the call. Winder's nearest unit, the half-trained District Brigade, numbered but two thousand. Charges and countercharges, orders, memos, pleas, and threats crisscrossed the bureaucratic channels of national and state governments with only one result: it was entirely clear that each state was going to care for itself, and Washington would have to survive as best it could.

While Washington fiddled, the Royal Navy schemed. The arrival of Ross's army gave Cochrane and Cockburn a perfect opportunity to cause the great diversion they wanted. They had three possible objectives: Barney's flotilla, the Washington-Alexandria area, and wealthy Baltimore, the home port of many privateers. Cockburn wanted a fast strike at Washington, then an overland march on Baltimore. The more cautious Cochrane, however, gave the destruction of Barney's gunboats first priority. Only then would an attack on Washington or Baltimore be considered.

On August 18 the British fleet moved. Ascending the Patuxent River, with Barney's flotilla fleeing in front of it, the task force anchored off Benedict, Maryland. The next day Ross's four regiments of regulars, a battalion of marines, and a detachment of sailors dragged three small cannons and landed, unopposed. With part of the fleet paralleling the line of march, the British column set off after Barney. The sun was scorching, the dust thick, and the ship-soft infantrymen suffered badly from thirst and heat exhaustion.

When the British landing became known, Washington seethed with activity, much of it unthinking and tardy. Finally, American troops began to move. Winder got two thousand men (regulars and District militia) to Wood Yard by August 22. Meanwhile, Ross continued his northerly march. On his flanks hung a party of American dragoons, whose commander was James Monroe, ex-colonel and Secretary of State turned chief scout. Ross feinted toward Wood Yard, then swung west. As they marched the British soldiers heard a series of explosions to the north. Cornered, Joshua Barney, on the orders of Secretary Jones, blew up his flotilla. His quarry gone, Ross halted at Upper Marlborough for about twenty-four hours to rest and plan his next move.

In the meantime, Winder's force had fallen back toward Washington and camped at the hamlet of Old Fields. The camp was a hotbed of rumors, alarms, and confusion. Many of the men were two days and long miles past their last sleep. They had no tents and scant rations. Many did not know where they were or what they were supposed to do. William Winder, their will-of-the-wisp commander, rode from Wash-

Wilmington
Susquehanna R.
Delaware River
New Jersey
Havre de Grace
Battle of North Point
Maryland
Baltimore
Fort McHenry
District of Columbia
Annapolis
Bladensburg
Washington
Oldfields
Upper Marlborough
Alexandria
Pig Point
Fort Washington
Woodyard
St. Michaels
Delaware
Delaware Bay
Cape Henlop
Lewes
Benedict
Potomac River
Rappahannock River
Virginia
Chesapeake Bay
N
York River
James River
Chesapeake Region
Hampton
Cape Charles
Cape Henry
Craney I.
Norfolk
Portsmouth
0
10
20
30
map by Thomas Coates

ington and back searching for advice and aid. After wearing out three horses, he injured himself by falling into a ditch on the night of August 23.

On the afternoon of August 23 Ross marched directly west toward Old Fields. Winder, believing himself outnumbered and still hoping to assemble a larger force, ordered a retreat, and his army stumbled back to Washington, eight miles away. Ross then swung directly north on the road to Bladensburg, Maryland.

Bladensburg, as early as the twenty-second, was defended by a Maryland militia brigade and artillery from Baltimore, commanded by Tobias Stansbury. Nestled between rolling hills, the pretty town rested on the east bank of the eastern branch of the Potomac. Directly west of the town a bridge spanned the river; from the bridge two roads branched off to the west and southwest, the first to Georgetown, the second to Washington. Stansbury's men, footsore and hot, were deployed west of the river near its banks and on a ridge commanding the Georgetown Road. An open field and orchard separated the infantry regiments from the guns and riflemen they were supposed to be supporting. The Marylanders numbered fourteen hundred, and more kept coming. Though not bad, their position was not as defensible as the Lowndes Hill complex east of the town.

The news on the twenty-fourth that Ross was headed this way disconcerted Stansbury. He believed the British to be an overpowering force and it appeared that Winder's force would not arrive before Ross. In the forenoon, however, Monroe rode up followed by more militia. The incoming troops received no central direction as they arrived; positions were chosen as the individual commanders thought best.

In Washington, amid the first symptoms of panic, Winder's regulars, Virginia militia, and the District Brigade marched toward Bladensburg. Left to guard the Navy Yard, Barney begged President Madison and Secretary Jones to be sent to the battle. At the last moment, they relented, and Barney marched. The President, after conferring with his shaken general and sulking Secretary of War, rode ahead with part of his cabinet. Behind his party, an explosion marked the end of the Navy Yard bridge, and wagons carrying official records began to leave the city.

The Battle of Bladensburg was fought in three stages. Though the Americans put two thousand more men and nineteen more guns on the field than the British, the flaws in their deployment, compounded by the disorganization of command and the men's rawness, allowed Ross to engage and defeat them in separate actions. There were too many American chiefs on the field. Monroe, for example, repositioned some Maryland troops to their disadvantage. Armstrong pressed Madison to place him in command, and the President himself nearly rode into the British lines. Winder, the man supposed to be directing the army, was near collapse. His one tactical contribution before the battle opened was to draw up his force on a ridge too far from Stansbury to aid the Marylanders.

Close to one o'clock Ross' column came over Lowndes Hill and streamed into Bladensburg. The Baltimore artillery opened fire. The leading British element, Colonel William Thornton's light brigade (the 85th Foot and the light infantry companies), pressed through the town and rushed the bridge. Thornton's men numbered over a thousand, the Marylanders on the river bank perhaps five hundred. The American fire dropped redcoats around the road, but Thornton drove forward. Deploying widely, his men moved north along the river where there were fords. The British, reaching the American side, scrambled into the woods and returned fire.

From behind a warehouse the first Congreve rocket, trailing flame, wobbled and gurgled toward Stansbury's position. The Congreve rocket was an uncontrolled, noisy, fear-inspiring precursor of the bazooka and the buzz bomb. When filled with explosives—as were the larger rockets fired from Royal Navy frigates—the Congreve was destructive. When used against men it was almost harmless, but decidedly nerve-racking.

Soon the British outflanked the guns and riflemen. The order to retreat—given by Major William Pinkney, the distinguished lawyer and diplomat—and the first touch of panic came at the same moment. Though rapid and disorderly, the retreat was short-lived, for the men rallied on Stansbury's second line.

The light brigade (all across the bridge by now) advanced directly on Stansbury, then slid toward his right flank, which rested on the Washington road. This tactic successfully separated Stansbury's troops from Winder. The trees of the orchard masked the British envelopment and Winder, who had joined Stansbury, did not see it. Stansbury's two thousand men fought alone, and for a while they fought well.

Winder, realizing that he must counterattack quickly, ordered the 5th Maryland Regiment to advance. Unsupported, the green militiamen marched forward, volleyed, and forced part of the light infantrymen back to the river. But the rockets and the British flanking movement turned the tide. Stansbury's other units, exposed on their hillside, broke and ran. Winder then ordered the artillery and the 5th to retreat. Under fire the Marylanders left the field with remarkable speed and considerable disorder. Though Winder planned to rally them on his third line, the troops fled down the Georgetown road, which quickly took them away from the battlefield.

The third engagement, begun thirty minutes after the first, was the bloodiest of the day. On a rise in the Washington road, Joshua Barney's navymen and five guns anchored Winder's line. With them were seven more cannon and three thousand militia. Thornton's men, excited by their earlier victories, charged Barney and were blasted backward by the big naval guns. Three times the light infantrymen came at Barney; three times they were repulsed. The 85th was badly cut up, Colonel Thornton wounded severely. At one point the sailors and marines fired toe-to-toe with the British and then—with cries of "Board 'em, board 'em"—launched a successful counterattack.

Ross, however, had advanced the 44th Foot on Winder's left flank. Though the District Brigade and the Maryland militia in Winder's line were not yet seriously engaged, the new threat destroyed Winder's desire to resist. Unaware that Barney was faring so well, he ordered a general retreat. The withdrawal, though rapid and confused, was not a frenzied "race." Only when Winder told General Smith's District Brigade to retreat beyond Washington did unit disintegration begin.

Though outflanked and outnumbered, the flotillamen stood fast until Barney, who was down with a bad wound, realized he was alone. Before the last British assault, delivered from three sides, reached the American position the sailors and marines were gone. Barney had fought well; captured, he was praised by Ross and treated with kindness and respect. The victory cost the British five hundred casualties, the Americans, one hundred.

In the early evening of August 24, Robert Ross, George

Cockburn, and two regiments in faded red hiked into a deserted Washington. North and west of the city streams of refugees–from President and Mrs. Madison to the lowliest clerks–fanned out in the evening haze. Winder's army, too, scattered. Unopposed, the British began to burn the public buildings. Though Ross would have preferred ransoming the city, he could find no one with whom to bargain. Using gunpowder and torches, the British ignited the Capitol, the White House, the War and Treasury buildings, the Greenleaf's Point arsenal and the office of the *National Intelligencer*, which was Cockburn's most acid critic. Flames glowed far into the night. A thunderstorm later checked the fires, but a violent tornado the next afternoon added to the damage. Though the conquerors helped themselves to an abandoned banquet at the Madisons', Washington was not kind to its conquerors. At Greenleaf Point, a magazine explosion reduced Ross's slim army by nearly a hundred casualties. The thunderstorm and tornado, having dampened the enthusiasm of the firebrands, Ross ordered a return to the Patuxent on the evening of the twenty-fifth. After an exhausting, disorderly march, his army re-embarked at Benedict on August 30.

Ross's expedition was a remarkable feat for British arms. His column forced the destruction of the Chesapeake flotilla, won a victory at Bladensburg, and burned the public buildings of Washington, all in the heart of enemy territory. Though the burning was condemned by both Americans and Britons, it was consistent wth the War Office's policy of creating war-weariness in the United States. But the effects of such an act were miscalculated. Reflecting the nature of American federalism, many Americans cared not a whit for Washington, but those who did, instead of being dismayed, became more determined to support the war.

The Royal Navy had not been idle while Ross's column was ashore. As a diversion to the Patuxent maneuver, a squadron of seven vessels worked its way up the Potomac and captured Alexandria on August 28. The only American fort in their path, Fort Washington, was obligingly destroyed by its commander. The city fathers ransomed their town, but the British, three days later, sailed off with the loaded Alexandria merchant ships as prizes. The trip back down the Potomac was harrowing, for the Americans plied cannon and fireboats against the squadron with some effect. Another diversion by the frigate "Menelaus" cost the life of its captain, mortally wounded by Maryland militia.

While Cochrane's fleet reassembled and Ross's soldiers rested, Baltimore raced to prepare itself for the attack its citizens were sure would come. Since its privateers had harried British shipping with a vengeance, Admiral Cockburn had consistently threatened that "the nest of pirates" would fall under his torch. In 1814 Baltimore was the fourth largest city in the United States. Its assets for war, compared with Washington, were enormous. First, it found a forceful, respected leader in Major General Samuel Smith, also a United States senator. Though only a militia officer, Smith used sheer bluff and political influence to wrest command of the city's defense from General Winder. Smith was a rarity: a sixty-two-year-old former Revolutionary officer who had neither forgotten his military education nor lost his taste for a fight. A peculiar twist of war placed willing, efficient subordinates under Smith's command. In Baltimore were no less a trio than Commodores John Rodgers, David Porter, and Oliver Hazard

Perry. They and their sailors, put on the bench by the blockade, were soon employed erecting fortifications, manning shore guns, and manning shallow-draft gunboats. At Fort McHenry, the city's principal defense works, George Armistead, major of artillery, commanded a determined unit of regulars, sailors, and volunteers.

Smith's army grew daily and his earthworks bloomed. He had ample artillery, and, as the Bladensburg veterans limped home and the militia mustered, he soon commanded some thirteen thousand men. All Baltimoreans rallied to the defense of their city. As Baltimore armed and Cochrane's fleet sailed north, the American government began to reassemble in Washington and Congress soon reconvened in a crowded room in the Post Office. When the President suggested a "temporary retirement," Armstrong, taking the hint, resigned on September 4. Monroe again took over the War Department.

Back at Baltimore, Samuel Smith moved to contest what he suspected would be Ross's route of march to the city. Patapsco Neck, a slender peninsula bordered by the Back and Patapsco rivers, ran twelve miles from Baltimore to Chesapeake Bay. To work in co-ordination with Cochrane's fleet, Ross must use this approach. While he did not expect his militia to best the British in an open fight, Smith believed he could offer sufficient opposition to discourage Ross from assaulting the city. Therefore, he sent John Stricker's 3d (Baltimore) Brigade to a narrow neck in the peninsula some five miles from Baltimore. There on September 11 Stricker deployed his five infantry regiments, placing four in two lines and one in reserve. His artillery consisted of six four-pounders.

Cochrane's fleet anchored off North Point and on the morning of September 12, Ross led his impatient regulars ashore.

The plan was to strike from land and sea. Ross's column, the Bladensburg veterans augmented with sailors and marines, took to the road as Cochrane launched his lighter frigates, gun brigs, bomb ships, and the rocket-firing "Erebus" up the Patapsco. As he marched toward Baltimore, Ross was in good spirits and so were his troops. Already it looked as though the typical American confusion had begun, for he received reports of captured cavalry scouts and fleeing militia.

To slow Ross's advance, Stricker detached a force of riflemen to harry the British. Though part of this force panicked on reports that it was flanked, the rest of the Marylanders took to the woods and ran into the scouting companies of the 85th Foot. The firefight roared up quickly with the British getting the best of it. It was hide and fire, load and run, for both sides. Well deployed, the 85th lapped around both American flanks. The riflemen began to run, but a few remained to fire a parting round. Ross moved out with his advance guard to reconnoiter. Two Baltimore boys, Daniel Wells and Harry McComas, took their last shot (for they both soon died) at a British officer on a white horse. Stricken, Ross fell into the arms of his aide and died. The news raced through the British column, stunning the men. The senior colonel, Arthur Brooke of the 44th, took command.

Stricker's stand at Godly Wood was more determined than the British expected. Brooke's lead element, the light brigade, again was forced to give ground when the Baltimore artillery opened fire. The British replied with Congreve rockets and shrapnel, but the militia stood fast. At a farm some haystacks caught fire, and behind the smoke Colonel Brooke launched his attack.

The 44th and 21st Foot, marines, and the seamen advanced

on Stricker's front while the 4th (King's Own) hit his left flank on Rock River. The firing grew hotter and an American regiment fled. Although the Marylanders held, their losses and their leakage to the rear reduced their numbers and Brooke now had four thousand on the field. Musket fire blazed between the lines. Just as the 21st Foot pressed in with the bayonet, Stricker ordered a retreat. The Americans fell back but quickly rallied behind the reserve regiment. There was no pursuit. Lasting an hour and a half, the sharp battle cost the British over three hundred men, the Americans, two hundred. General Smith had made his point: Baltimore would be an expensive conquest. The British bivouacked for the night.

On September 13, Cochrane's bombardment fleet anchored off Fort McHenry and opened fire as Brooke moved against Smith's fieldworks. Neither effort succeeded. Throughout that day and night the Royal Navy threw mortars, rockets, and shells in fiery paths at Fort McHenry and Covington and the other waterfront batteries. The American guns replied briefly but were outranged. For twenty-five hours the American garrisons endured nearly eighteen hundred shells and in doing so, lost forty men. A British landing party made for Fort Covington but was repulsed. Ashore Brooke feinted twice, but became convinced that the American works would not be easily taken. After conferring with Cochrane, he pulled his army back, and the same day, September 14, the Royal Navy ended its bombardment. Plainly, Baltimore was not worth the effort the British would have to make to take it.

Aboard a small vessel, Francis Scott Key, a prominent Washington lawyer, watched the siege throughout the night of September 13–14. Key had come to the British fleet to arrange for the discharge of an American prisoner of war, Dr.

William Beanes. At dawn Beanes asked if the flag was still there. Caught up by the inspiration of the moment, Key jotted down the first draft of some verses. Later revised and later still entitled "The Star Spangled Banner," these verses were set to the tune of an old British drinking song, "Anacreon in Heaven," and eventually became the American national anthem.

During 1814 the war's familiar pattern continued: both sides were able to defend themselves but neither was strong enough or willing enough to mount a successful invasion. Cochrane's repulse at Baltimore and the much more important American victory at Plattsburg a few days before blunted Great Britain's offensive. Before the end of the year the stalemate had spread to the Niagara frontier also. Only the South remained an active theater.

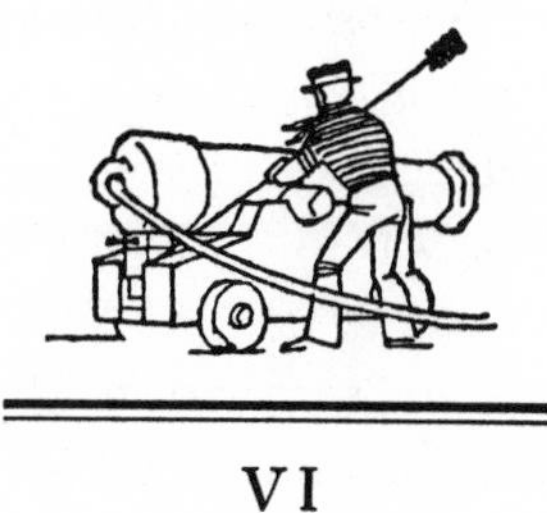

VI

Jackson and the War in the South

Though the stage sets and the actors were very different, the central theme of the drama played out in the South bore striking resemblance to that in the North. In both areas seapower played a leading role, in both there were the same insuperable obstacles of movement and supply, and in both there was the strange contrast between primitive American and modern European methods. The Indian clothed only in war paint fought side by side with (and sometimes against) the British professional in parade dress. Weapons ranged all the way from tomahawks and clubs to the latest Congreve rockets. Frontiersmen, regulars, Creoles, pirates, and free men of color pitted their skill and stamina against some of the most famous units of the British army.

Even in its broad outlines the war in the South resembled that in the North: a short-lived offensive phase, a war against the Indians, and a successful defense against large-scale invasion. In other words, Spanish Florida was to the South what British Canada was to the North, the hostile Creeks were the counterpart of Tecumseh's northern confederacy, and the Battle of New Orleans was to the South what Plattsburg was to the North.

The offensive phase was cut short, not by enemy resistance, as along the Canadian border, but by administration politics and policy. Spanish Florida could have been taken by force of arms any time before, during, or after the war. At the beginning of hostilities, President Madison sought authority from Congress to occupy East Florida, but a combination of Federalists and anti-Madison Republicans blocked any such authorization. Later, after the failure to invade Canada and the offer of Russian mediation, the administration regarded occupation as inexpedient.

The campaign against the Creeks was total war on a small scale: the United States attempted not only to kill as many hostile Indians as possible but also to destroy their capacity to resist. The conquest of the Creeks was as necessary as it was savage. Had the United States failed to clear out this pocket of resistance in the heart of the Southwest, the British could have landed anywhere on the Gulf, marched inland with the aid of their Spanish and Indian allies, and descended upon New Orleans from the north. If this had happened, no American commander, not even Jackson, could have saved New Orleans or any part of the Mississippi Valley the British might have chosen to appropriate.

THE SPANISH BORDERLANDS

Spain, of course, was a friendly power but she was allied to an enemy of the United States. To refer to Spain as a "power" in the period 1808–14 is a mere courtesy, for that unfortunate country was torn asunder by the Napoleonic struggle. As part of his design to subdue the entire Continent, Napoleon defeated the Spanish armies and set up his brother Joseph as king. But not even Napoleon could subdue the Spanish people who rose in revolt. A junta in Cadiz directed the activities of the resistance and enjoyed the support of the British. Napoleon had under his power not only his brother but also the legitimate ruler, Ferdinand VII, who was his prisoner. In these circumstances the United States recognized no Spanish government though it dealt unofficially with the Chevalier de Onis, who represented the junta.

The Spanish authorities at Mobile, Pensacola, and St. Augustine remained at their posts but they exercised only nominal control over their far-flung dominions. Amelia Island, near the coast of Georgia, was a haven for smugglers, while to the west the Indians could strike the outlying American settlements and escape into the privileged sanctuary of Spanish territory. In March, 1812, General George Mathews took possession of Amelia Island and St. Mary's River. Whether or not General Matthews exceeded his instructions is a matter of debate. In any case he was disavowed by the President. For some months, however, United States troops continued to occupy these Spanish borderlands.

When the war was declared against Great Britain the President was anxious, according to his latest biographer, "for authority to occupy East Florida, primarily to thwart a British occupation but under full expectation of securing the province as reparation for spoilation of American commerce." Anticipating congressional approval, on October 12, 1812, Madison asked the governor of Tennessee for fifteen hundred volunteers and informed Major General Thomas Pinckney, commanding the Southern Department, that a force was to be embodied "for offensive operations, preparatory to the entire possession of East Florida."

The prospect of occupying Florida met with hearty approval not only in Georgia but Tennessee as well. The people of both states were convinced that the hostile activities of the Indians were aided and abetted by Spanish authorities in Florida. In addition, the Tennesseans were hopeful that a shorter route to the Gulf could be established through the rivers of West Florida. On December 10, 1812, Major General Andrew Jackson, head of the Tennessee militia, assembled two thousand volunteers in Nashville. Having heard that certain militia had stood on their constitutional rights and refused to cross into Canada, Jackson informed Secretary of War Eustis that his men had "no constitutional scruples, and if the Government orders, will rejoice at the opportunity of placing the American eagle on the ramparts of Mobile, Pensacola, and Fort St. Augustine."

Displaying an energy unmatched in any other theater of war, Jackson by the middle of February had his army at Natchez where he was ordered to halt by General James Wilkinson, commanding the Seventh District, with headquarters in New Orleans. Jackson had no means of knowing that between October, when the call for volunteers went out, and February the whole atmosphere in Washington had changed. The offensive moves against Canada had failed one after another in 1812 and General Harrison, with his second Northwestern Army, had suffered an additional setback at the River Raisin early in 1813. Congress seemed determined to continue politics as usual and military failure had nourished factionalism. On February 12 Congress passed a bill authorizing occupation of Florida west of the Perdido (the area to which the United States had already asserted its rights under the treaty acquiring Louisiana), but withholding the authority to occupy East Florida. Accordingly, John Armstrong, who had taken over as Secretary of War from Eustis, wrote both Generals Pinckney and Jackson that there would be no invasion, and they could dismiss their troops "with thanks," but without pay or rations and without transportation or even medicine for the sick.

The government in Washington might casually abandon brave men, but Jackson would not. Furious, he posted a proclamation in his camp announcing his intention of marching his army home "on my own means and responsibility." And that is precisely what he did. A stern disciplinarian, Jackson made no effort to court popularity with his troops. But seeing that he shared the privations and the difficult work of the homeward journey some of his men remarked that he was tough as hickory. From that time onward, Jackson was known respectfully, if not affectionately, as "Old Hickory."

In the strictly limited border war there was little honor to be won and that little was garnered by James Wilkinson. Under the act of February 12 the President was authorized to occupy Florida west of the Perdido. Since part of the area was already occupied, this meant, in practical terms, the port of Mobile. Orders went to General Wilkinson, who on April 15 made with efficiency and dispatch the only permanent addition of territory resulting from the war. Wilkinson was ready and anxious to march on to Pensacola but, as we have already seen, he was ordered to the lakes. Armstrong explained that "the mission to Petersburg and the instructions to our envoys put a barrier between you and Pensacola." The troops which had occupied Amelia Island and St. John River since March, 1812, were finally withdrawn in May, 1813, thus ending the first phase of the war in the South.

THE CREEK WAR

In 1812 the southern states west of the Appalachians still had numerous Indians. The whole eastern bank of the Mississippi from the mouth of the Ohio to the Gulf was occupied by the Chickasaws and the Choctaws. The Creeks held most of present-day Alabama, and the Cherokees resided in the mountains and valleys of western Georgia and eastern Tennessee, one of the most beautiful and salubrious areas in the world. The Chickasaws and Choctaws took little or no part in the war and some of the Cherokees sided with the United States. Only the Creeks developed a sizable hostile faction. The growth of a war party among the Creeks was the result partly of real grievances, partly of Tecumseh's activities, and partly of accident.

The bases of discontent of the southern Indians were roughly the same as those in the North. Between 1802 and 1805 the Creeks had parted with extensive lands in the center of Georgia and later federal troops had laid out a horse path through part of the Creek lands. In the period immediately preceding the war, however, there seem to have been no fresh provocations of any importance. According to the prevailing standards of white men the Creeks were relatively "civilized." They derived their livelihood primarily from agriculture rather than the chase, they had a workable form of tribal and intertribal government, and they had a national history preserved in myth and legend. Contacts with the outside world were few for most of the Creek towns were remote and surrounded by vast stretches of wild and untamed country. The agent of the United States government among the Creeks was Benjamin Hawkins, against whom the Indians had no complaint. Hawkins was a rarity: an honest agent who had the best interests of his wards at heart.

Tecumseh, of course, wanted to bring the southern Indians into his confederacy and to that end he made a visit in 1811. To certain young Creeks steeped in a tradition of past glories, Tecumseh's vision of a united stand against further white encroachment had appeal. Furthermore, the sorcerers whom Tecumseh brought with him mixed with and indoctrinated certain of the Creek prophets. But the elders of the tribe, among whom was Big Warrior, remained unconvinced and even denounced Tecumseh. Having little else on which to rely, Tecumseh resorted to magic and made various predictions. In the months after his visit nature came to his aid in the form of a comet, a shower of meteors, and even an earthquake. The supernatural powers of Tecumseh and his prophets seemed confirmed.

When he returned to the Creek country in 1812, Tecumseh had not only the signs and portents in his favor, he had something quite tangible: military victory. He told how the Indians and their powerful allies, the British, had vanquished the armies of the Americans at Detroit and he promised that the southern Indians would receive aid from both the Spanish and the British. This put an entirely new aspect on matters and the dire warnings of the old men were brushed aside. Among the leaders of the young warriors, or Red Sticks, was thirty-year-old William Weatherford, a nephew of the famous chief Alexander McGillivray. Weatherford, or Red Eagle, had Scottish, French, Spanish, and Creek ancestors but he boasted "not one drop of Yankee blood." Intelligent, bold, and devoted to his cause, he was a worthy lieutenant of Tecumseh in the southern theater.

The chapter of accidents which played into the hands of the war party began to unfold late in 1812 when Chief Little Warrior led a band of some thirty Creeks all the way to Canada, where they participated in the River Raisin massacre. On their way home these Indians murdered some isolated white families living near the mouth of the Ohio. The Chickasaws, fearing they would be held responsible, sent messengers to the Creeks demanding punishment of the murderers. The old chiefs complied with these demands: the offenders were hunted down and killed. The Creeks were divided into two main settlements: those living along the lower Chattahoochee and Apalachicola rivers were known as the Lower Creeks, while those living in the higher valleys of the Gulf Coast streams were known as the Upper Creeks. Outraged by the execution of Little Warrior and his followers the Upper Creeks determined to avenge his death by attacking the Lower Creeks and any whites within striking distance. Thus the conflict in the South differed from that in the North in that it was partly a civil war and partly a war of jealous half-breeds.

In July, 1813, a half-breed chief, Peter McQueen, and the Red Stick prophets, Josiah Francis and High Head Jim, decided to take a group of Creeks to visit Pensacola. Their purpose was to deliver a letter from the British authorities at Malden to the Spanish governor and to dispose of booty they had acquired in raids on outlying settlements. At Pensacola the Indians were received by the Spanish governor, who, according to McQueen's own story, gave the visitors "a small bag of powder each for ten towns, and five bullets for each man."

The governor professed to regard these gifts as mere tokens of friendship, useful only for "hunting purposes." American frontiersmen, who were already hurrying into log forts, were unable to regard the matter in this light. As they returned to their towns, the Indians were intercepted by a band of whites at a place called Burnt Corn, about eighty miles north of Pensacola. Most of the Indians escaped but they lost a part of their ammunition and their pack mules.

Among the leaders of those who attacked the Indians at Burnt Corn were two half-breeds, Captain Dixon Bailey and Major Daniel Beasley. After their encounter these two men repaired to Fort Mims, a stockade about forty miles north of Mobile. The fort contained 550 persons, including some 175 militia under Beasley, and civilians of both sexes and all ages. Under the leadership of McQueen and Weatherford, the Indians attacked this poorly guarded stronghold on August 30 and quickly overcame its defenses. Some Negroes were spared to be slaves and about seventeen whites escaped, but all the others, including women and children, were massacred. The Fort Mims massacre aroused the whole country and might have created real alarm but for Perry's victory that came only a few days afterward. Actually the naval victory on Lake Erie sealed the ultimate fate of the Indians, both north and south, but this was by no means clear at the time. Six months of hard fighting was ahead before the frontier settlements considered themselves secure.

Major General Pinckney, who commanded the Department of the South, organized an expedition under Brigadier General John Floyd which was to move westward from Georgia. Brigadier General F. L. Claiborne, brother of the governor of Louisiana, was to come in from the west with one thousand

Mississippi volunteers and the 3d U.S. Infantry. The legislature of Tennessee voted to call up twenty-five hundred volunteers and appropriated $300,000 for immediate expenses. One column of Tennessee troops was to move south from Nashville and another southwest from the Knoxville-Chattanooga region.

What made the conquest of the Creeks a formidable military task was neither the size of their forces nor their skill in combat but the inaccessibility of their habitations. The total number of hostile warriors is seldom estimated at more than four thousand, and it is doubtful they ever mustered more than one thousand in any one battle. Though the Creeks possessed great personal bravery and fanatical devotion to their cause, they had no artillery and made only limited use of firearms. If they carried a musket into battle they usually fired it once and then resorted immediately to their ancient and trusted weapons, bows and arrows, tomahawks and clubs. Fighting the Creeks was not so much a problem as moving and supplying an army in their territory. The heart of the Creek country, the sacred Hickory Ground, was 150 miles distant from any base that could furnish supplies.

When news of the Fort Mims massacre reached Andrew Jackson, he was in bed recovering from a wound received in a brawl with the Benton brothers, Thomas Hart and Jesse. But death alone could have stayed the hand of the general. Immediately he issued orders for volunteers to rendezvous at Fayetteville, in south central Tennessee, on October 4. Among those who assembled was Jackson's best friend and ablest lieutenant, John Coffee, who led the cavalry. Further down in the ranks was Ensign Sam Houston, who, after the war, was to become governor of Tennessee and president of the Republic of Texas. Also on hand was that product of the wild frontier, Davy Crockett, whom one of the old chroniclers describes as "the merriest of the merry, keeping the camp alive with his quaint conceits and marvelous narratives."

In characteristic fashion Jackson opened his campaign with several rapid movements. Passing through the site of present-day Huntsville, Alabama, he marched to the Tennessee and where the river makes its southernmost bend established Fort Deposit, hoping to fill it with supplies. Continuing south he crossed Raccoon Mountain, which, though not as "tremendous as the Alps" as one of the soldiers naïvely thought, was nevertheless a rugged barrier. On the upper reaches of the Coosa River, Jackson built Fort Strother, which became his base for several months.

There soon followed two minor engagements, one at Tallushatchee on November 3 and another at Talladega on November 9. The former was actually fought by General Coffee, but it was indicative of the kind of warfare Jackson proposed to conduct. Using tactics similar to those employed by Hannibal at the Battle of Cannae, Coffee arranged his troops in a semicircle and sent forward a small body of troops to entice the Indians to attack. When the Indians were within the circle the advance troops retreated, the ends of the semicircle were brought together and over 180 Indians were killed. According to Coffee, "not one of the warriors escaped to tell the news." At Talladega Jackson attempted to apply the same methods, but on this occasion his lines gave way and about 300 of 700 Red Sticks were killed.

Had Jackson been able to follow up these initial strokes with a general offensive, he might have ended the Creek war in short order. But his slim resources were already spent. The twin evils of a shortage of supplies and short-term enlistments threatened now to end the campaign before it really began.

Jackson was depending on both supplies and reinforcements to come down the Tennessee River from the eastern part of his state. The river was low and no supplies came. Some troops under Major General John Cocke did reach Creek territory but their only contribution to Jackson's campaign was to attack the Hillabees, a tribe of friendly Indians, on November 18.

Part of Jackson's army consisted of one-year volunteers who had been enlisted on December 10, 1812. These were the men who had been released to their homes after the useless expedition to Natchez and then called back into service. Had replacements been available, probably they would have been allowed to go home. But determined not to abandon his campaign until his mission was accomplished, Jackson took the position that the four months the men had spent at their homes did not count. When one company started to march off, Jackson, still unable to lift a musket because of the bullet in his shoulder, placed his gun across the neck of his horse and threatened to shoot the man who made the first move. Sullenly the men abandoned the road to Nashville, but this was by no means the end of Jackson's trouble with the militia.

As the year drew to a close the Creek campaign threatened to bog down on all fronts. The expedition coming west from Georgia under Brigadier General John Floyd with about one thousand militia attacked the village of Autossee, twenty miles above the Hickory Ground on November 29. Though Floyd claimed to have killed two hundred Creeks, he was obliged for lack of provisions to retire to the Chattahoochee River. The troops under Brigadier General Claiborne marched into the Creek country from the south. They succeeded in capturing Weatherford's own town and in killing some thirty Indians but they too were soon without provisions. On Christmas Day the troops feasted on parched corn. With the terms of his Mississippi volunteers about to expire, Claiborne could do nothing but retreat. Thus as the year ended the Creek country had been invaded from four different directions but only minor raids had been carried out. The heart of Creek resistance had hardly been touched.

To Governor Willie Blount of Tennessee the whole undertaking seemed, for the moment at least, hopeless. He therefore wrote General Jackson recommending, but not commanding, a withdrawal. Added to all his other troubles Jackson had the faintheartedness of his civilian superiors. In a long letter designed to stiffen the governor's spine Jackson exhorted: "Arouse from yr lethargy . . . with energy exercise yr functions–the campaign must rapidly progress or . . . yr country ruined." Suspecting the governor had succumbed to the great weakness of all politicians, Jackson wanted to know, "Are you my Dear friend recommending to me to retrogate to please the whims of the populace. . . . Let me tell you it imperiously lies upon both you and me to do our duty regardless of the consequences or the opinions of these fireside patriots."

There was no further suggestion that Jackson retreat, and he did not. Some sixty-day troops arrived in January and Jackson threw them against the Creeks in indecisive engagements. The tide did not turn until February when reinforcements from Tennessee brought the army to a total of about five thousand men. Especially important was the arrival of the 39th U.S. Infantry which gave Jackson the means of coping with undisciplined militia. Breathing a sigh of relief the general remarked that the regulars "will give strength to my arm and quell mutiny."

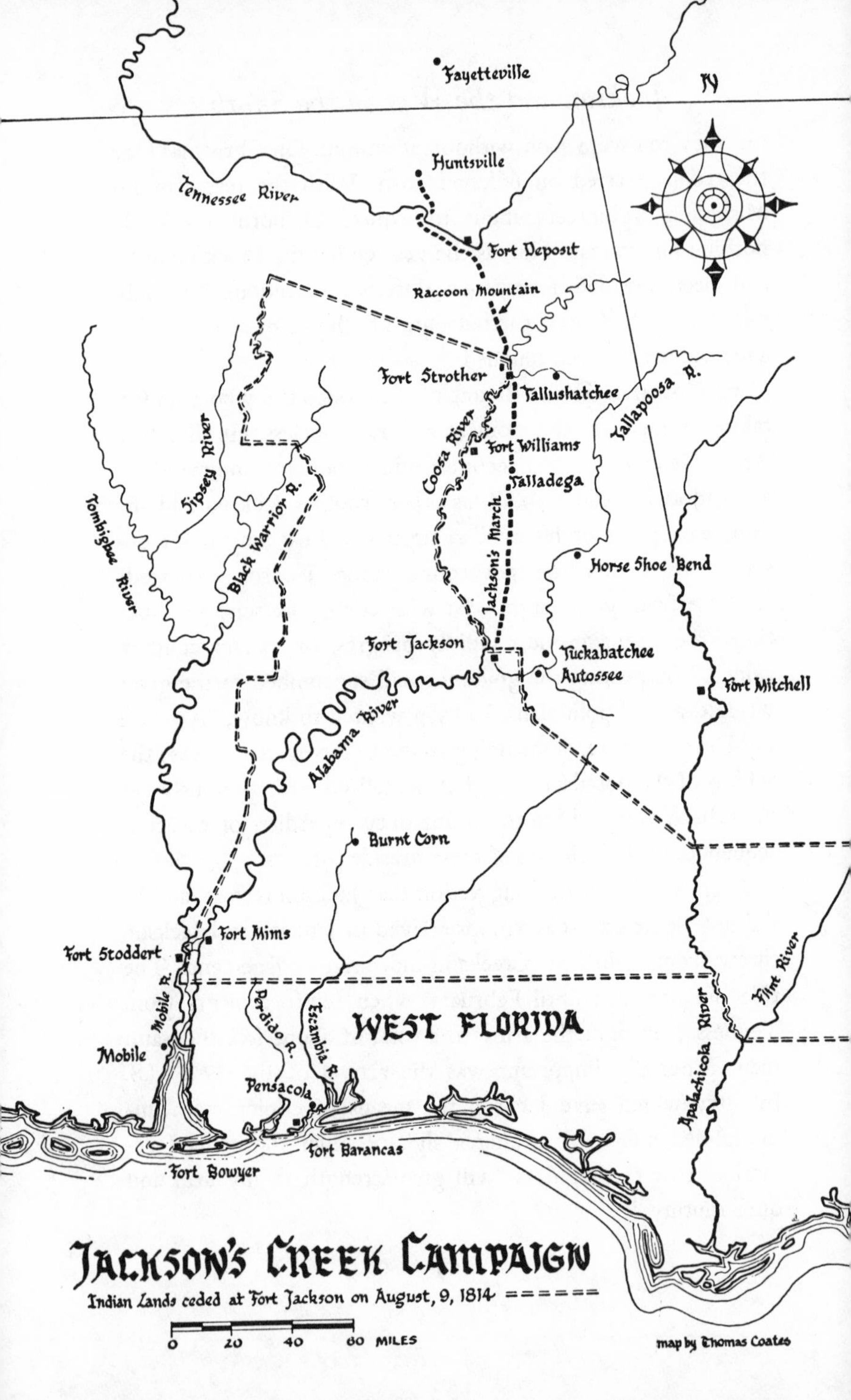

Fayetteville
N
Huntsville
Tennessee River
Fort Deposit
Raccoon Mountain
Fort Strother
Tallushatchee
Tallapoosa R.
Sipsey River
Coosa River
Fort Williams
Talladega
Tombigbee River
Black Warrior R.
Jackson's March
Horse Shoe Bend
Fort Jackson
Tuckabatchee
Autossee
Fort Mitchell
Alabama River
Burnt Corn
Fort Mims
Fort Stoddert
Mobile R.
Perdido R.
Escambia R.
WEST FLORIDA
Flint River
Apalachicola River
Mobile
Pensacola
Fort Barancas
Fort Bowyer
JACKSON'S CREEK CAMPAIGN
Indian Lands ceded at Fort Jackson on August, 9, 1814
0 20 40 60 MILES
map by Thomas Coates

When friendly Indians brought information that a large number of Creeks had fortified a position on the great bend of the Tallapoosa River, Jackson prepared at last to strike into the heart of the Creek country. Leaving a strong garrison at Fort Strother he sent his supplies down the Coosa on flatboats and marched about two thousand men toward Tohopeka, or Horseshoe Bend. The position consisted of a peninsula of about one hundred acres formed by the bend of the river. Across the narrow neck of the peninsula the Indians had constructed a zig-zag row of logs five to eight feet high with portholes arranged so that an attacker would be subject to cross fire. Along the river the Indians had placed hundreds of canoes in case they had to retire from their fortified enclosure. Jackson's plan was simple: Coffee, with the cavalry and about two hundred Cherokee allies, was to gain the high ground along the river and close off any means of escape. Jackson himself would lead the assault against the breastworks in front.

Action began on the morning of March 27. The Cherokees swam the river and brought the canoes to Coffee's side. These were used to cross the river and attack the Indians from the rear. Jackson opened up on the breastworks with his six-pound cannon. Unable to effect a breach by noon, he ordered the 39th Infantry to storm the palisade. Once inside the wall the battle broke up into many small pockets but Jackson steadily closed the ring. About 2:30 P.M. he sent a messenger to the main island of resistance in the middle of the horseshoe offering clemency to those who surrendered. The warriors, still urged on by the surviving prophets, answered by nearly killing the messenger. The slaughter went on until after sundown. The next morning 550 dead Indians were counted within the bend and many others were killed in the river. Probably not more than two dozen Indians escaped with their lives. Jackson's loss was about 50 killed and 150 wounded.

The retribution for Fort Mims was terrible, but Jackson was not done. Moving south he built a strong fort (Jackson) near the confluence of the Coosa and Tallapoosa rivers. Though he scoured the country he could find only a handful of hostile Creeks. Many fled into Spanish territory and a few came in to surrender. Among the latter was William Weatherford, who offered his person in exchange for food for the starving women and children. Admiring Weatherford's courage, Jackson granted him amnesty on condition that he try to persuade the remaining hostiles to make peace.

After the resignation of William Henry Harrison, Jackson was made a brigadier general in the regular army. On May 28, 1814, he was promoted to major general and made commander of the 7th Military District which included Tennessee, Louisiana, and Mississippi Territory. In his new position one of his first duties was to conclude a treaty with the Creeks, and by the first of August he was at Fort Jackson for this purpose. Since most of the hostiles had by this time fled into Florida, those Indians at the parley represented primarily those friendly to the United States. To their astonishment these warriors soon learned that the innocent were to be made to suffer along with the guilty. Jackson demanded the cession of twenty-three thousand acres comprising a broad strip west of the Coosa and north of Spanish Florida. The object was to separate the Creeks from the Chickasaws and Choctaws on one side and from the Spanish on the other. When the friendly chiefs protested, Jackson said they could either sign or move into Florida. The treaty by which the Creeks gave up one-fifth of Georgia and three-fifths of what was later Alabama was signed August 9. In a letter to his wife, Rachel, Jackson said that the "disagreeable business" was done, and "I know your humanity would feel for them."

CLEARING THE GULF COAST

When Secretary of War Armstrong heard of the Battle of Horseshoe Bend he decided that the war was over on the southern front. He wrote Jackson that rumors of the Spanish or British inciting the Indians were incredible and the "report of a British naval force on our southern coast . . . is nearly of the same character." Fortunately, Jackson did not depend on Washington as his sole source of information. During the whole of the Creek campaign he had never lost sight of what he considered the main threat: the possibility that the British might establish bases in Spanish Florida. As soon as he completed his disagreeable business at the Hickory Ground, he therefore marched toward Mobile, where he found his worst fears confirmed. Arriving on August 27, he learned that, two weeks before, Colonel Edward Nicholls with about two hundred troops had landed at Pensacola and was occupying Fort Barrancas. Realizing that Mobile would be next on the British timetable, Jackson spent the day of his arrival organizing and dispatching 160 men to strengthen Fort Bowyer on the end of a sand spit guarding the entrance to the bay.

Fort Bowyer was originally constructed by Wilkinson shortly after he had occupied Mobile in 1813. While possessing twenty cannons its mud walls, gun platforms, and magazines had been allowed to fall into disrepair, or were never completed. Under the direction of Major William Lawrence, one of the best junior officers in the regular army, repairs and construction went forward rapidly.

While the Americans shored up their defenses the British engaged in a lark. During the southern campaign the British were guilty of the same type of wishful thinking that the Americans had indulged in during their Canadian campaign: the notion that they could cause the inhabitants of the area to aid their activities. One group the British felt confident they could rally to their cause was the Baratarian pirates, commanded by Jean Laffite. This merry collection of outlaws operated from a harbor a few miles to the south of New Orleans, occasionally capturing Spanish vessels, continually violating the American customs regulations. Governor W. C. C. Claiborne attempted to terminate this affront to his authority but enjoyed little success because of the tolerant attitude of the citizens of Louisiana to the pirates. The governor's efforts, however, had resulted in the capture of one of the three Laffite brothers. With knowledge of these developments, the British at Pensacola dispatched the sloop "Sophie" under command of Captain Nicholas Lockyear to Barataria Bay to negotiate with Laffite. An amnesty was offered if the freebooters would surrender their ships and their stronghold to the British and join in an attack on New Orleans. Laffite requested fifteen days to think over the offer. The "Sophie" waited a few days near the harbor, then stood off to the east, rejoining three British vessels off Mobile on September 12.

The four British vessels were under command of Captain Sir William H. Percy, while the land forces consisting of about sixty marines and a hundred Indians were under Major Edward Nicholls. The land forces came ashore on the twelfth in the rear of Fort Bowyer. Grapeshot kept them at a safe distance. Several days were spent maneuvering the naval vessels through the narrow shoals of the harbor entrance and in the end only the "Sophie" and the "Hermes" were able to bring their guns within range of the fort. In an exchange of shots on September 16 the flagship "Hermes" had her cable cut by a shot. Drifting into the full raking fire of the American batteries, her crew sustained twenty-five casualties. When she drifted farther into shoal water her captain set her afire and blew her up. The remainder of the British squadron withdrew to Pensacola and the marines marched overland to the same destination.

As the British beat their retreat Jackson waited impatiently north of Mobile. From Washington he hoped to receive authorization to march into territory nominally Spanish; from Tennessee he hoped to receive the troops to carry out his attack. Permission to invade Spanish territory never came; a letter dated October 28 *forbidding* action was received only after the war was over. On October 25, however, General Coffee arrived with twenty-eight hundred mounted infantry. With his trusted lieutenant at hand, Jackson ignored the silence from Washington and took his line of march. By November 6 he was before Pensacola with approximately four thousand men. His first move was to send the Spanish governor, Don Matteo Gonzales Manrique, a demand for the surrender of Forts Barrancas, St. Rose, and St. Michael "until Spain can preserve unimpaired her neutral character." Neither expecting nor receiving a satisfactory reply Jackson prepared his attack. Seven British vessels, mounting over one hundred guns, guarded the western, and usual, approach to the city. On November 7, Jackson dispatched five hundred men to make a feint from that direction while the main body of his troops bypassed the city through the woods and attacked from the east. After some heavy fighting in the outskirts of the city, the governor surrendered. Jackson made preparations for the capture of the adjacent Fort Barrancas and, he hoped, the British arms and men contained therein. But the British denied him this opportunity by blowing up the fort and withdrawing. Nicholls fled eastward toward the Apalachicola, taking his Indian allies with him. Jackson completed the neutralization of Pensacola by blowing up Fort St. Michael, which guarded the western approach to the city, and withdrew. Arriving at Mobile on November 11, he sent Major Blue and a thousand troops to the Apalachicola to destroy the British arms depot which had been supplying the Indians.

Jackson's foray into Spanish territory has been much criticized. But Mobile and Pensacola were logical steps after Horseshoe Bend, for these actions thoroughly demoralized the remaining hostile Indians and convinced them that their British allies were unreliable. Even the Spanish, though they had perforce to conform to local changes in the power structure, were unlikely in the future to give active help to their allies. Manrique, who a few months before addressed Jackson in haughty tones, now signed himself "your most faithful and grateful servant, who kisses your hands." As the morale of the Indians and Spaniards declined, the confidence of American troops rose. In fact the inhabitants of the whole Gulf Coast now had new faith in their leader.

It is true of course that almost to the last moment Jackson did not expect a direct attack on New Orleans from the sea. He did not expect it because he could not believe that any commander would be so foolish as to undertake such a thing. "A real military man, with full knowledge of the geography of this country," he wrote, "would first possess himself of that point [Mobile], draw to his standard the Indians, and march direct to the Walnut Hills [present-day Vicksburg] . . . and being able to forage on the country, support himself, cut off all supplies from above and make this country an easy conquest." Though he oversimplified the problems of movement and supply, essentially Jackson was right. There were a dozen ways of defending New Orleans against an amphibious invasion: at worst one could fire the city and retreat up the Mississippi. There was always hope for an army as long as it could maintain communication with the back country. But once a strong enemy placed himself above the city and cut off supplies coming down the river, there was no defense. Jackson was justified, therefore, in emphasizing the security of his eastern front. The Duke of Wellington himself advised against a direct attack from the sea and there is good reason to believe that as late as October the British expected to land at Mobile.

THE BATTLE OF NEW ORLEANS: FIRST PHASE

What were the motives of the British and how did their plans develop? One thing is clear: after they had won the European war and were free to take the offensive the British did not propose to repeat the strategical errors of the American Revolution. The experiences of that conflict were sufficient to convince them that little could be accomplished by taking cities along the east coast. True, in 1814 Vice-Admiral Sir Alexander Cochrane was authorized to strike at cities in the Chesapeake area but his force was not intended "for any extended operation at a distance from the coast." New Orleans was important not just as a city but because it was the key to the whole trans-Appalachian area.

The government at first planned to dispatch a very large force to the Gulf area under Sir Rowland Hill, Wellington's second in the Peninsula campaign. This force was to have been assembled at Bermuda or the Barbados. Shallow-draft Dutch vessels for use in the shoal waters of the coast were to be procured, and supplies were to be forwarded from Europe to the base selected. A cover plan provided for a landing on the Georgia coast to draw attention to that area.

Developments in both Europe and America resulted in major alterations in these plans. Admiral Cochrane, who had been in London during the winter of 1814 and had participated in the planning, arrived in Bermuda in April to take command of the British naval forces in North American waters. One of his first acts was to send Captain Hugh Pigot in the frigate "Orpheus" to the mouth of the Apalachicola River to arouse and arm the Indians. Encouraged by the report brought back by Pigot, Cochrane estimated that three thousand British troops, with the aid of Indians and disaffected French and Spaniards, could drive the Americans entirely out of Louisiana and Florida. The British historian Sir John Fortescue remarks that Cochrane's estimate was "a piece of folly so childish that it ought to have warned British Ministers against listening to any of his projects. Listen they did, however. . . ."

The British ministers listened because Admiral Cochrane was telling them what they wanted to hear. Because of conditions in Europe they had already decided to reduce the commitment to the New Orleans expedition to six thousand troops who would be under General Ross instead of under Lord Hill. (Later still, the expedition was reinforced until eventually there were probably around ten thousand troops.) The purpose of this reduced but still formidable commitment was described as "First, to obtain command of the embouchure of the Mississippi, so as to deprive the back settlements of America of their communication with the sea; and, secondly, to occupy some important and valuable possession, by the restoration of which the conditions of peace might be improved, or which we might be entitled to exact the cession of, as the price of peace."

On matters having political implications Lord Bathurst was quite explicit to Ross. The general was not to encourage inhabitants to place themselves under British dominion, but should he find "a general and decided disposition to withdraw from their recent connection with the United States, either with the view of establishing themselves as an independent people, or of returning under the dominion of the Spanish Crown, you will furnish them with arms and clothing. . . ." Those displeased with the rule of the United States should be made to understand, however, "that Great Britain cannot pledge herself to make the independence of Louisiana or its restoration to the Spanish Crown, a *sine qua non* of peace with the United States."

Not only was the expedition reduced in size, but there were other alterations in the original plans. The advance base was changed from Bermuda to Jamaica and the shallow-draft vessels as well as provisions were to be purchased in the West Indies instead of Europe. All these changes compromised security. The purchase of supplies locally not only drove prices out of sight but advertised the dimensions of the undertaking. Under such conditions the cover landing was useless.

The army and navy commanders were to meet no later than November 20 but otherwise tactical details were left entirely to the discretion of those in the field. The army and navy commanders were at liberty to strike directly at New Orleans, to land at Mobile or some other suitable place along the Gulf and march overland, or to abandon the expedition entirely, if such a course seemed desirable. When Ross was killed in the attack on Baltimore, Sir Edward Pakenham, brother-in-law of the Duke of Wellington, was put in charge of the troops. He was to follow the directives given to Ross.

On November 22 Jackson began to move west toward New Orleans, 130 miles from Mobile. The government in Washington had received word of British intentions and from Pittsburgh had dispatched by flatboat four thousand stands of arms. Governor Blount had seen to the organization of twenty-five hundred Tennessee militia who, commanded by Major General William Carroll, left Nashville November 20. Additional troops were to be sent from Kentucky. Still unsure of the British place of landing, but hoping to provide for any eventuality, Jackson left one thousand troops at Mobile and sent General Coffee with two thousand mounted riflemen to Baton Rouge, from whence they could be used in the defense of either Mobile or New Orleans. The remaining troops, some two thousand in number, accompanied the general to New Orleans, where they arrived December 2.

New Orleans was blessed by its environs in that it was a remarkably defendable position. Located on a spit of dry land on the east bank, about a hundred miles above the mouth of the Mississippi, the city was almost surrounded by swamps filled with moss-covered cypress trees, huge marsh reeds, and reptiles. For an invader, therefore, there were many roads leading to New Orleans, but no good ones. West of the mouth of the Mississippi there were Bayou Lafourche, which was quite narrow and easily obstructed, and Barataria Bay behind which were swamps traversed only by small bayous, best known to the pirates. The great river itself was guarded by two forts, St.

Philip, about thirty miles from the mouth, and, about forty miles farther up, St. Leon, located at a sharp, almost S-shaped bend of the river known as English Turn. A sailing vessel riding a breeze that would carry it north to this turn would have to wait for a change of wind direction before it could proceed farther, a feature which often resulted in several days' delay for merchant vessels heading inland. The fort was so located that it could destroy any approaching English ships as they stopped at the bend. Two connecting lakes, Borgne and Pontchartrain, lie east and north of the city. Lake Borgne stretches within eight miles of the city but it is so shallow that a man-of-war could get no closer than sixty miles. North of this approach was an even shallower passage leading into Lake Pontchartrain. From this large body of water bayou St. John led south into the city, but this narrow avenue was guarded by Fort St. John. Troops landed at the western end of Lake Borgne could take a road, called Chef Menteur, leading along a narrow stretch of dry land, called the Plain of Gentilly, to the city. Flanked by swamps and occasionally narrowing down to one hundred yards, this road promised an easy defense. Rejecting this obvious approach, troops could attempt to follow one of the many small bayous draining plantations along the east bank of the Mississippi, flowing eastward into Lake Borgne. Most of these bayous had the peculiar characteristic of swamp streams whereby they deposit sediment on either side of their course, creating their own banks. Thus they provide a useful course for flat-bottom barges and also paths for marching soldiers.

Within a day of his arrival Jackson set about preparing the physical defenses of the city and organizing its human resources. Essentially, he had four basic tasks. One was to strengthen the various forts guarding the strategic and obvious approaches to the city. Another was to render impassable the many small bayous leading into or near the city. A third was to position his troops so that they could be quickly concentrated at whatever point the British decided to make their attack. The fourth task was the gathering of intelligence, both of the British movements and of the topography of the area around the city. The last advice he had heard from Washington concerning the British intentions had been received some sixty days earlier, informing him only that a large British force was preparing to attack either through the Mobile or New Orleans area. Since that less-than-new news nothing had been heard from Washington. A more effective source of information concerning the British movements along the coast were the various privateers operating in these waters and Laffite's pirates stationed on numerous coastal islands. The pirates were also very useful in providing information relating to the hidden bayous within the Delta, though Jackson remained loath to accept their services officially. Such maps as he received were drawn up by Major A. Lacarrière Latour, the principal engineer for the New Orleans area, which was technically a naval port commanded by Master Commandant Daniel T. Patterson. Latour had received his training while in the service of Napoleon's army and repeatedly provided Jackson with the most accurate intelligence of both the topography and of the various British movements in and around the city.

Besides the troops Jackson brought with him, New Orleans had already raised the two battalions of free Negroes commanded by Major Pierre LaCoste and Louis Daquin. A third battalion was organized by Major Jean Plauché, made up primarily of the well-dressed sons and brothers of the New Orleans aristocracy. A fourth group of "New Orleans Sharpshooters" was commanded by Major Thomas Beale. The state militia was commanded by General David Morgan. One other group that was to contribute much in the coming battle was made up of Choctaw Indians commanded by Major Pierre Jugeat. LaCoste's colored battalion was sent to guard the Chef Menteur Road, the most obvious approach to the city, while Plauche's uniformed companies were sent north of the city to strengthen and guard Fort St. John and Fort Petites Coquilles guarding the Lake Pontchartrain approach. Morgan's troops were sent south of English Turn to the west side of the river to await developments. Beale's Sharpshooters, Daquin's colored battalion and Jugeat's Indians were kept in the city, from which they could be moved in any direction. All available men and the slaves of the various plantation owners were put to work obstructing the various small bayous by felling trees across them and, where possible, filling them with mud. Finally, Jackson learned from Commodore Patterson that Lake Borgne itself was guarded by five of Jefferson's gunboats commanded by Lieutenant Thomas Ap Catesby Jones. Conceivably these small boats could delay the sending of troop-laden barges across Lake Borgne. At the very least they could warn Jackson of a British approach from that direction.

Having taken care of these various preparations, Jackson descended the Mississippi to Fort St. Philip, where he and Commander Patterson saw to the commencement of the construction of two additional batteries and a general strengthening of the fort. Returning to the city six days later on December 10, he went to Chef Menteur to check up on its defenses. While he was there, word came that British forces were operating off Cat Island at the mouth of Lake Borgne.

It will be recalled that the expedition was under orders to sail from Jamaica by November 22. By that date neither of the senior army commanders, Generals Pakenham and Lambert, had arrived. The fleet waited four days and then sailed without them. Since General John Keane, the acting commander, was much inferior to Admiral Cochrane in age, service, and prestige, the navy made the decision on the time and place of landing. In all probability Cochrane decided to strike New Orleans directly after he heard of Jackson's activities at Mobile and Pensacola. He was told that New Orleans was weakly defended, which was correct, and that the Creole inhabitants were thoroughly disaffected, which was not altogether correct. With the negotiations at Ghent three months old and the winter season rapidly approaching, there was obvious need for haste. Fortescue tells us: "It is easy to see that the choice of New Orleans as an objective was due to naval advice and that this advice was due chiefly to the desire for prize money. . . . Prize-money had for nearly two centuries been the motive for all amphibious operations recommended by the Navy." Making some allowance for Fortescue's pro-army bias the accusation is still not without foundation. Piled up in New Orleans were commodities from the whole trans-Appalachian area estimated to be worth four million pounds sterling. That Admiral Cochrane intended to collect some prize money is suggested by the fact that he included in his fleet several barges for carrying off the loot.

Whatever the motives, the decision was made to attack through Lake Borgne directly from the east. Approaching the mouth of the lake, the men-of-war soon ran out of water. Shallow-draft barges rowed by sailors would have to transport the troops the remaining sixty miles to New Orleans. Such an action required the removal of the gunboats which the British observed on the lake.

On the night of the twelfth, forty-five rowboats, manned by twelve hundred sailors and marines, were sent in to capture the five gunboats. Utilizing their sails, the gunboats fled east, attempting to take word of the British arrival to Jackson. Unfortunately, during the night of the thirteenth, they were becalmed and by noon of the fourteenth the hard-rowing British caught up. Pausing just beyond the gunboats' range, the troops had lunch and then moved into battle. The ten-to-one ratio in both ships and men soon enabled the British to capture all of Commander Jones's boats and men. Though having rowed for thirty-six straight hours, the British were able to turn around and return to the fleet to report their victory. The bearer of this news was Captain Lockyear, who hoped this would make up for his failures in dealing with the pirates and in trying to take Fort Bowyer. Upon hearing the news, Keane gathered together the advance units to be ferried to Pea Island some thirty miles inside the lake.

The next seven days were spent rowing the troops in to this miserable bar of sand. The round trip took about three days, which meant that the soldiers had to spend upwards of a day and a half huddled in the barges while the exhausted sailors fought the wind and tide of the lake. Once on the island, they found it to be made up primarily of sand, marsh reeds, alligators, and snakes. Every afternoon during this period there was a drizzling rain followed by an evening fog and a severe frost during the night. Without shelter, the troops never could get dry and had the unpleasant experience of their clothes freezing to their bodies every night. One thousand Jamaican Negroes, unaccustomed to such weather and without proper clothing, were put *hors de combat.* That any troops survived to go on to New Orleans is a credit to their stamina.

By December 22 all the troops, exclusive of Lambert's not-yet-arrived battalion, were on Pea Island and General Keane made ready to advance across the next thirty-mile stretch of water to the Delta itself. Scouts had gone to the end of the lake and checked the various bayous flowing into it. Most were obstructed, but they had found one, Bienvenue, that was unblocked and unguarded. Bayou Bienvenue led out into a wide plain directly beside the Mississippi River, a few miles south of New Orleans. Keane saw to the loading of twenty-four hundred soldiers on the naval barges and proceeded to the mouth of this bayou marked by a red flag tied to a tree. A group of American pickets was discovered near the fishing village, two of whom were captured while three others ran into the swamp. Proceeding up the bayou to the canal and following the canal east toward the river, Keane soon saw the cypress trees and swamp give way to the dry and level ground of the Villeré plantation. American troops stationed in the plantation house were surrounded and captured without a shot being fired, though the son of the owner of the plantation escaped and spread the alarm.

Keane now had to decide his next move. Colonel Thornton, who accompanied him, had led the successful advance on Bladensburg and he advised marching on New Orleans immediately. Keane could see he had found an admirable battleground, nearly one mile wide from the Mississippi River bank to the edge of the swamp. This plain stretched northward, narrowing at places, toward the city. Sixteen hundred men had already poured out of the swamp to stand on the plain beside him and some eight hundred more stretched back along the five-mile route between the shores of Lake Borgne and his position. It was noon and thus he had several hours of daylight left to make his attack. On the other hand, he had earlier questioned some of Laffite's men, and they had led him to believe that at least fifteen thousand troops were garrisoned in the city. The captured sailors of the gunboats had confirmed this figure, as had two of the pickets who had returned to surrender after struggling around in the swamp for a while. In fact, Jackson had no more than twenty-one hundred troops in the city at this time. Even so, tactics favor the defensive, and General Keane might have seen his army destroyed in sections were he to attempt an attack with only one-third of his forces. Accordingly, he decided they would spend the night at this plantation and await the arrival of the other British troops from Pea Island. A weak line was formed to the north of their camp beginning at the woods and extending to within a few hundred yards of the levy holding back the Mississippi.

Thus between December 15 and 22 the British were able to enter Lake Borgne in force, to discover a bayou leading to solid ground, and to land over two thousand men within nine miles of New Orleans without Jackson's having any intelligence of their movements. Why Bayou Bienvenue was left unobstructed in defiance of written orders is still a mystery. Though ignorant of his enemy's movements Jackson had not been idle. He had learned of the destruction of his gunboats on the lake on the evening of the fifteenth while inspecting works north of the city. Hurrying back to headquarters he dictated orders steadily for a day and night. General Coffee was summoned from Baton Rouge and express letters went to Generals Carroll and Thomas, wherever they might be on the river. Several suggestions were made to the legislature. When it refused first to draft seamen for the ships "Carolina" and "Louisiana" and then to suspend the writ of *habeas corpus* Jackson's patience, never abundant, was exhausted. On December 16 he declared martial law and took all defense matters into his own hands.

To this point the Laffite brothers had refused to join the British and Jackson had just as steadfastly refused to accept the services of a band he called "hellish banditti." Edward Livingston, however, whom Jackson respected as a lawyer and patriot, kept up his entreaties in behalf of his clients and Jean Laffite paid a personal visit to Jackson's headquarters. Why the general relented is not known, but the fact that Laffite had a large supply of powder, ammunition, and flints and about one thousand men ready to fight may have had something to do with his decision. With this addition to his ranks, Jackson was able to man the guns of the "Carolina" and "Louisiana." By December 20 General Coffee encamped a few miles north of the city with twelve hundred men, having marched 135 miles in three days. This day also saw the advance units of Carroll's army float into the city on barges which they had requisitioned during their journey. By so traveling, Carroll had outrun the messengers he had sent during his trip, and he had also come upon a barge loaded with eleven hundred muskets dispatched in August from Pittsburgh. The merchant to whom they had been entrusted had been trading with the various river communities as he floated in a leisurely fashion down the Mississippi. The muskets were much needed to supplement those acquired from the Baratarians. Hinds's Mississippi Dragoons also rode into the city. Jackson immediately dispatched Carroll's troops to back up those of LaCoste guarding the Plain of Gentilly to the east. Coffee and Hinds were retained in the city. Plauché, guarding Lake Pontchartrain north of the city, was ordered to hold it to the last man.

When, on the twenty-third Jackson learned that Keane's troops were pouring into the Villeré plantation, he immediately ordered a night attack. The first Battle of New Orleans drew upon the resources of the troops Jackson had kept in the city for just such an occasion. A pincer movement was planned using the two regular units near the river, Daquin's colored battalion in the middle, Beale and Hinds's troops to the left, with Coffee's troops, dismounted, attacking from the far left, near the woods. The "Carolina" was to open the action by shelling the British encampment from the river. Relieved of the necessity of being seaworthy, the "Carolina" had been loaded with many guns so as to increase her broadside greatly. Guns were in plentiful supply in New Orleans, many having been shipped there by the War Department for installation in Jefferson's gunboat fleet. Since only a few of these gunboats had been built the cannon lay in the armory until Jackson and Laffite made use of them. By 7:00 P.M. it was dark enough for the "Carolina" to drop down the river and approach the British camp. The shelling of the camp began at 7:30 and Jackson attacked at 8:00.

The British soldiers had been making themselves comfortable for the first time since they had left England. Compared to their cramped ship quarters or Cochrane's barges or the desolate Pea Island, the mud flats of the Villeré plantation were heaven. Wood had been gathered and fires blazed all around the area. A few attempted to extinguish the fires, but most ran toward the river to gain shelter near the protecting levy. Jackson's attack found them in this disorganized condition. The "Carolina" ceased fire so as not to hit Jackson's men, and pitch blackness fell over the area as Jackson moved down along the levy. Coffee, accompanied by the Choctaw Indians, moved south along the woods and then wheeled to the right and began to fight his way toward the river. In the darkness, the battle became a lieutenant's war with small squads of men operating without any contact with the rest. Soon hand-to-hand combat became the main method of fighting, with British bayonets meeting tomahawks and knives. The British began to push Jackson's forces back. Jackson ordered a withdrawal and by 9:30 silence settled over the area. Jackson had entered the battle with two thousand men against British troops numbering twenty-four hundred. His losses in killed, wounded, and captured amounted to 213, the British, 228. Though indecisive, the battle was a decided advantage to the Americans, for the British never quite recovered from their shock and surprise. The British troops were denied a good night's sleep by the sniping of Beale's Sharpshooters and the "Carolina" resumed shelling of their position. During the night, however, they had the pleasure of seeing the second wave of troops from Pea Island arrive, boosting their number to forty-seven hundred. Jackson withdrew about one mile back toward the city, stopping at a point where the woods narrowed the plain down to a width of about six hundred yards.

Daylight, the day before Christmas, found Jackson calling to the city for shovels for the purpose of creating a strong defensive position, but nevertheless he held LaCoste and Carroll on the Chef Menteur Road lest the British be making a mere feint at the Villeré plantation. A bend in the river prevented Keane from being able to see Jackson's position. All he knew for sure was that he had been attacked at night by about two thousand men. A principle of war dictates that no general risks a night action unless he has considerable reserves behind him. Jackson's sudden attack confirmed in Keane's mind that he was faced with an army of at least fifteen thousand and, accordingly, he decided to wait until all the British troops had been ferried over from Pea Island. The third wave of troops that arrived on Christmas brought General Pakenham, who expressed some surprise at finding his army committed to an action that required an advance of what amounted to a narrow defile. However, Cochrane and Keane pointed out that the Plain of Gentilly was even more narrow, as were all the other approaches to the city. Cochrane expressed regret that his massive fleet could be of no assistance in the forcing of the city, but stated his confidence that two thousand of his sailors could quickly scatter the "dirty shirts." Pakenham felt that he could not make an advance on the city without first removing the "Carolina" as a threat to his flank and, accordingly, several large cannons that had already been rowed to Pea Island were hastened to the camp. Dragging the cannons through the bayou, a passage that was already rapidly deteriorating owing to the heavy traffic it had sustained, the sailors had them mounted on the levy by the twenty-seventh and began firing heated shot. A strong head wind prevented the "Carolina" from escaping, and it soon caught fire and exploded. The guns were then trained on the "Louisiana" farther upstream, but crews in rowboats were able to tow it out of range. Pakenham was now free to attack against an enemy about whose size and position he knew almost nothing. He spent the remainder of the day organizing his troops for the advance and, by December 28, he was ready to take the city.

The War of 1812

BATTLE OF NEW ORLEANS: SECOND PHASE

The time Pakenham spent dragging up the cannon could serve only to help Jackson. Rodriquez Canal was deepened, the mud from its bottom being thrown up on its north bank, creating a wall. Trees were hacked out of the swamp and stacked corduroy fashion along the north bank before being covered with more mud, thereby giving the wall some shape. The rampart was extended into the swamp some two hundred yards, then curved back toward the city to prevent a flanking movement on that side, but this work had just begun when the British attacked.

Retiring to the Villeré plantation, Pakenham set about considering his next move. The unsuccessful attack was entered in his diary as a reconnaissance in force. This time it seemed to him that the artillery on Jackson's line had been his most deadly foe, and he decided that he must have heavy guns from the fleet. Sixty miles the cannon were rowed. By this time Lambert's troops were beginning to arrive and each soldier was given a cannon ball to carry through the five miles of swamp. One unfortunate boatload of soldiers thus burdened with cannon balls in their knapsacks turned over during its passage across Lake Borgne, and they all disappeared beneath the waves without a sound. Arriving at the passage through the swamp the remaining soldiers found the sides of the bayou beginning to collapse, causing many of the barges to become grounded in the mud. Some of the barges thus had to be dragged by ropes through the five miles of swamp. Nevertheless, by the night of the thirty-first, Pakenham could order the cannon to be moved forward toward the American line, there to be set up in protected batteries for action at dawn.

Five batteries were set up, the first with seven cannons aimed toward the river, seventeen other cannons distributed among the other four batteries. Great difficulty was experienced by the British in finding enough mud with which to form protective walls for their cannon. If they dug more than a few inches into the soil, the hole quickly filled with water, and so dirt had to be hauled from a fairly wide area. Barrels of raw sugar that had been found on the plantation were used as walls of the batteries in the hope that they would serve as sandbags. By New Year's morning, Pakenham was ready to begin the artillery duel.

Jackson too had been utilizing this time. While the attack of the twenty-eighth found him with five cannon in position, by the morning of the first he had twelve cannon in the line and three more located on the west bank of the river. Attempting to calculate what he would do were he in Pakenham's position, Jackson saw that the far side of the river could offer a means to defeat his line. While the river was approximately a mile wide, British cannon on that side could fire into Jackson's line from behind and make Jackson's position untenable. Accordingly, on the twenty-ninth he sent his engineer, Latour, across the river to construct a line opposite his. The Louisiana militia under Morgan were assigned to build and defend the line and to protect Patterson's guns located there. On his own side of the river, Jackson saw his mud wall built up to a height of eight feet from the base of the canal, five feet high on its back side. The part of the line extending into the swamp was also built up. Carroll's troops were released from guarding the Chef Menteur Road and took up a position near Coffee in the swamp. Jugeat's Choctaw Indians took up the farthest left position, concealing themselves among the cypress trees. It was during these preparations that the famous cotton bales were brought into play when they were used as gun embrasures for Jackson's cannon.

On New Year's morning, Jackson was preparing to review his troops when the fog lifted and the assembled warriors found themselves faced by the secretly constructed British batteries. Amid a rain of shot, Jackson's men scattered to their positions along the wall. The British opened their barrage without bothering first to get the range of the target. Consequently, much of the shot which had been most laboriously carried from the fleet to their position was wasted in the fields behind Jackson's position. The American artillery, notably Battery No. 1 commanded by Captain Humphrey of the regular army and Battery No. 3 commanded by the pirate Dominique You, took the time to fire a few practice shots, finding the range of their target before opening with all their cannon. Within a very short time the American guns were tearing the British batteries apart. Patterson's two cannon across the river soon swept from the top of the levy the British battery aimed in his direction. You's cannon tore the British sugar barrels to pieces which, in the drizzle that developed during the artillery duel, soon made a sticky quagmire of the British positions. Concentrating on the heaviest guns first, You and Humphrey soon had smashed or dismounted the most effective portion of the British artillery. By noon Pakenham had to order another retreat. Considering that in both weight of shot and number of cannon the British enjoyed an advantage over the Americans, this victory was one of the most significant indications of the superiority of the American artillery. During the duel the British attempted another advance against Coffee's section of the line, but by this time the line had been improved and

Coffee's men, combined with the Choctaw Indians hidden in the swamp, easily repulsed them. Pakenham retired to Villeré to consider his next move.

The following days of quiet left Jackson completely puzzled. The British could hope to gain nothing by further delay and it seemed only logical to him that they must be preparing to withdraw and attack from a new direction. Accordingly, he spent much of this time rechecking the Chef Menteur Road and the St. John Bayou north of the city. Little more could be done to strengthen his line, though the cotton bales, which had revealed an unfortunate characteristic of catching on fire from the cannon blasts, were pulled out and replaced with mud. The only further use they were to serve in the battle was as beds for the troops behind the line, a welcome alternative to the muddy ground. On January 3 Thomas's Kentucky troops arrived but without guns. Upon hearing of this, Jackson is reported to have exclaimed, "I don't believe it. I have never seen a Kentuckian without a gun and a pack of cards and a bottle of whiskey in my life." History has not recorded whether they came without the latter two items, but certain it is that they had no guns. A search of the city managed to dig up a few rusty Spanish muskets and, armed with these, half of them were ordered to the west bank of the river to support General Morgan, who was being less than effective in his preparations. Contrary to the advice of Latour, he selected a position to defend at one of the widest sections of the plain running along the west side of the river, thereby causing his line to be stretched out very thinly. In addition, he was a very indecisive man who was not able to command the respect of his troops. Thus the back-breaking work of digging the mud and throwing it up into a wall went very slowly. Jackson, for his part, began the construction of a second line two miles closer to the city to fall back upon in case the British were to breach his first line.

The British on their part had indeed decided to attempt to cross the river. This was to be but one aspect of a renewed attack upon General Jackson's line. By this time, all of Lambert's troops had reached the British camp and Pakenham now had in excess of nine thousand against Jackson's five thousand. Colonel Thornton was to take fourteen hundred of the British troops across the river and attack up that side in conjunction with a renewed British advance on the east bank. For the transport of the troops, the canal running across Villeré plantation to the levy was to be widened so as to allow the passage of heavy barges. The levy itself was to be pierced, permitting the barges to enter the Mississippi and subsequently cross it. Hopefully Thornton could capture Patterson's guns and turn them against Jackson's line. The British plans do not seem to have gone very far beyond this. Had they decided to send a substantial body of men across the river with heavy cannon, they might have forced Jackson to attack, or at least divide his rather weak forces. Based on the results of Jackson's attack of the twenty-third, such a move into the open might have been fatal for his army. Fortunately he never had to resort to this.

The night of the seventh was spent by the British in frantic preparation for an all-out assault in the morning. The only new factor favoring the British was the arrival of Lambert's troops, and evidently this was enough to make Pakenham think that he could succeed, though all his previous assaults had been repulsed. Working against Pakenham was the growing strength of Jackson plus the increasing demoralization of his own troops. Their many nights spent sleeping in the mud and living on low rations, their repeated defeats, the constant threat of the silent Indians, the continual shelling of their camp by Patterson's guns, and, finally, the overheard despairing complaints of their officers, including Pakenham, had had their effect on the British troops. Preparations for the assault included the bundling up of fascines of sugar cane with which to fill the canal in front of Jackson's line and the construction of ladders with which to climb the wall of that line. Plans called for the 44th Regiment, commanded by Colonel Mullens, to lead the attack bearing the ladders and fascines. The British force was to be divided into two columns. The left arm, led by Rennie, was to attack along the levy and its adjacent road. The right arm, led by General Gibbs, was to attack along the edge of the swamp. General Keane was to follow the second arm and go to the aid of whichever one seemed most to require it. General Lambert and his troops were held in the rear as reserves. The plan called for an attack just before daybreak so as to minimize the effectiveness of the Tennessee rifles. Thornton was to be across the river with fourteen hundred men in position to attack Morgan at the same time. The transfer of Thornton's troops was to suffer the first of many fatal delays. During the night the levy was breached in the hope of raising the water level in the canal through which Thornton's troop barges were to be dragged. The river level had dropped during the night, however, and, when the levy was pierced, Thornton was amazed to see the water level in the canal drop rather than rise. This, in combination with the constantly collapsing mud banks, caused many of the barges to be mired, and only with the greatest of effort was Thornton able to get one-third of his troops across the river, some three miles below Morgan's position, by daybreak.

Meanwhile, in the predawn darkness, Pakenham began to move his troops forward. Batteries were again set up within seven hundred yards of Jackson's position and again great difficulties were encountered in gathering enough mud for the protection of these batteries. Mullen's troops marched forward to the point where he thought they would find the fascines and ladders only to find that they were located some three hundred yards back. Accordingly, Mullen's troops double-timed to the rear, gathered their bundles, and staggered back toward the front. While they were still in the process of regaining their position in the line, Pakenham fired the rocket signaling the beginning of the advance.

Jackson had observed the British activities during the day and knew that the attack was planned for the following morning. His line was ready. The Kentucky militia still on his side of the river, now commanded by General Adair, as General Thomas had fallen ill, had been positioned to support Carroll along the swamp end of the line. The colored troops of LaCoste and Daquin held the center, while the 7th Infantry and Plauche's New Orleans troops held the levy end of the line. Coffee and the Indians remained in the swamp to his left. Along the entire length of the line, the troops stood four deep.

With Pakenham's rocket signal, all eyes strained as they attempted to pierce the heavy fog lying along the mud flat before them. Suddenly a breeze began to break patches in the fog and it lifted, unmasking the British advance now not more than 650 yards away. Stretching back as far as the eye could see were the British troops. Their red uniforms with the white cross-belts, occasionally broken by the bright green uniforms of the Rifle Corps, stretched like a carpet. As the British passed the five-hundred-yard mark, Jackson's cannons opened fire, beginning the decimation of the advancing troops. The British cannons were no more effective this day than they had been before. As the advance came within the range of the long rifles, Jackson ordered some of the cannon to cease firing so that their smoke would not spoil the aim of the keen-eyed woodsmen. With orders to aim just above the breastplate, paying particular attention to any mounted officers, the riflemen fired as one, a sheet of orange flame rippling down the length of the line. The first rank then stepped back to reload while the second rank took its place, then the third, then the fourth. Thus a steady fusillade tore apart the approaching British columns. Mullen's troops found themselves behind the first part of the advance rather than leading with the fascines and ladders. As they drew near the deadly wall of mud, panic seized their ranks and they threw down their bundles and began firing wildly at the line. The troops in front of them found themselves being shot at from two directions and they too broke. Gibbs, whose section of the line was suffering the most devastating effects of the accurate rifle fire of Carroll, Coffee, and Adair, spurred his horse forward, attempting to rally his line. As he came within range, four bullets tore through his body. Pakenham urged his horse forward, caught up with Keane, and ordered his troops to the aid of Gibbs's column. As they drew near, Pakenham's horse was shot under him. He swung himself up on another and was immediately shot through the neck and stomach. General Keane was similarly cut down, but his wounds were not fatal. To add to the misery of the now leaderless right column, the Choctaw Indians and some of Coffee's troops began to move against them, firing from behind the trees of the swamp.

The left wing along the levy succeeded in capturing a re-

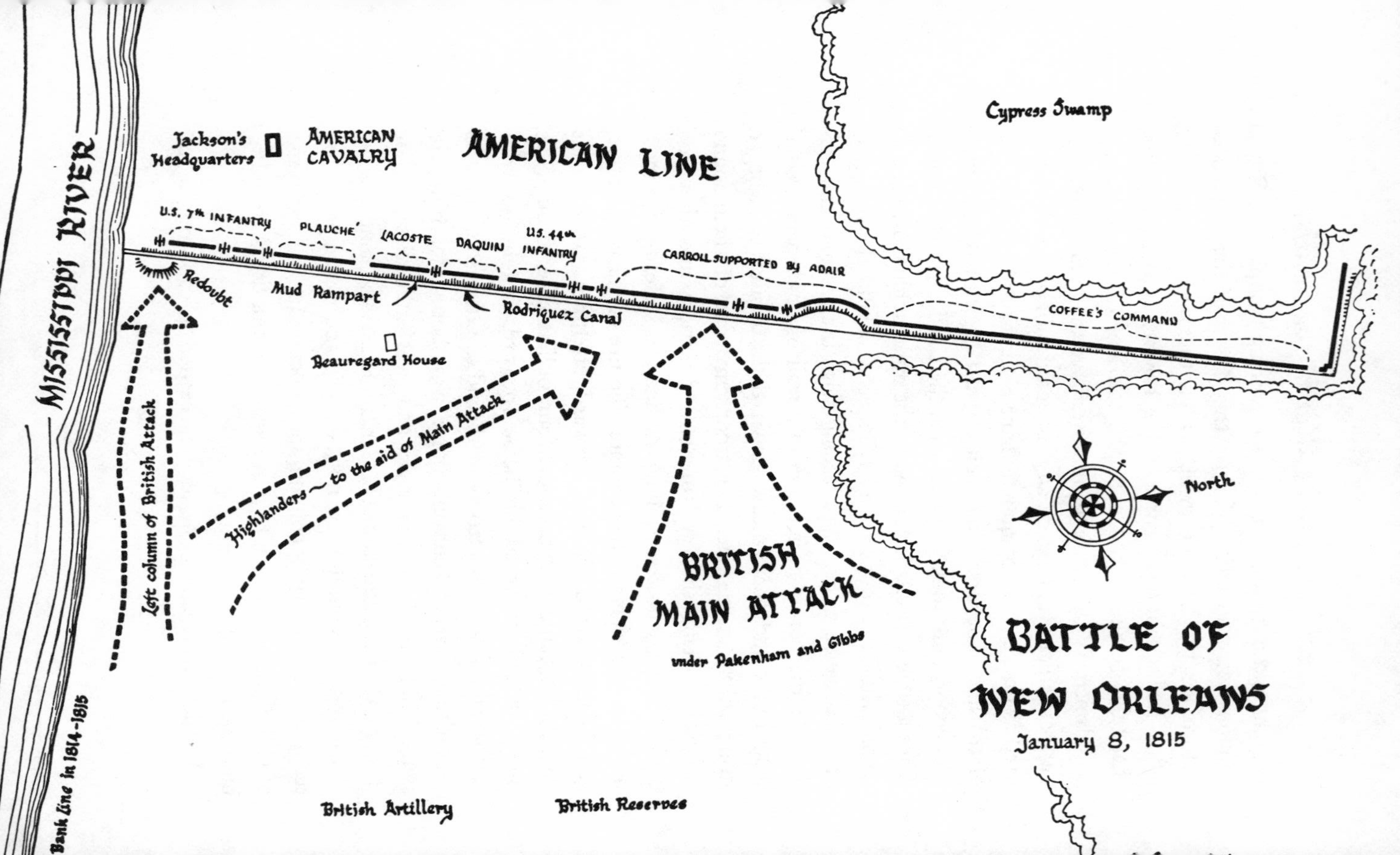
BATTLE OF NEW ORLEANS
January 8, 1815
Cypress Swamp
Jackson's Headquarters
AMERICAN CAVALRY
AMERICAN LINE
MISSISSIPPI RIVER
U.S. 7th INFANTRY
PLAUCHE'
LACOSTE
DAQUIN
U.S. 44th INFANTRY
CARROLL SUPPORTED BY ADAIR
COFFEE'S COMMAND
Redoubt
Mud Rampart
Rodriquez Canal
Beauregard House
Left column of British Attack
Highlanders ~ to the aid of Main Attack
BRITISH MAIN ATTACK
under Pakenham and Gibbs
North
British Artillery
British Reserves
Bank line in 1814-1815

doubt and a few soldiers, including Rennie, managed to clamber up the sides of Jackson's wall only to die there. Instead of supporting the left wing Keane ordered the 93d Highlanders to oblique across the field in support of Gibbs's column. The brave Highlanders lost five hundred men, including their commander, Colonel Dale, in a futile attempt to save the day. Rennie's men, unable to advance from the outwork to the breastwork and suffering terrible losses from the artillery batteries near their end of the line, retreated. Lambert, far to the rear, received word from the retreating troops that all his superior officers had been killed and he was now in charge. Viewing the scene before him, he saw one-third of the British army lying in terrible heaps before the American line. Another third was streaming past him in complete disarray. Though his troops were still fresh, he could see no wisdom in renewing the attack and the retreat was sounded. By 8:30 in the morning, the firing had ceased and Jackson's men could look over their parapet and see a once-brown field now red with the bodies of over two thousand British troops, many still living though horribly wounded.

Meanwhile, on the west bank of the river, Thornton, who had proved his mettle at Bladensburg, was enjoying considerable success. Pakenham's rocket had caught him far from the American line and he did not approach the advanced forces until the battle on the east bank was well under way. Morgan's first line was quickly put in retreat and Thornton advanced on to the low, partially complete main line of the Louisiana general. This too was quickly breached and Patterson was forced to spike his guns and join the run to the rear, but not before his cannons had aided Jackson by contributing to the slaughter of Rennie's left wing. In the attack on the American lines

Thornton was so badly wounded that he had to turn over his command to a less experienced lieutenant colonel. The fully-to-be-expected destruction of the guns by Patterson denied their services to the British troops, freeing Jackson of the unpleasant experience of having his line subject to a raking fire from the right. By this time, the battle on the east bank had nearly ended, but the British continued the pursuit of Morgan's fleeing troops, the latter being encouraged in their flight by three hearty cheers from Jackson's men across the river. Three miles behind their original position, Morgan's men rallied and formed a line while the British paused to await orders.

The situation on the west bank became a source of great anxiety to Jackson but he kept his wits about him. When, during the afternoon of the eighth, General Lambert requested a cease fire for the purpose of burying the dead Jackson agreed, but *only* for the east bank. The ruse worked: during the night Lambert ordered his troops on the west bank to recross the river, thus forfeiting his one advantage. The next day the surviving British soldiers were permitted to come forward and carry the wounded back to the Villeré plantation, where army surgeons were feverishly amputating injured limbs. It was while on one of these grisly missions that the British soldiers learned that Jackson's line had sustained a loss of only seven killed and six wounded.

Though the British line had been badly mauled, discretion dictated that Jackson not take his raw woodsmen over the wall to attack the remainder. Discretion also dictated that the wall remain fully manned until the British threat was far distant. By the eighteenth Lambert had organized his forces enough to begin the unhappy retreat back through the swamp to the shore of Lake Borgne, then the long passage by rowboat to the desolate wastes of Pea Island. By January 27 the last of the now almost starved Britons had quit the shores of the Mississippi Delta. Mrs. Pakenham, waiting on one of Cochrane's ships for the signal to enter New Orleans as the governor's wife, instead saw with horror her husband's body loaded aboard the ship preserved in a barrel of rum. She was not the only wife to be deprived of her husband. Between December 23 and January 8 the British lost twenty-four hundred men. Cochrane attempted to save some face by mounting an attack on Fort St. Phillip, but three days of bombardment saw only the improvement of the fort's resistance as its aim became more accurate with practice. In his frustration, Cochrane then moved to Mobile and captured Fort Bowyer, but this triumph was without effect.

On January 23 Jackson marched his troops back to receive the plaudits of the Crescent City. Maintaining martial law until the middle of March, he also kept the various volunteers in their militia organizations until he received official word of the signing of the peace treaty with England. This, plus other actions irritating to certain citizens, caused the Louisiana Senate to omit his name from the list of officers to whom they extended their thanks for saving the city.

It is often stated that the Battle of New Orleans was useless because it was fought after the signing of the peace. Before accepting this simplistic judgment we might ask ourselves what were British war aims, particularly with regard to the South, and how these aims were affected by the signing of the peace.

The British may have provoked the war but they did not start it. The Americans started it and the British, forced to fight, decided they should get some tangible results from their efforts. American aggression against Canada in the future could best be prevented by limiting the growth of the trans-Appalachian settlements. Eschewing direct annexation of territory, the British planned to create a large Indian buffer state in the Northwest which would begin at the old Greenville Treaty line in Ohio and sweep indefinitely westward. In the Southwest, New Orleans would be seized in order to deprive the back settlements of their communication with the sea.

Conditions in Europe and England's alliance system made it inexpedient to annex Louisiana outright. Great Britain, allied to Spain, had taken the view that the treaty by which Napoleon sold Louisiana to the United States was illegal. Pakenham, therefore, was to "rescue" Louisiana. Accompanying the expedition was a complete civil government staff, including a customs collector, an attorney general, an admiralty judge, a superintendent of Indian affairs, and others. Included in General Pakenham's dispatch case was a commission from the Colonial Office making him governor of Louisiana and a proclamation declaring the sovereignty of Great Britain in behalf of Spain "over all the territory fraudulently conveyed by Bonaparte to the United States." General Pakenham and, later, Spain would of course regulate the trade going out of the mouth of the Mississippi in accordance with Britain's interest and security. Thus hemmed in by the Indians on the northwest and the Spanish on the southwest, and with no outlet for surplus agricultural products, the growth of the American West would be effectively stifled.

These were optimum benefits that Great Britain hoped to gain from her vast expenditure of blood and treasure. Should the fortunes of war go against her, or should her position on the Continent deteriorate, she was not prepared to fight indefinitely for territorial gains in America. Hence, as we have already noted, Pakenham was warned that "Great Britain cannot pledge herself to make the independence of Louisiana, or its restoration to the Spanish Crown, a *sine qua non* of peace with the United States."

Did the Peace of Ghent materially alter these aims and plans? The available evidence, if by no means conclusive, is suggestive. In the first place the treaty had been signed, but by its own terms it was not to go into effect until ratifications were exchanged. Pakenham was under orders to continue to prosecute his offensive until a special emissary from the Prince Regent reached him. Anthony St. John Baker, who had been secretary of the British commission at Ghent, was appointed chargé and sailed for the United States on January 2, 1815. Baker had instructions on when and under what conditions he was to exchange ratifications but what these instructions were, we do not know. We do know that a week after he sailed, heavy reinforcements for Pakenham were ordered from Canada and Great Britain. We know also that as late as February 28 Lord Liverpool wrote Wellington that "It is very desirable that the American war should terminate with a brilliant success" at New Orleans. If the ministry intended to restore Louisiana to the United States, why did they intensify their efforts to ensure success? It may have been a mere matter of pride, but one doubts it.

To return to Anthony St. John Baker: He arrived at New York on February 11 and was greeted with news of Jackson's victory and Pakenham's death. If he had contingent instructions they were obviously set aside by these events. Ratifications were exchanged on February 17.

New evidence may some day shed additional light on British

intentions. What will forever remain a mystery is what the ministry would have done if Pakenham had won. In other words, even if we knew beyond any doubt that the British intended to hold Louisiana in spite of the treaty, we have no means of knowing that the ministry would have adhered to those intentions. One development that might have made them change their minds, even in the face of victory in New Orleans, was Napoleon's escape from Elba on February 26. But this is mere speculation. The fact is that Jackson hurled back into the Gulf of Mexico one of the mightiest invasion forces ever assembled down to that time. That action settled the future of Louisiana and, ultimately, of Florida as well.

VII

Peace Without Victory

Word of the victory at New Orleans was received in Washington February 4, 1815; ten days later the government received a copy of the Treaty of Ghent. The psychological effects of these events were enormous. Everywhere there was at least relief and in most places, especially the South and West, rejoicing that backwoodsmen under Jackson had defeated veterans of the Napoleonic wars. The great victory at New Orleans tended to blot out the memory of the frustrations, reverses, and defeats that had gone before. In the American mind it obliterated the true character of the war. In February, 1815, the whole country rejoiced in an exultant new nationalism forgetting that, six months before, the Treasury had been empty, the government powerless to raise an effective army, and the Union threatened with dissolution.

The War of 1812

LACK OF MEN AND MONEY

Let us return briefly to the financial situation. For reasons we have already noticed, Congress relied mainly upon borrowing as a means of financing the war. To be sure Congress in 1812 had doubled the import duties and in 1813 it had revived some of the old Federalist excise taxes and imposed direct taxes on dwellings and slaves. But after 1813 imports fell off greatly and the internal taxes produced a very inadequate revenue. In order to enable the Treasury to obtain cash in advance of collections and in anticipation of receipts from long-term loans, Congress authorized the issue of short-term Treasury Notes. Though these were neither legal tender nor redeemable in specie, the Treasury accepted them for all payments due the United States.

In 1814 Congress authorized more borrowing than in the two previous years: $20 million in short-term Treasury Notes and $28 million in long-term stock. To a generation accustomed to hear of annual government expenditures in terms of billions of dollars this may seem a trifling sum. In that day, however, it represented five times the annual peacetime expenditures of the federal government and the task of raising so much money was enormous. After the first year of the war the only way the Treasury could borrow money was to sell its stock at greater and greater discounts. A congressional committee after the war estimated that of more than $80 million borrowed from 1812 to 1816, the government actually received in specie value only about $34 million.

The summer and fall of 1814 marked the lowest ebb in the financial history of the United States. Soon after the British burned Washington, the banks from New York to New Orleans suspended specie payment. This did not hurt the banks, since they remained open and continued to transact business, many of them at handsome profits. There were, however, many side effects which greatly hampered the war effort. After the suspension, notes issued by the state banks became practically the only currency, and they began to fluctuate in value. But depreciation of the currency was only part of the problem. When the First Bank of the United States went out of existence in 1811, Secretary Gallatin arranged for the state banks to take on the Treasury's business. They were a poor substitute. All the Treasury's operations were nationwide in scope but there was no national administrative machinery. Forced to deal with a bewildering variety of institutions, the Treasury found it difficult to make quick loans or even to transfer its deposits with facility. Henry Adams writes: "The Treasury had no means of transferring its bank deposits from one part of the country to another. . . . Thus while the government collected in the Middle and Southern states millions in bank-notes, it was obliged to leave them in deposit at the local banks where the collection was made, while its debts in Boston and New York remained unpaid. The source of revenue was destroyed."

Many historians tend to blame the financial failure on refusal of Congress to renew the charter of the Bank of the United States in 1811. That the absence of a central authority, the chartering of many unsound state institutions, and depreciation of bank currency, all added to the difficulties and embarrassments of the government cannot be denied. Yet the causes of the trouble lay not just in the refusal to recharter the national bank, but in the whole system of Republican finance and especially in Congress's timidity in using the taxing power in support of the rapidly expanding debt. Had the state banks followed sounder practices, they might have been even less willing to buy government securities backed by such a weak tax structure. Congress' refusal to legislate a sufficient revenue soon enough and in the amounts necessary was a mistake that might have been remedied.

Less subject to remedy was another fundamental cause of the government's financial difficulties: the nature and location of the opposition to the war. It happened that those sections of the country which had the most cash also were those most opposed to the war. A variety of economic factors—some of which we shall notice in connection with the Hartford Convention—combined to make New England the one section that profited from the war. In Massachusetts alone the specie holdings jumped from $1,709,000 in June, 1811, to $7,326,000 in June, 1814. Opposed to the war from the beginning, the New England Federalists hoped to bring about peace by withholding financial and other support. Harrison Gray Otis, a Boston Brahmin, was a director of several banks. His biographer, Samuel Eliot Morison, says that "Otis's correspondence gives indubitable proof that an excellent understanding existed between the financial powers of both cities [Boston and Philadelphia] to withhold subscriptions to government loans until peace was assured."

Another factor contributing to financial weakness was unsteady leadership. Because of factional opposition in Congress and disharmony in the cabinet, Gallatin left in May, 1813, to go abroad as a member of the peace mission. The Treasury was left in the hands of Secretary of the Navy Jones. In March, 1814, Jones left the government and George Washington Campbell became Secretary of the Treasury. As a Senator from Tennessee Campbell was supposed to have friends in Congress but he had limited, if any, influence in the financial community. Admitting failure, he resigned in October, 1814, to be succeeded by Alexander James Dallas. The new Secretary, an able administrator, reported a few days after assuming office that not even the interest on the public debt had been paid punctually and a large amount of Treasury Notes had been dishonored. "The hope of preventing further injury and reproach in transacting the business of the Treasury is too visionary to afford a moment's consolation," he said.

It should be noted that neither the empty treasury nor the manpower shortage can be blamed on New England exclusively. Adams remarked that "Except New York, Kentucky, Tennessee, and perhaps Ohio, no state gave to the war the full and earnest cooperation it needed." Actually sentiment in New England was divided and despite the opposition of state governors and other officials many patriotic men enlisted in the regular army. In fact some of the best regiments were recruited in New England. It was the Massachusetts 9th and 21st, the Vermont 11th, and the Connecticut 25th that did some of the hardest and most skillful fighting at Chippewa, Lundy's Lane, and Fort Erie. In the number of recruits furnished the regular army Massachusetts was second only to New York.

Nevertheless the manpower problem, like the money problem, reached the crisis stage in the fall of 1814. Earlier in the year Congress made efforts to establish a regular army that could be depended upon for the duration. The term of enlistment was extended from one to five years, bounties were tripled, and by various laws the paper strength of the regular army was raised to sixty-two thousand men. None of these measures, however, sufficed to put an effective force in the field: by the end of September the actual strength was but thirty-four thousand men. This, at a time when one hundred miles of the coast of Maine were in the hands of the British; when a great naval and military force was known to be headed toward the Gulf Coast; and when a force of twenty thousand men were gathering at Kingston to attack Sackett's Harbor. After the burning of Washington, Secretary of State Monroe again assumed the duties of the War Department in addition to those of his own department. The House Committee on Military Affairs asked him how an army might be raised. Monroe replied that all other expedients having failed, the time had now come to resort to conscription, and he described in detail how such a plan might be put into operation. Anticipating the furor that such a drastic measure would cause in Congress, Monroe presented three alternatives. The last of these—the one Monroe considered least desirable—was to continue the existing system with an increase in the land bounty. This was the alternative adopted. The new provisions encouraged desertions for the purpose of re-enlistment but otherwise had little effect. The government had to carry on as best it could with thirty-four thousand regulars and the six-month militia.

With the federal government unable to raise an effective national army and with the danger of invasion daily mounting, the state governments began to take matters into their own hands. Massachusetts, Connecticut, Pennsylvania, Maryland, Virginia, South Carolina, and Kentucky took steps to form state armies or had plans to that end. It looked as though the federal government had reached the end of its resources and the very existence of the Union hung in the balance.

Peace Without Victory

THE HARTFORD CONVENTION

The convention that met in Hartford in December, 1814, was both a symptom and a cause of the government's weakness. The New England Federalists were opposed to the war on principle and they cannot be charged with inconsistency. Two issues seem to have transformed passive opposition to active obstruction: the threat to war profits and the fear of invasion.

Unable to prevent the declaration of war, the Federalists had decided to give minimum support and extract maximum profit from the conflict. In the early stages of the struggle, it will be recalled, many New England shippers took advantage of British licenses to help supply the allied armies on the Iberian Peninsula. Later, as privateers, many of these same shippers attacked British commerce. Since the commercial blockade did not extend north of New York until after the defeat of Napoleon, New England for a while had a monopoly of the import business. Furthermore, her geographical position made smuggling and supplying the enemy easy. Illicit traffic reached such proportions, in fact, that at the close of 1813 Congress passed an act absolutely forbidding the coastal trade. The very word "embargo" was anathema in New England. Within a short time the whole section was alive with town meetings which sent forward memorials condemning the act. As long as Great Britain was fighting Napoleon, the Federalists could cloak their profiteering in a mantle of righteous indignation. Napoleon represented tyranny, atheism, and wickedness, the New England clergy constantly reminded their parishioners. But after April, 1814, the anti-Christ had been exiled to Elba, and the hated embargo on coastal trade was repealed.

By this time, also, Great Britain, if she meant to win the

war—which she certainly did—could no longer exempt New England from its effects. After the defeat of Napoleon, it became part of British policy to extend the blockade to include the New England coast and to make raids along the coast bringing the war home to the people. In July Moose Island and Eastport, Maine, were captured and their inhabitants forced to take an oath of allegiance to George III. The first week in September Lieutenant General Sir John C. Sherbrooke, the governor of Nova Scotia, entered the Penobscot and in the name of His Majesty took formal possession of all of Maine from that river to New Brunswick. Until this time the New England Federalists had recommended relying upon the magnanimity of their British cousins rather than force of arms. When they were told that Sherbrooke's forces would soon descend upon Boston, they began to wonder. They wondered even more when they learned that the inhabitants of Alexandria, Virginia, a city as staunchly Federalist as Boston, after surrendering to the British, had been forced to surrender also their shipping, merchandise, flour, and tobacco. (The low-paid British sea captains had an unquenchable thirst for prize money.)

Though a part of his state was occupied by the enemy and his capital threatened, Governor Caleb Strong steadfastly refused to yield on the militia issue. Informed of the plight of Massachusetts, the national government offered to maintain the militia if it were placed under command of regular army officers. Governor Strong's answer was an offer to call out the militia *to defend Boston*, provided the state retained command, and the United States paid the bill. At a special session of the General Court in October, the state of Massachusetts' defenses was discussed. John Holmes, the Jeffersonian leader of the state Senate, reminded the Federalists: "You took the defense of the State out of the hands of the General government. You would not permit them to decide on the danger. You refused them the means to repel it, and now, forsoothe you complain you are left defenceless." Ignoring the fact that they were at least partly responsible for their own woes, the Federalists persuaded the General Court to send out an invitation to other New England states to meet at Hartford for the purpose, among other things, of concerting measures of interstate defense.

The Hartford Convention met in secret session from December 15 to January 5, 1815. Delegates from Massachusetts, Connecticut, and Rhode Island attended. Vermont and New Hampshire declined to participate although two counties in Vermont and one in New Hampshire sent delegates. Harrison Gray Otis, at whose suggestion the convention was called, and George Cabot, who became its presiding officer, were considered moderates. Their program called for a strong and united expression of New England's grievances, for defense carried out by the states but financed by revenues of the national government, and "a radical reform in the national compact." The report of the convention, drawn up with the object of carrying out these designs, set forth the doctrines of interposition and nullification and suggested no less than seven amendments to the Constitution. Though the dissolution of the Union "should if possible, be the work of peaceable times, and deliberate consent," there was the implication that if these amendments were not adopted and if New England's grievances became permanent, the ultimate solution was secession. Thus the program actually adopted by the Hartford Convention was "moderate" in the sense that it fell short of the program advocated by the Essex Junto and some of the other extremists who were insisting that the Union was already dissolved and that a separate peace with Great Britain should be sought. Three "ambassadors" were appointed to carry the report of the convention to Washington. As they approached the capital the news of the Peace of Ghent became known and their mission was made ridiculous. Fortunately for the United States, Great Britain knew nothing of the Hartford Convention until after a peace treaty had been signed. Nevertheless, the conditions which gave rise to the convention were well known and they helped to encourage the British to prolong the peace negotiations.

THE PEACE OF CHRISTMAS EVE

Before discussing the negotiations leading to the treaty of Ghent we must first ask ourselves what had each country hoped to gain by resorting to arms. In other words, what were their war aims—which is a question very distinct from the causes of the war. The Americans began by hoping to gain much from the war and then, after early military defeats, narrowed their demands. Specifically, the United States initially desired to gain Canada, to secure the repeal of the Orders-in-Council and abandonment of impressments, and ended by advocating peace on the basis of *status quo ante bellum*. The British began by offering an armistice on the basis of the repeal of the Orders-in-Council, then, secure in Europe, demanded a large Indian buffer state and other extensive territorial cessions, receded from this to an offer of settlement on the basis of *uti possidetis* (state of possession at the end of hostilities), and ended by accepting the *status quo ante bellum.*

The process by which the demands diverged and then came

together is an interesting one. When Britain repealed the Orders-in-Council in June, 1812, about one-half of the war aims of the United States were accomplished without the firing of a shot. Thinking the Americans might be satisfied with half a loaf, the British ordered Admiral Warren to attempt to negotiate a cease fire. In view of the fact that negotiations immediately before the war had emphasized the Orders-in-Councils as a grievance, the British were entirely justified in believing that repeal would serve as a basis for ending hostilities. Secretary of State Monroe, however, informed Admiral Warren that since the United States regarded impressment as an outrage, it must cease before negotiations could begin.

About the same time that Monroe was turning down overtures from Admiral Warren, Tsar Alexander of Russia made an offer to mediate the Anglo-American dispute. John Quincy Adams, U.S. minister to Russia, promptly transmitted the offer but it did not arrive in Washington until March, 1813. By this time, with one attempt to invade Canada having ended in total defeat and another mired in the great swamps of northwestern Ohio, the United States was pathetically anxious to talk peace. Without waiting to see whether the British would accept Russian mediation, President Madison appointed Albert Gallatin, his Secretary of the Treasury, and James Bayard, a Federalist, as peace commissioners. Leaving in May, Gallatin and Bayard set out for St. Petersburg, where in co-operation with John Quincy Adams, they were to conclude peace.

In spite of the fact that the war had not gone well for the United States, Monroe instructed the commissioners to make no agreement that did not contain a formal renunciation of impressment. Other promises with regard to the rights of neutrals in future wars were to be extracted also. When, during the spring, the military situation improved, these instructions were modified so as to extend American demands. On June 23, 1813, Monroe wrote Gallatin and Bayard that York (Toronto) had been taken and British forces had been driven from the Strait of Niagara, the recruiting service was doing well, and the war was becoming popular. "These successes ought to have a salutary influence on your negotiations," he said, "it might be worthwhile to bring to view the advantages to both Countries which is promised by a transfer of the upper parts and even the whole of Canada to the U.S."

Arriving in St. Petersburg in July, the American plenipotentiaries learned that the Emperor was at the front directing his troops and little disposed to give attention to American concerns. With nothing to do, Bayard and Gallatin lingered in Russia until January, 1814. At last Britain gave a polite but firm refusal to the offer of mediation on the ground that impressment was a domestic question.

Not wishing to seem to bar all paths to peace, Britain indicated to the United States that she would be willing to negotiate directly. Whereupon President Madison added Henry Clay and Jonathan Russell to the American delegation. In writing to the five commissioners on February 14, 1814, Monroe again emphasized that they were to make no treaty that did not have a stipulation on the abandonment of impressments.

Leaving St. Petersburg, Gallatin and Bayard, through their friend Alexander Baring, obtained permission to enter England in April. Their object was to hasten the negotiations. Having just triumphed over Napoleon, the British were not anxious to speed negotiations, but they did agree to Ghent as a suitable meeting place. Since the United States had refused earlier peace overtures on the basis of the repeal of the Orders-in-

Council and since England had pulled down what they considered the greatest tyrant since Alexander, the attitude of a large part of the British public was that "Jonathan should be given a good drubbing." In writing to a kinsman Bayard said that he and Gallatin had arrived in London "at a very inauspicious moment. The Allies were at Paris and they had just received the news of the abdication of Bonaparte. The whole nation were delerious [*sic*] with joy which was not indulged without bitter invectives against their remaining enemies the Americans. The time of declaring war had stung them more than the act itself. They considered it as an aid given to their great enemy at a moment when his power was most gigantic. . . . They thirst for a great revenge and the nation will not be satisfied without it."

Not only must the thirst for revenge be assuaged, reasoned the ministry, the upstart republic must be taught a lesson. If the notion got abroad that Britain shrank from small wars, dealings with other small nations might be annoyingly difficult in the future.

Reports of the British temper began to filter into Washington by June. Gallatin advised his government not to insist on the impressment issue. By dropping it the United States would put the British in the position of prosecuting the war for territorial acquisition only, a type of war they might support for a while but not indefinitely. At a cabinet meeting on June 27 the gloomy news from London, the empty state of the United States Treasury, and various other items were discussed. It was therefore decided to seek peace without any stipulations on impressment and the new instructions reached the American commissioners as the negotiations got down to serious business in Ghent early in August. From the beginning the Americans possessed a tremendous advantage in knowing precisely what they wanted: peace with no concessions. Concerning the abilities of the American delegation Henry Adams writes, "Probably the whole British public service, including Lords and Commons, could not at that day have produced four men competent to meet Gallatin, J. Q. Adams, Bayard and Clay on the ground of American interests."

The British commission was inferior to the American both in clarity of its instructions and in the ability of its individual members. It was headed by Admiral Lord Gambier, whose chief claim to fame was that he had assisted in the burning of Copenhagen in 1807. The second ranking member was Henry Goulburn, a fiercely anti-American Tory, thirty years of age, who was Under-Secretary for War and the Colonies. Having worked closely with his superior, Lord Bathurst, he was familiar with the problems of the colonists, particularly the fur traders. The last member was William Adams, a Doctor of Civil Law, whose academic attainments were supposed to assist the deliberations in various ways. That the British commissioners were mere messengers is indicated by Goulburn, who wrote in his autobiography that "constant contact was kept up with the Foreign Office, the seals of which were, with the absence of Lord Castlereagh at Vienna in the hands of Lord Bathurst and with Lord Castlereagh himself by means of messengers who were dispatched regularly twice a week. Nor did we present any note until it had been transmitted and received the approval of the Foreign Office."

At the beginning the British announced that their Indian allies must be included in the treaty as a *sine qua non.* They also expected a cession of territory in eastern Maine and northern New York and between Lake Superior and navigable water on the Mississippi. A permanent Indian dominion to consist of all the Northwest beyond the line of the Treaty of Greenville of 1795 was to be created. The right of Americans to dry fish on British shores in the North Atlantic, guaranteed by the Treaty of 1783, was declared to be forfeited, to be revived only by granting an equivalent.

The American commissioners had not the slightest intention of granting any of these demands. They drafted a masterful reply, intended to influence opinion at home and on the Continent, and rather ostentatiously prepared to leave. Bayard, who had opposed the declaration of war, wrote privately to a friend: "I trust in God that when the character of the war is so totally changed and when we are not simply contending for the honor of the nation but driven to fight for its existence—the Federalists will prove themselves, what I have always believed them to be the true and faithful friends of their Country. As to the origin of the war we are all agreed. But when peace is refused upon just and moderate terms and the most extravagant pretentions are advanced, what is left for us but to fight manfully or submit to disgrace and ruin."

In advancing what Bayard called "extravagant pretentions," the British of course did not expect that they would be accepted. It was obvious to all that they were stalling for time and expected their armies in the field to accomplish what their diplomats at the conference table could never hope to do. Still the government did not want the negotiations broken off; they would yield just enough ground to keep the Americans talking. When news of the fall of Washington reached London on September 27, the British government had already decided to abandon the Indian buffer state. Completely confident of the success of British arms they suggested *uti possidetis* as a basis of settlement. Rejecting *uti possidetis* just as firmly as the Indian buffer state, the Americans again made ready to leave Ghent. Toward the end of October news of the naval battle of Plattsburg, Prevost's retreat into Canada, and the repulse at Baltimore reached London. Though shaken by these unexpected reverses the cabinet resolved to remain firm in their demands. Bathurst informed Goulburn that the military developments had not affected the government's plans, but "had Lord George Prevost kept Plattsburg . . . we would have had a better case of it."

The cabinet might attempt to ignore the situation in America, but they could not remain indifferent to their own internal situation and the unending power struggle on the Continent. Prevost's retreat meant that the American war, which had already cost far more than anyone had contemplated, would have to be continued another year at an estimated cost of £10 million. To raise such a sum the hated property tax, due to expire within a few months, would have to be extended, and the chances of being able to secure such an extension were negligible. The war was an expensive nuisance in many ways. Because of the activities of American privateers insurance rates in the Irish Sea were three times as great as at the height of the war with France.

So far as the European situation was concerned, the whole picture changed dramatically between May and October. Britain's freedom from perils proved to be remarkably short-lived. In May the allies had been united in victory; by October they had fallen apart and western Europe was troubled by, among other things, the new power of Russia. The Congress meeting at Vienna was making no progress and Castlereagh began to feel uneasy with some of the best regiments of the British Army in far-off America.

Hoping at one and the same time to get Wellington out of Paris, where they feared for his life, and to rid themselves of the war, the British cabinet asked the Duke to assume command in America. Serving as ambassador to France since the end of hostilities, Wellington had long since become the cabinet's chief adviser not only on military matters but on nearly all important questions of policy. In reply Wellington said he had no objections to going to America, but he could not promise much success there. "That which appears to me to be wanting in America is not a general, or a general officer and troops, but a naval superiority on the Lakes." Since a military solution was so unpromising why not simply end the war on the best terms possible, he suggested. "In regard to your negotiation, I confess that I think you have no right, from the state of the war to demand any concession of territory. . . . Why stipulate for the *uti possidetis?* You can get no territory; indeed the state of your military operations however creditable does not entitle you to any."

Not only was the greatest soldier of the empire pessimistic, everywhere the ministry might turn there were symptoms of war weariness. Parliament assembled on November 8 and soon opposition to the war was openly expressed. The position of those opposed to continuing the war was strengthened when details of the early negotiations became public knowledge. Assuming the British would break off the talks, the American commissioners sent copies of all correspondence with the British from the beginning of the negotiation down to August 20 to President Madison. Outraged at the extensive territorial demands but realizing their propaganda potential, Madison had the correspondence published, as President Adams had done in the XYZ Affair. When copies of the documents reached England on November 18 even newspapers that had once advocated giving Jonathan a good drubbing were displeased. The liberal opposition in Parliament now had what they considered proof of their allegations that the government had made excessive demands. Though the government affected to be outraged by a breach of diplomatic usage, Castlereagh had in fact predicted that the documents would be published. In the House of Lords, the Marquis of Lansdowne said that while he was willing to support the dictum of perpetual British allegiance and of the right of impressment, he would not support a war for conquest or territory, for the lakes, or the Indians.

Actually the ministry needed no urging. Having made up their minds to terminate the miserable affair they lost no time. On November 18 Lord Liverpool wrote Castlereagh they had determined not to continue the war for the purpose of securing territory. The reasons he alleged were: the lack of progress in the negotiation at Vienna, the "alarming" situation of the interior of France, the state of finances, the difficulties of continuing the property tax, the opposition in Parliament, and the views of the Duke of Wellington.

We need not concern ourselves with the details of the last month or so of negotiations except to say that having forced back the British inch by inch, the Americans fell to quarreling among themselves. Albert Gallatin, who by his patience and wisdom had become the real head of the delegation, had to assume responsibility not only for treating with the British but also keeping peace among his own countrymen. After months of exhausting labor the treaty was finally signed on Christmas Eve, 1814. It was simply a cessation of hostilities; both sides agreed to the *status quo ante bellum.* In order to make it appear that the British had not abandoned their Indian allies completely, there was an innocuous provision that both the United States and Britain would grant amnesty to the Indians and regard them as in the same status they occupied in 1811. The questions of rights in the fisheries, the navigation of the Mississippi, armaments on the lakes, and boundary questions were referred to commissions for future settlement.

The treaty said nothing of the alleged causes of the war—the rights of neutrals and impressments. Failure to mention maritime grievances did not mean that the United States had abandoned its principles; it only meant that the United States lacked the military strength to win recognition of those principles. The United States might be said to have vindicated what it considered its rights only in the sense that it was willing to fight for them.

If the men at Ghent ignored principles and postponed substantive issues, they were right in doing so. The war having produced only stalemate, neither side had grounds for attempting to impose its will on the other. With good sense both countries decided to settle what could be settled in an atmosphere of peace and to leave the rest to time.

WHY NOBODY WON

The diplomats at Ghent accomplished little of a positive nature because the soldiers in the field failed to achieve a decision. Militarily the War of 1812 was a draw. Though each side was able to win minor victories on its opponent's soil, neither was capable of carrying out a large-scale, decisive offensive. What accounts for the inability of either side to achieve its objectives by resort to arms?

Part of the answer is simple. Until April, 1814, Britain was confronted with a two-front war. Wisely and consistently she gave prior attention to Europe until the greater enemy was defeated. During the whole of this time Canada was expected only to hold her own, and it should be emphasized that the defensive phase of the war was conducted with great skill. During the early phases of the war Brock's leadership was superb, and Governor-General Sir George Prevost showed considerable competence in many respects. In a province that contained many American sympathizers Brock conciliated the opposition, used the Indians to best advantage, and succeeded in reversing a highly unfavorable military situation. Had Brock lived he might have passed over to the offensive, but General Procter succeeded only in losing what Brock had won. Sir George Prevost has been criticized and even vilified for his conduct of the war. For the Plattsburg campaign Sir George deserves criticism, but there are elements in the larger picture that should not be ignored. Sir George deserves credit for winning over the French-Canadians and in converting their possible opposition to active co-operation. Early in the war, upon being informed that no specie could be spared from England, he successfully guided the Army Bills Act through the parliament of Lower Canada. This act created a paper currency without which the war could not have been financed in Canada. Sir George was also successful in maintaining the neutrality and even a remarkable degree of active co-operation from New England. In all these matters he was carrying out the expressed desires of His Majesty's government. It was when he attempted to pass from the defensive to the offensive phase of the war that Sir George's limitations as a soldier became manifest. He simply was not the aggressive, swashbuckling type of soldier needed for the job. But General John Burgoyne had been, and faced with the same task as Prevost, he had failed even more miserably over thirty years before.

Reasons for the failure of the United States to exploit British weakness during the first two years we have already noticed: poor preparations, poor civilian and military leadership, lack of unity, and bad strategy. Perhaps it need only be emphasized that these factors were related one to another and were mutually supporting. President Madison was about the equal of Prevost as a war leader. In the realm of political theory the President had no superior and few equals in his day. His real weakness stemmed not from his ignorance of military affairs—a defect which with his excellent mind he could easily have overcome—but from the fact that he was not an effective politician. He could control neither his cabinet nor his party. To be a successful commander-in-chief a President must first demonstrate that he is the politician-in-chief. In explaining war aims to the rank and file of citizens, in the everyday rough and tumble of politics, in parliamentary maneuver Madison was somewhat less than mediocre. There are, however, at least two achievements to his credit: he never panicked and he remained tolerant of his domestic enemies. The capacity of the administration—and the country—to absorb disappointment and even disaster was impressive. This ability to pick up the pieces and to try again was indicative of the basic soundness of the social fabric. No wartime President has ever been subjected to so much invective and abuse as Madison. Though the provocation was extreme, he never suggested measures abridging freedom of speech or press. The absence of repressive legislation enabled the country quickly to unite after the war with a minimum of bitterness and resentment.

The President's chief civilian advisers were of very uneven quality. After ridding himself, belatedly, of the incompetent Paul Hamilton, Madison had a good Secretary of Navy in William Jones. Of the Secretaries of War Monroe was by all odds the best. Armstrong was certainly an improvement over Eustis and he deserves credit for infusing more energy into his department. But essentially he was a schemer rather than a planner and by attempting to exercise command in the field he showed a faulty concept of his proper role. His approach to strategy was amateurish: he could dream up ideas but he had not the foggiest notion of how to put them into effect. Finally, he allowed personal prejudices and puerile squabbles to fetter his judgment and destroy his usefulness. Monroe, on the other hand, showed increasing capacity to deal with the larger problems of planning and administration. He developed a sound strategic plan and had the war lasted another year he would probably have put it into effect.

Fortunately for the United States the quality of military leadership improved more rapidly than the civilian leadership. Winfield Scott, Jacob Brown, and Alexander Macomb demonstrated their abilities early and they were advanced in rank. These men were among the best officers ever to serve in the U.S. Army and the soldiers they trained were of high quality. Andrew Jackson was the counterpart to Brock in energy and ability. But the most any of these officers could do was to defend his country against invasion or win minor victories on foreign soil. Why were their military achievements so circumscribed?

The answer seems to be that both sides were attempting to carry out operations that were simply beyond the technical means of the day. In Canada to a degree, and much more so in the United States, there was much brute strength but nowhere did there exist either the private or public means to organize resources and bring them to bear in an effective war effort. The art of administration had not developed sufficiently to solve the problems at hand. In the United States individual shipbuilders and contractors for the army did remarkably well, but their efforts were unequal to the demands. Individual ship captains and generals of the army fought well and won victories but their accomplishments did not add up to a decision.

During the debates on the declaration of war John Randolph warned the war hawks that nature would prove to be their greatest enemy. Like George III, Randolph had fits of insanity but there were occasions, such as this, when his insight was sharp and prescient. In the older, settled parts of the eastern seaboard transportation had improved considerably since the American Revolution. In the western and southern parts of the country, however, where most of the fighting was destined to take place, inland transportation was poor indeed. In the interior, supplies had to be moved over roads—usually mere trails—that were primitive at best and impossible at worst. Surveying the whole situation Leonard White, the foremost authority on the administrative history of the United States, recently reached the same conclusion as Randolph: "Given the state of the means of communication, 1800–1830, it may be doubted whether it would have been physically possible to mount an effective campaign on any substantial scale. Even where integrity, good will and harmony of purpose prevailed, nature, not yet subdued by man, interposed stupendous obstacles."

Not only were communications slow and difficult, distances were immense. For the government in Washington to attempt simultaneously to carry out operations along the Great Lakes and the Gulf of Mexico would be roughly equivalent to a government for the whole of Europe trying from a headquarters, say in Brussels, to carry on one major campaign in the Balkans and another along the border between Russia and Prussia.

We have noted many examples of supply and transportation difficulties. Hull's campaign failed partly because of inability to bring forward supplies; his successor, Harrison, for over a year spent most of his time, not in leading his army in battle, but in trying to feed it. Jackson, when he plunged southward from Tennessee in 1813, was supposed to depend on supplies coming hundreds of miles down the winding Tennessee River. The result was that Jackson and his men lived off the land and lived so poorly that the army threatened to desert *en masse* and Jackson's already delicate digestive system became permanently impaired. Even with all his tremendous energy it was not until March, 1814, that Jackson was at last able to strike at the heart of Creek resistance.

The system of communications in Canada, though simpler than that of the United States, was more vulnerable. All the main settlements, all the points of major strategic importance were on one continuous water route: the St. Lawrence River and the Great Lakes. As Canadian historian C. P. Stacey points out, the frontier to be defended and the line of communication were one and the same; and nearly the whole length of the communications was exposed. As long as Britain ruled the seas, communication from the ports of England to the head of navigation at Montreal presented few problems. In summer, that is. In winter the St. Lawrence was frozen and supplies had to travel by sledge. Iron traveling over this route ended up with the value almost of gold. When the war was nearly over, Sir George Prevost wrote Lord Bathurst that forty 24-pounders intended for the fleet on Lake Ontario, hauled on the snow 400 miles from Quebec to Kingston, had cost £4,800; a cable hauled from Sorel to Kingston, a distance of 250 miles, had cost £1,000. Even in summer, especially above Montreal, where there were numerous falls and rapids, there were great difficulties. Workmen, laborers, and voyageurs were nearly always hard to obtain. In August, 1813, General Procter wrote from Sandwich: "Being situated at the extremity of a long line, I do not feel the full effect of his Excellency's consideration for me; the aid intended never reaches me undiminished from some circumstance or another."

Early in the war the British had few troops to send to Upper Canada. Later they had the troops but not the supplies. By October, 1814, Prevost had from 13,000 to 14,000 troops idle in Montreal. Knowing that Sackett's Harbor was weak at that time he wished very much to attack that port. He traveled to Kingston to plan such an attack but found that supply difficulties made it impossible.

Henry Adams writes that in proportion to population, the effort put into the Civil War was ten times greater than the War of 1812. If this is so, it is largely because a transportation revolution had taken place in the intervening years. Roads were improved vastly, hundreds of canals and the development of steamboats made transportation of men and supplies much easier, especially in the West, and, most important, railroads crisscrossed the country in a system that made travel swifter and easier than ever before in the history of man. Yet Allan Nevins writes that "Lincoln presided over a weak government which suddenly had to be made strong. And behind the government lay a largely inchoate society. . . . Where were the technicians in 1861? Where were the efficient business administrators? Where were the thousand organizations, industrial, commercial, financial, professional, to lend them support? Where were the principles and precedents?" If this was so in 1861, how much more was it true in 1812.

VIII

Epilogue

Wars may have consequences, good or bad, that have no relation either to their causes or to the aims of the belligerents. In both the United States and Canada the War of 1812 initiated or hastened the development of many trends of a psychological, economic, and political nature. Both countries emerged from the conflict stronger than they entered and with a quickened national spirit.

In Great Britain, on the other hand, the war has never held high place and its consequences were not profound. The war was for the most part accepted as an incident of the larger struggle, an additional burden that must be borne. Contrary to the impression that one might receive by reading the works of Theodore Roosevelt or Henry Adams, the Royal Navy gave a good account of itself. For the most part the American frigate victories, and victories on the lakes as well, were won by heavier ships with greater fire power. By the end of the war the blockade of the American coast was effective and the small American navy was practically neutralized. Nevertheless, while the war lasted, the Royal Navy lost reputation and was rudely shaken from its complacency, which, for its own sake, was probably a good thing. On land, the war added nothing to the reputation of British soldiers or statesmen. When news of the peace reached the British army off Mobile Bay Sir Harry Smith wrote: "We are all happy enough for we Peninsula soldiers saw that neither fame nor any military distinction could be acquired in this species of milito-nautico-guerrilla-plundering warfare." One has to dig deeply to find anything at all on the War of 1812 in British military annals.

If the war was little more than an added burden to Great Britain, it was far more to Canada. The Loyalists, especially, who had been harried from the land during the Revolution felt strongly about the issues. To them it seemed the armies of the United States were attempting to follow them into exile and to deprive them of their homes. But all Canadians, whether of Anglo-American or French origin, felt that they were fighting for life and liberty, and the war did more than any other single event to reconcile the two peoples to each other.

Even though the United States was unable to break Canada's single line of communications, the war brought home in a very forceful way this strategic weakness. Some years after the war the British government began the construction of a more defensible line remote from the American frontier. The new line consisted of a system of canals which allowed the passage of vessels drawing nine feet from Montreal to the city of Ottawa and from there to Lake Ontario. The Ottawa-Rideau canal, which cost the British taxpayers about $2.5 million, was one of the most extensive pieces of military construction in North America.

Though improvements were made in logistics as a result of the war, nothing was done about the manpower problem. The militia system of Canada, like that of the United States, created a huge army on paper but provided nearly nothing in the way of effectual training and preparation. In spite of its defects, the militia played a significant role in the defense of Canada. Unfortunately, the contributions became exaggerated in the popular mind, the dominant role played by the regulars was overlooked, and a myth was created that the militia were almost wholly responsible for saving the country. As an effect of this popular belief, an inadequate militia system was left unchanged for nearly half a century. But myths can be beneficial. Since the successful defense of the nation created a common national heritage there can be little doubt that Canada emerged from the contest much stronger than she entered.

The same is true to an even greater degree of the United States. The blunders and defeats had a sobering effect; delusions were swept away and many changes, especially in the administration of military affairs, resulted. Before detailing these it might be well to point out first what did not change. There was no fundamental alteration in American attitudes toward war. A high degree of individualism and antimilitarism remained a basic trait of the American character. Although the regular army and navy were strengthened immediately after the war, not even the disgraceful defeats could destroy the myth that the best reliance in time of national danger was the militia.

Americans were simply not ready to accept either the idea of a large standing army or even sweeping reforms of the militia system. In justice to the political leaders of an earlier generation it must be acknowledged that the social and political conditions of the country imposed limitations on what could be done about the manpower problem. Even after some of the worst defeats Jefferson wrote: "It is nonsense to talk of regulars. They are not to be had among a people so easy and happy at home as ours. We might as well rely on calling down an army of angels from heaven." The aging Jefferson and youthful Daniel Webster saw few political questions alike, but on this they agreed. "Unlike the old nations of Europe," said Webster, "there are in this country no dregs of population fit only to supply the constant waste of war and out of which an army can be raised for hire any time and for any purpose. Armies of any magnitude can here be nothing but the people embodied; and if the object be one for which the people will not embody there can be no armies."

Though there were no fundamental changes in manpower policy, the disclosure of military weaknesses did bring about the first major reorganization of the federal administrative system in the history of the United States. The establishment of the army general staff, the formation of a board of navy commissioners, and the reform of the system of accountability of the army and navy did much to correct old errors and to form the basis for yet other improvements. The reorganization of the army staff, which came about in 1813 as a result of the early failures in the Northwest, did not create a general staff in the modern sense of that term. Composed of the adjutant general, the inspector general, the quartermaster general, the commissary general of ordnance, the paymaster, and the assistant topographical engineer, the general staff was concerned with management or with what might simply be called housekeeping duties. It did not act as a unit and it did not concern itself with broad matters of planning, strategy, and policy. The Board of Navy Commissioners, created in 1815, consisted of three regular naval officers of the rank of captain or above and its duties were to advise the civilian secretary on such matters as the building, repair, and equipping of vessels and the superintendence of the naval yards, naval stations, and dry docks. The Secretary retained direct control of such functions as the appointment of officers, movement of ships, and the discipline of personnel. Despite its limitations the new legislation made provision for relieving the civilian secretaries of much routine detail and, more importantly, they would henceforth have professional advisers at least on the technical aspects of their duties. No longer would the army and navy departments consist only of a Secretary and his clerks.

The war also demonstrated, as the Revolution before it had, the futility of applying the European military system without modification to the American scene. If the Americans failed to learn from the Revolution and even expanded on some of their mistakes, so did the British. Sir Edward Pakenham's columns steadily advancing across the cane stubble in the face of the withering fire of Jackson's frontiersmen was Bunker Hill reenacted on swampy southern soil. The Americans proved themselves exceptionally good at gunnery, whether with rifle, musket, or cannon and whether on land or on sea. The American rifle, though it was used only on a restricted scale, again showed itself a superior weapon.

Finally, the war gave impetus to the development of scientific engineering in the United States. None of the works constructed by the West Point engineers was captured by the enemy, and it has been estimated that during the campaign of

1814 the system of fortifications doubled the capacity of the small American army. West Point, which was reorganized and professionalized soon after the war, was to influence engineering education throughout the nineteenth century.

The economic and political effects of the war were probably more far reaching than the military. As in all wars, certain individuals and certain communities suffered, but the same geographical conditions that made large-scale victories so difficult also saved the country from widespread physical devastation. To be sure, the Niagara frontier was ravaged and small coastal towns from Maine to Georgia succumbed to the torch and sword but, excepting Washington, no large city was occupied. The blockade had stopped commerce and a large part of the harvests of two seasons remained in the hands of the producers or was piled up in overcrowded warehouses. But the moment the blockade was lifted, rice, cotton, tobacco, grain, and other products were rushed to the waiting European market.

Three factors provided considerable stimulus to the growth of manufacturers during and after the war. In the first place the ground had been prepared by a long list of technological developments. The spinning jenny, the cording machine, the steam engine, automatic milling machinery, the slide lathe, better casting methods, and the concept of the assembly line and interchangeable parts had preceded the war. During the war the demand–and hence prices–for finished products was increased by the dropping off of imports and the ever increasing needs of the war effort. Also, for a variety of reasons, capital flowed into New England during the war. This capital, concentrated in the hands of knowledgeable entrepreneurs, found its way into profitable manufacturers. From 1807 to 1815 the number of spindles in cotton mills increased at least sixteen-fold while the value of factory-made woolens increased from an estimated $4 million in 1810 to $19 million in 1815. In short, the war was followed by an economic boom, a boom that ended eventually in a bust—another story entirely.

The political effects were no less important than the economic. By opposing the war and obstructing its prosecution, the Federalists ruined their party beyond all hope of recovery. Everywhere in 1816 the Jeffersonians triumphed, but it was a Pyrrhic victory, for they were forced to accept the principles of the vanquished. The War of 1812 was the great watershed of Jeffersonian democracy. The old Jeffersonians hated war and avoided it as long as they could because they foresaw that it would bring on those centralizing tendencies—a strong army and navy, high taxes, a bureaucracy, manufacturing, industrial cities—which they wanted to avoid. Even before the war a new generation of Republicans began to question some of the old tenets. But it remained for the war itself not only to expose the internal weaknesses of the Jeffersonian system but to hold them up to cruel caricature. To many young congressmen, including Clay and Calhoun, the experiences of the war were deeply humiliating. Though they might differ on means, the statesmen of the Old Republic were united in a strong desire to see self-government succeed. When the noble experiment came close to ignoble failure they began to examine their assumptions. Even Jefferson decided that an equilibrium between agriculture, manufactures, and commerce might be a good thing. Though the postwar Republicans were by no means of one mind, a majority of them did pass laws continuing the high tariffs of the war period, establishing a second national bank, and providing for certain internal improvements. These measures were both a reflection of, and a stimulus to, the new spirit of nationalism which found expression also in certain historic decisions of the Supreme Court.

The very process of growth and expansion ushered in by the war brought with it new problems that in time would divide the country. State rights, strict construction of the Constitution, and local interests were not dead issues; they are perennial issues, indigenous to the federal system. But nationalism was firmly enough planted that, though it might be assailed, it could never be uprooted. Alexander James Dallas, who in matters of finance at least was a hard-headed realist, described the conflict as "a holy war" that advanced the nation "a century in power and character."

The War of 1812 has sometimes been called the Second War of American Independence and, rightly understood, this concept has merit. It was not a second war of independence in the sense that Great Britain was again trying to reduce the states to colonial status. Though there was much contempt for the republican form of government and, among certain interests, much jealousy of American commercial enterprise, Great Britain as a whole accepted American independence. But the war did mark the end of American dependence on the European system. For the United States, no less than Europe, 1815 marked a turning point. From the founding of the Republic until the final exile of Napoleon the primary concerns of public policy were foreign affairs and defense. Again and again American foreign relations were conditioned by, and sometimes determined by, the shifting power structure and the almost continuous wars in Europe. From the Revolution onward a basic aim of American statesmen had been to achieve freedom of action so that the United States could choose war or peace as its interests might dictate. With the settlement of 1815 this aim became a reality to a degree that the early statesmen had hardly dared to hope.

In 1812 the nationalistic young Republicans regarded the Royal Navy with its insistence on the right of impressment as the chief affront to American independence and honor. Yet after the war it was British seapower that enabled the United States to turn its entire attention to internal development and territorial expansion. And this was not the happy circumstance of a day or even a decade. For a century after the Peace of Ghent the Royal Navy was the main shield of the American Republic against the distresses of Europe.

Important Dates

1812 The United States declares war on Great Britain, June 18
Hull enters Canada, July 12
Fort Michilimackinac surrenders to the British, July 17
Fort Dearborn massacre, August 15
Hull surrenders to Brock at Detroit, August 16
The "Constitution" defeats the "Guerrière," August 19
Brock is killed at the Battle of Queenston Heights, October 13
The "Wasp" (U.S.) defeats the "Frolic" (British), October 18
The "Wasp" captured by the "Poictiers," October 18
The "United States" defeats the "Macedonian," October 25
William Eustis resigns as Secretary of War, December 3
Monroe serves as Secretary of War, December 3 to February 5, 1813
The "Constitution" defeats the "Java," December 29
Paul Hamilton resigns as Secretary of the Navy, December 29

1813 William Jones assumes his duties as Secretary of the Navy, January 12

Important Dates

River Raisin massacre, January 23

John Armstrong becomes Secretary of War, February 5

The "Hornet" defeats the "Peacock," February 24

Captain David Porter of the "Essex" rounds Cape Horn and sails into the Pacific to prey upon British whaling ships, March

Oliver Hazard Perry arrives at Presque Isle, Pennsylvania, to assume responsibility for constructing a fleet on Lake Erie, March 27

British naval forces raid in the Chesapeake Bay area, March to December

British blockade extended from Long Island to the Mississippi, March 30

Wilkinson occupies Mobile, April 15

Americans capture York (Toronto), April 27

Siege of Fort Meigs begins on May 1 and ends on May 5

Americans capture Fort George, May 27

British forces repulsed at Sackett's Harbor, May 29

The "Shannon" defeats the "Chesapeake," June 1

Detachment of Americans defeated at Stoney Creek, June 6

Major Croghan successfully defends Fort Stephenson against British attack, August 1

Perry gets his fleet over the bar at Presque Isle and into the lake, August 4

Fort Mims massacre, August 30

Battle of Lake Erie, September 10

Harrison lands in Canada, September 27

Battle of the Thames, October 5

Battle of Chateauguay, October 25–26

Battle of Tallushatchee, November 3

Battle of Talladega, November 9

Battle of Chrysler's Farm, November 11

Fort George evacuated and Newark burned by Americans, December 10

Fort Niagara occupied by British, December 18

Lewiston, Fort Schlosser, Black Rock, and Buffalo destroyed by the British, December 19–31

1814 Battle of Horseshoe Bend, March 27

The "Phoebe" and the "Cherub" defeat the "Essex," March 28

Important Dates

The "Orpheus" (British) defeats the "Frolic" (U.S.), April 20

The "Peacock" (U.S.) defeats the "Epervier" (British), April 29

The British extend the blockade to include New England, May 30

The "Wasp II" (U.S.) defeats the "Reindeer" (British), June 28

Battle of Chippewa, July 5

Battle of Lundy's Lane, July 25

The Creeks sign a treaty at Fort Jackson ceding much of their land, August 9

Siege of Fort Erie begins August 13 and ends September 21

The British land near Benedict, Maryland, August 19

Battle of Bladensburg, August 24

The British burn Washington, August 24 and 25

British capture Alexandria, Virgina, August 28

Prevost moves south toward Plattsburg, end of August

Armstrong resigns and Monroe takes over as Secretary of War, September 4

Battle of Lake Champlain, September 11

Prevost retreats to Canada, middle of September

British repulsed at Mobile, September 12–16

Fort McHenry, near Baltimore, bombarded, September 13–14

British abandon attempt to take Baltimore, September 14

Jackson seizes Pensacola, November 7

Jackson returns to Mobile, November 11

Jackson leaves for New Orleans, November 22

British fleet sails from Jamaica for New Orleans, November 26

British overwhelm American gunboats on Lake Borgne, December 14

British land their troops below New Orleans, December 23

Jackson attacks in a surprise night battle, December 23

Peace of Ghent signed, December 24

1815 Battle of New Orleans, January 8

Ratifications of the Peace Treaty exchanged and President Madison declares the war at an end, February 17

Suggested Reading

GENERAL

The War of 1812 has not inspired so much writing as the American Revolution, the Civil War, or the two world wars. To a degree, however, the quality of the historical literature compensates for its lack of quantity. Still useful, especially for the details of battles large and small, is Benson J. Lossing's *Pictorial Field Book of the War of 1812* (New York, 1868). Though his 1,000-page book inevitably contains some inaccuracies, Lossing had an excellent command of contemporary accounts and the sketches he made of persons and places in the 1860's are fascinating.

More professional in tone, and with a much better grasp of larger issues are the histories of Theodore Roosevelt, Henry Adams, and Alfred Thayer Mahan. The best general history is still Adams's *History of the United States in the Administrations of Jefferson and Madison, 1801–1817* (9 vols., New York, 1889–91). Harvey A. De Weerd edited and reprinted the military chapters of Adams's work as *The War of 1812* (Washington, 1944). This single volume is useful but the reader must go back to the nine-volume edition for a full account of the background, legislation, diplomacy, and aftermath of the war. Based on extensive use of original materials in the United States, Great Britain, and France the *History* is unsurpassed for its thoroughness, sophistication, and literary charm. But Adams had a dislike of the British, a contempt for western Americans, and a hatred of Virginians, and these prejudices are subtly woven through the whole fabric of his work. Many of Adams's distortions have been corrected by Irving Brant in his biography of James Madison, especially the volumes entitled *Secretary of State, 1800–1809* (Indianapolis, 1953); *The President, 1809–1812* (Indianapolis, 1956); and *Commander-in-Chief, 1812–1836* (Indianapolis, 1961). One suspects, however, that Brant, with his strong pro-Madison bias, has introduced some oddities of his own.

The best account of naval affairs is Mahan's *Sea Power in Its Relation to the War of 1812* (2 vols., Boston, 1905). On general strategy, on the role of seapower on the lakes, and on the blockade Mahan is excellent. I have, however, ventured to differ with his contention that the United States should have concentrated on heavy ships of the line with auxiliary vessels to match. Readers who object to Mahan's sometimes stilted prose will delight in Theodore Roosevelt's clarity and directness. His *Naval War of 1812* (New York, 1903), begun while he was an undergraduate at Harvard, presents a spirited narrative and a penetrating analysis of operations, marred only by a tendency toward jingoism.

Roosevelt wrote his books in order to correct what he considered the errors of fact and interpretation in William James's *Naval Occurrences of the Late War between Great Britain and the United States of America* (London, 1817). James was prejudiced against Americans and the same fault characterizes his *Full and Correct Account of the Military Occurrences of the Late War between the United States and Great Britain* (2 vols., London, 1818). Both titles are still valuable, however, not only because they represent a contemporary British view but also because in their long appendixes, many contemporary documents are reprinted. Understandably, anti-American bias is to be found also in Canadian accounts such as Gilbert Auchinleck's *A History of the War Between Great Britain and the United States of America* (Toronto, 1855) and James Hannay's *History of the War of 1812* (Halifax, 1901). None of these earlier historians were more anti-American, however, than Sir John Fortescue, who in his monumental *History of the British Army* (13 vols., London, 1911–35), has several chapters of the War of 1812. Sir John's prejudice extended not only to America but to all forms of democracy. Nevertheless he had a sturdy honesty, a real talent for analyzing a battle, and a good sense of proportion. C. P. Lucas's *Canadian War of 1812* (Oxford, 1906) represented a decided improvement over all previous histories. Based mainly on printed sources Lucas's book is fair to both sides and remains the best account of Canada's part in the war.

The publication of several excellent histories before World War I possibly discouraged further work. Ralph D. Paine's volume in the Chronicles of America series, entitled *The Fight For a Free Sea* (New Haven, 1920), is a popular summary of Mahan. William Wood's volume in the Chronicles of Canada series, entitled *The War with the United States* (Toronto, 1921), is based upon an intimate knowledge of original sources but it suffers from lack of proportion.

After the first world war historians were concerned primarily with the causes of the war. Nothing further of importance of a general nature appeared until A. L. Burt's *The United States, Great Britain, and British North America* (New Haven, 1940). While Burt does not attempt to deal with operations battle by battle he undertakes to explain the significance of what happened. His analysis is excellent but he is concerned, of course, only with the war as it affected Canadian-American relations. In 1949 Francis F. Beirne published *The War of 1812* (New York), a well-written general account relying mainly on Lossing and Henry Adams. In 1954 Glenn Tucker, making extensive use of newspapers, published a lively narrative entitled *Poltroons and Patriots* (2 vols., Indianapolis). A recent general naval account is C. S. Forester's *The Age of Fighting Sail: The Story of the Naval War of 1812* (Garden City, N. Y., 1956). As one would expect, the creator of Hornblower tells a good story; he also makes good use of Wellington's *Supplementary Dispatches*, but otherwise adds little to the older accounts.

Abbott Smith, "Mr. Madison's War," *Political Science Quarterly*, LVII (1942), 229–46, develops an interesting thesis on the relationship of Madison to the war hawks. Marcus Cunliffe's article in Ernest May's (ed.) *The Ultimate Decision: The President as Commander-in-Chief* (New York, 1960) sets forth the good and bad points of Madison's wartime leadership. *After Tippecanoe*, edited by Philip P. Mason (East Lansing, 1963), contains useful essays by both American and Canadian historians.

One of the most original recent contributions to the history of the period is a study in administrative history, Leonard D. White's *The Jeffersonians* (New York, 1959). No serious student can afford to ignore this excellent book. The legislative branch of the government played an active role in the war and this aspect has been treated in some detail by William Barlow in his unpublished Ph.D. thesis, "Congress During the War of 1812," The Ohio State University, 1961. Edward Wagner treats "State-Federal Relations During the War of 1812," in his unpublished Ph.D. thesis, The Ohio State University, 1963.

CHAPTER I

Some comments on historiography of the causes of the war are made in the text. The principal items referred to are as follows: Roger Brown, *Republic in Peril* (New York, 1964); Louis M. Hacker, "Western Land Hunger and the War of 1812: A Conjecture," *Mississippi Valley Historical Review*, X (1924), 365–95; Reginald Horsman, *The Causes of the War of 1812* (Philadelphia, 1962); Lawrence S. Kaplan, "France and Madison's Decision for War, 1812," *Mississippi Valley Historical Review*, L (1964), 652–71; Margaret K. Latimer, "South Carolina–A Protagonist of the War of 1812," *American Historical Review*, LXI (1955–56), 921–29; Bradford Perkins, *Prologue to War: England and the United States, 1805–1812* (Berkeley and Los Angeles, 1961); Julius W. Pratt, *Expansionists of 1812* (New York, 1925); Julius W. Pratt, "Western Aims in the War of 1812," *Mississippi Valley Historical Review*, XII (1925), 38–50; Norman K. Risjord, "1812: Conservatives, War Hawks, and the Nation's Honor," *William and Mary Quarterly*, 3d ser., XVIII (1961), 196–210; George R. Taylor, "Agrarian Discontent in the Mississippi Valley Preceding the War of 1812," *The Journal of Political Economy*, XXXIX (1931), 486–505; George R. Taylor, "Prices in the Mississippi Valley Preceding the War of 1812," *Journal of Economic and Business History*, III (1930–31), 148–63.

Suggested Reading

CHAPTER II

For the Canadian side of the story Ferdinand B. Tupper, *The Life and Correspondence of General Sir Isaac Brock* (London, 1847) is indispensable. This book contains not only a narrative of events but also extensive quotes from Brock's correspondence with his family. Lady Matilda Edgar's *General Brock* (Toronto, 1909) and other biographies of Brock seem to be based largely on material in Tupper. The best set of original documents is Ernest A. Cruikshank's *Documents Relating to the Surrender of Detroit* (Ottawa, 1913). A compilation entitled, "Documents Relating to Detroit and Vicinity, 1805–1813," *Michigan Historical Collections,* XL (1929), contains useful correspondence from Hull to Dearborn, Eustis, and others. For this and all the chapters on operations John Brannan (comp.), *Official Letters of the Military and Naval Officers of the United States During the War With Great Britain in the Years 1812, 13, 14 & 15* (Washington, 1823) is invaluable.

The best contemporary account on the American side of the campaigns of 1812 and 1813 is Robert B. McAfee's *History of the Late War in the Western Country* (Lexington, 1816). The best recent account is Alec R. Gilpin's *The War of 1812 in the Old Northwest* (East Lansing, 1958). Milo M. Quaife, in his article "General Hull and His Critics," *Ohio State Archeological and Historical Quarterly,* XLVII (1938), 168–82, maintains that General Hull's military abilities were mediocre and so were those of all his subordinates. Quaife also edited a good eye-witness account, *The Chronicles of Thomas Vercheres de Boucherville* (Chicago, 1940).

Morris Zaslow in *The Defended Border: Upper Canada and the War of 1812* (Toronto, 1964) edits and reprints several articles useful for this and Chapters IV and V. This book also contains an excellent bibliography.

CHAPTER III

The general naval histories dealing with the war on both the high seas and the lakes are discussed above. Special phases of naval power are treated in Howard I. Chapelle, *The History of the American Navy: The Ships and Their Development* (New York, 1949); George Coggeshall, *American Privateers and Letters of*

Marque . . . (New York, 1856); John Philips Cranwell and William B. Crane, *Men of Marque: A History of Private Armed Vessels out of Baltimore During the War of 1812* (New York, 1940); Bruce Grant, *Isaac Hull, Captain of Old Ironsides* (Chicago, 1947); Charles O. Paullin, *Commodore John Rodgers* (Cleveland, 1910); Charles O. Paullin, "Naval Administration Under Secretaries of the Navy Smith, Hamilton, and Jones, 1801–1814," *United States Naval Institute Proceedings*, XXXII (1906), 1289–1328; Charles H. J. Snider, *The Story of the "Nancy" and other Eighteen-Twelvers* (Toronto, 1926); Charles H. J. Snider, *Under The Red Jack: Privateers of the Maritime Provinces of Canada in the War of 1812* (Toronto, 1928); Gomer Williams, *History of the Liverpool Privateers . . .* (Liverpool, 1897).

CHAPTERS IV AND V

Though it fails to come up to modern standards of documentary publication, Ernest A. Cruikshank's *Documentary History of the Campaign Upon the Niagara Frontier* (9 vols., Welland, Ont., 1896–1908) contains an amazing variety of source material. Logan Esarey's (ed.), *The Messages and Letters of William Henry Harrison* (2 vols., Indianapolis, 1922) and *The Public Papers of Daniel D. Tompkins, 1807–1817* (3 vols. New York and Albany, 1898–1902) are sources of prime importance. Many useful items may be found on the building of the Lake Erie fleet in "The Dobbins Papers," Buffalo Historical Society *Publications*, VIII, 257–379. On the battle itself Charles O. Paullin's *Battle of Lake Erie* (Cleveland, 1918) is the best collection of documents. John Armstrong, *Notices of the War of 1812* (2 vols., New York, 1840) gives his views of the campaigns along the Canadian border and elsewhere. John Richardson's *War of 1812*, edited by A. C. Casselman (Toronto, 1913), is a valuable account by a British officer. Some of the latest evidence on the capture of York is given in Edith G. Firth (ed.), *The Town of York, 1793–1815* (Toronto, 1962). John S. Moir in "An Early Record of Laura Secord's Walk," *Ontario History*, LI (1959), 105–8, summarizes the old and gives one piece of new evidence on a legendary incident of the war.

Louis L. Babcock's *The War of 1812 on the Niagara Frontier* (Buffalo, 1927) is a good secondary account. Max Rosenberg's

The Building of Perry's Fleet on Lake Erie (Harrisburg, Pa., 1950) is also reliable. Neil H. Swanson's *The Perilous Flight* (New York, 1945) is a detailed account of the events in the Baltimore-Washington area, August-September, 1814.

There are many biographical studies among which the following are especially useful: Freeman Cleaves, *Old Tippecanoe; William Henry Harrison* (New York, 1939); Charles J. Dutton, *Oliver Hazard Perry* (New York, 1935); Charles W. Elliott, *Winfield Scott* (New York, 1937); James R. Jacobs, *Tarnished Warrior: Major General James Wilkinson* (New York, 1938); and Glenn Tucker, *Tecumseh: Vision of Glory* (Indianapolis, 1956).

There are many good articles on special phases of the war and the following are especially useful: Allen Dale, "Chateaugay," *Canadian Geographical Journal*, XI (1935), 33–41; J. Mackay Hitsman, "Sir George Prevost's Conduct of the Canadian War of 1812," Canadian Historical Association, *Report, 1962*, pp. 34–43; W. B. Kerr, "The Occupation of York," *Canadian Historical Review*, V (1925), 9–21; John K. Mahon, "British Command Decisions in the Northern Campaigns of the War of 1812," *Canadian Historical Review*, XLVI (1965), 219–37. Howard S. Miller and Jack Alden Clarke, "Ships in the Wilderness: A Note on the Invasion of Canada, 1813," *Ohio History*, LXXI (1962), 124–28; Howard H. Peckham, "Commodore Perry's Captive," *Ohio History*, LXII (1963), 221–27; George F. G. Stanley, "The Indians in the War of 1812," *Canadian Historical Review*, XXXI (1950), 145–65; and three articles by Charles P. Stacey, "Commodore Chauncey's Attack on Kingston Harbour, November 10, 1812," "The Ships of the British Squadron on Lake Ontario, 1812–1814," and "Another Look at the Battle of Lake Erie," in the *Canadian Historical Review*, XXXII (1951), 126–38; XXXIV (1953), 311–23; and XXXIX (1958), 41–51, respectively.

CHAPTER VI

Accounts by British participants include the following: John H. Cooke, *A Narrative of Events in the South of France and the Attack on New Orleans* (London, 1835); George R. Gleig, *Subaltern in America* (Philadelphia, 1833); and William Surtees, *Twenty-five Years in the Rifle Brigade* (Edinburgh, 1833). An excellent account by a participant on the American side is A. Lacarrière Latour's *Historical Memoir of the War in West Florida and Louisiana* (Philadelphia, 1816). There is material in John S. Bassett (ed.), *Correspondence of Andrew Jackson* (Washington, 1926–35).

The old biographies, James Parton's *Life of Andrew Jackson* (3 vols., New York, 1860) and John S. Bassett's *The Life of Andrew Jackson* (2 vols., New York, 1911), contain much useful information. For sustained narrative interest no account of the southern campaigns surpasses Marquis James's *Andrew Jackson: the Border Captain* (Indianapolis, 1933). On the details of the Battle of New Orleans, Alexander Walker's *Jackson and New Orleans* (New York, 1856) was considered standard for years, but this older account has been updated and largely replaced by Charles B. Brooks's *The Siege of New Orleans* (Seattle, 1961). On strategy see John K. Mahon, "British Command Decisions Relative to the Battle of New Orleans," *Louisiana History*, VI (1965), 53–76. Nearly all the accounts mention the role of the pirates, but Jane L. de Grummond devotes a whole volume to the subject in *The Baratarians and the Battle of New Orleans* (Baton Rouge, 1961).

The naval phases are treated by Walton L. Ainsworth in "An Amphibious Operation that Failed," *United States Naval Institute Proceedings*, LXXI (1945), 193–201, and by Wilburt S. Brown in his unpublished Ph.D. thesis, "The Amphibious Campaign for New Orleans, 1812–1814," the University of Alabama, 1963.

CHAPTERS VII AND VIII

Curtis P. Nettels in *The Emergence of a National Economy, 1775–1815* (New York, 1962) gives a succinct account of the main economic aspects of the war. His bibliography is excellent. Raymond Walters, Jr.'s *Albert Gallatin* (New York, 1957) treats the career of this important Jeffersonian both as Secretary of the Treasury and as peace commissioner. Alexander Balinky's *Albert Gallatin: Fiscal Theories and Policies* (New Brunswick, 1958) is original and suggestive. On the manpower problem Marvin A. Kreidberg and Merton G. Henry's *History of Military Mobilization in the United States Army, 1775–1945* (Washington, 1955) is standard. Samuel Eliot Morison's *Life and Letters of Harrison*

Suggested Reading

Gray Otis (2 vols. Boston, 1913) is still the best account of the events surrounding the Hartford Convention.

The latest scholarly treatment of the peace negotiations is by Bradford Perkins, *Castlereagh and Adams: England and the United States, 1812–1823* (Berkeley, 1964), which unfortunately came out too late to be used in this volume. The standard account is Frank A. Updyke, *The Diplomacy of the War of 1812* (Baltimore, 1915). Samuel F. Bemis's *John Quincy Adams and the Foundations of American Foreign Policy* (New York, 1949) relates the peace issues to the larger picture. Fred L. Engleman's *The Peace of Christmas Eve* (New York, 1962) is a popular account. On both the peace negotiations and their aftermath George Dangerfield's *The Era of Good Feelings* (New York, 1953) is excellent.

Acknowledgments

Several of my friends, including Robert H. Bremner, George Coder, Foster Rhea Dulles, Philip P. Poirier, John Resch, Robert Seager, Lester W. Smith, Albert Weinberg, and H. O. Werner, have read parts of the manuscript and offered many helpful suggestions. Students in my seminar in the early national period of American history explored various topics and I have not hesitated to incorporate some of their findings. I am especially grateful to Allan R. Millett and Timothy Kahrl who helped me with Chapters V and VI, respectively. As a result of the assistance given me the manuscript was much improved, but of course I am entirely responsible for all the weaknesses, omissions, and errors that remain. I wish also to acknowledge the assistance of Thomas Sheahan in compiling the index and the excellent typing service furnished gratis by the office of the Dean of the College of Arts and Sciences of the Ohio State University.

Index

NOTE: Forts will be found alphabetically under the general heading of "Forts."

Index

Index

Index

Index

Index

Index

Index

Index

Index